Introduc

If we had gone with our capital into a c   ]
unproductive desert we might have (?
that has been inflicted upon us. But w̲ ̲ ̲.̲ ̲.̲ ̲ ̲.̲.̲.̲.̲.̲y̲ ̲.̲.̲.̲.̲ ̲.̲.̲.̲.̲.̲.̲.̲ ̲.̲.̲.̲ ̲ ̲.̲.̲.̲y̲
over three million passengers and over one-and-a-half million of goods per
year. It was not, therefore, folly that took us to this country with our capital,
but the invitation we received and the faith our predecessors had in the
equitable treatment we should receive from the Brazilian Government.

Follett Holt, GWBR chairman.
Ordinary General Meeting, 28 February 1923

The push to modernise Brazil in the second half of the nineteenth century rested squarely on the British-owned railways that took produce from the interior to the coast. Nevertheless, this was a double-edged sword for the country, as Richard Graham argues in his book *Britain and the Onset of Modernization in Brazil*. The fact that the British at this time controlled many of the railways, as well as the major import-export trading houses, the ocean-going and coastal navigation companies, the insurance firms, and the banks that had capital to invest - all of this contributed to cancel out any effort to reduce Brazil's dependence on imports from Britain. "On the other hand, the very fact that Brazil did begin to industrialize suggests that the grip was not a stranglehold. There were significant areas of productive activity which the British did not dominate, and there were some points at which [...] they even fostered industrialization."[1]

Nevertheless, investments from abroad were mainly speculative in nature, perhaps especially so in the case of the railways. The Brazilian historian Josemir Camilo de Melo points out in his study of British railways in the cane fields of the northeast of Brazil (*O trem inglês nos canaviais do nordeste*) that "the railways, in fact, seemed to stray from their aim - the transport of agricultural produce - seeking a better financial return, at least for the banks, both British as well as national. With guarantee payments paid promptly, the railways were a fertile field for investment, not only of big investors, but even of such ordinary citizens as priests, lawyers, students, and even unmarried girls in England whose parents gave them shares as dowries."[2]

As we shall see in this book, all these judgements are true: British pre-eminence in key sectors did help set in motion the modernisation of Brazil, but then, somewhat in contradiction, the resulting dependence on British expertise and merchandise actually held back the country's development. While the plan was to promote a national railway network, integrating the vast country, the mechanism by which the government paid 7 per cent guaranteed interest each year over the capital invested in order to attract foreign capital meant that British businesses dominated the early period of railway construction, and this initial objective was lost, arguably forever. Railway companies were incorporated in London expressly to take advantage of the generous concessions offered, not out of altruism. In the early decades of their operation these companies were attractive to British investors on account of the guarantee of return on investment, paid in gold in London, and passed on as dividend payments to shareholders. The companies had no real stake in seeing agricultural produce rise or even in contributing to regional or national development in Brazil. For example, it took three decades for the railway lines to reach the cotton producing belt in the interior of the north-eastern provinces.

In his research paper *Public Policy and Private Initiative: Railway Building in São*

Paulo 1860-1889, Colin M. Lewis stresses that "the expectation that railways in Brazil were inherently profitable was current for much of the imperial period, despite the depressing evidence of the companies' insatiable appetite for government guarantee payments."[3] The fact is that the railways started to live off the guarantee of interest and other subsidies and privileges granted by the government. They also acted as a magnet for other British investments. Writing in 1887, John Casper Branner noted in his article *The Railways of Brazil* that: "Where the [rail]roads are owned or operated by English companies, the railways' supplies have been brought from England without exception, and when the contractors have been Englishmen, the supplies have come from England."[4]

At the same time, the early development of railways in Brazil would have been absolutely impossible without British knowhow and rolling stock - and the resilience of the British engineers. Railway construction in this period was no easy matter, especially in the face of the challenges presented by building in a tropical country, even for the British who dominated the railway engineering achievements around the world in the nineteenth century. In 1949, the Brazilian historian Estevão Pinto wrote that "the construction of the [rail]roads demanded, as a general rule, immense sacrifices - it was necessary to conquer the mangroves, the lakes, the rivers, the valleys, the washing away by floods, the precipices, the forests - which demanded of the engineers, apart from their professional ability, the temperament of pioneers and of frontiersmen. Add to this the dangers of other kinds, the malaria and the yellow fever, for example, which decimated, by preference, the foreign workers."[5]

And there were significant gains for Brazil. One significant and generally overlooked contribution made by the British railway companies, starting in the northeast of Brazil, was to help hasten the abolition of slavery. Before railways started to be constructed in Brazil, the only defined social classes that existed were the *senhores de engenho* (sugar planters) and the slaves, backed by the battalions of poor rural whites that had resulted from natural demographic growth. The railway phenomenon contributed to the transition from the dominance of this rural oligarchy to an embryonic local bourgeoisie and middle class made up of engineers and technicians, men who formerly had sought work as civil servants on public works, and this promoted social mobility. Undoubtedly, the influx of foreign workers for railway construction and the operation of the railways helped to make salaried work more dignified, and they brought new ideas that challenged the prevailing status quo.

Over time, railway workers came to see themselves as a class and as a force for change. The strikes and protests, initiated by disaffected workers in the northeast on the Recife and São Francisco Railway (later part of the Great Western of Brazil Railway network), greatly contributed to the creation of an organised workers' class in Brazil. Josemir Camilo de Melo notes that: "One of the most important influences caused by the railways over the organisation of the local labour market resides in [planting] the embryo of the working class conscience [...] as a practice in the fight for better salaries and working conditions."[6] But it would be wrong to see these British companies solely through the prism of employer-worker conflict, although there certainly was plenty of that. The Great Western of Brazil Railway, for instance, was the first company in Brazil to introduce a social security plan for its employees, in 1923.

This book sets out to tell the fascinating history of one of the best-remembered railway networks in Brazil, the Great Western of Brazil Railway Company Limited, popularly known as the *Gretoeste*, which came to dominate more than 1,700 kilometres of railway in four States of the north east of Brazil, and lasted (along with the ancestor lines that

The Great Western of Brazil Railway

William Edmundson

Steam locomotive manufactured by Swiss Locomotive and Machine Works, Winterthur, Switzerland, in 1922, one of two identical engines acquired by the Great Western of Brazil (numbers 224 and 225). This locomotive originally burned wood but was converted to fuel oil after arriving in Brazil.
Works Photograph, courtesy Swiss Locomotive and Machine Works. Author's collection.

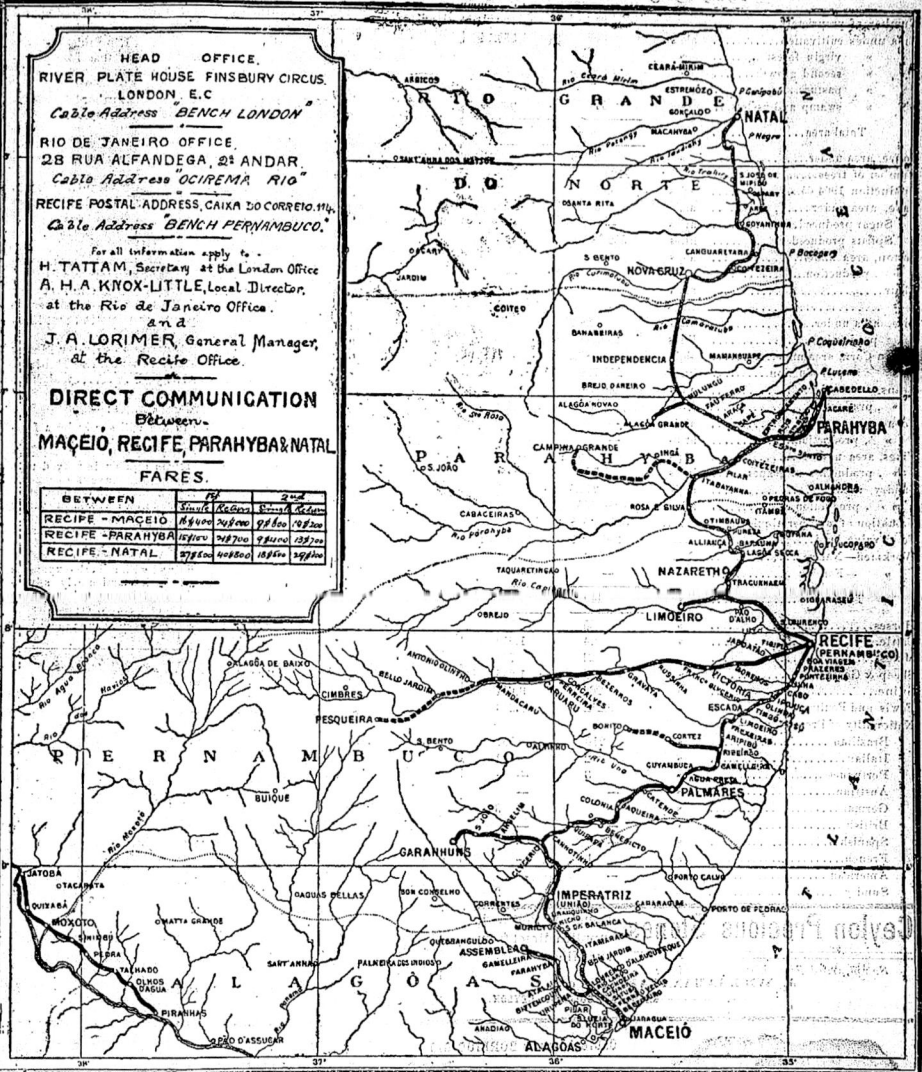

it absorbed) as a British company for nearly one hundred years until nationalisation in 1950. The name 'Great Western' derived from the generally western direction taken by the original line belonging to this company in the then province of Pernambuco. Without doubt, the choice of this name was also to make it attractive to British investors, given its famous namesake, the Great Western Company in Britain, engineered by the legendary Isambard Kingdom Brunel, which operated its first train in 1838. This railway linked London with Bristol and later dominated the south-west and west of England and most of Wales. The epithet 'great' was commonly used in the naming of railways in the early period; examples in Britain include The Great Northern, The Great Eastern, The Great North of Scotland, and The Great Central Railway, and the Great Western name was carried to many countries abroad apart from Brazil.[7]

This book is the product of intensive study of both primary and secondary sources. Finding the former poses problems. As D. C. M. Platt affirms in his archive report on *The British in South America*, there are "special problems of locating archives in Latin America," given that these countries "are concerned, in every respect, far more with the present and future than with the past, and this attitude is reflected in an indifference towards archives. [...] Legal requirements alone tend to guide firms in the preservation of their archives, and once the span of years laid down by the law has been accomplished, businessmen are only too happy to use the terms of the law itself as a general directive for destruction."[8] This tendency is exacerbated by the decline and, in many sectors, the disappearance of British commercial involvement in Brazil since 1945. Nevertheless, there is a good deal of primary documentation available related to the history of the Great Western. The Arquivo Público de Pernambuco in Recife possesses an extensive collection of original documents relating to railway companies in north east Brazil, catalogued by the historian Josemir Camilo de Melo. The archive can be accessed in the annex building of the public archive at Rua Imperial 1069 in Recife, and the archive staff is very helpful. The archivists in the Fundação Joaquim Nabuco in Recife are also very obliging, and are keen to help with research in the Biblioteca Central Blanche Knopf. The rare books in this reference library and archival photographs in the excellent photographic library were important tools in the preparation of this book.

Much valuable primary material is also now available on the internet. This includes the texts of key Brazilian laws and decrees; the *Diário Oficial da União* in its original format; the Hemeroteca Digital Brasileira of the Fundação Biblioteca Nacional with scanned and searchable copies of old newspapers (including such English language periodicals in Brazil as *Wileman's Brazilian Review* and *The Rio News*) and the annual reports of the provincial presidents. There are also paid sites in Britain for searching old newspapers - *The Times*, for example, is particularly useful for publishing and commenting on the copious minutes of railway company board meetings - as well as copies of significant periodicals of the period such as *The Railway Times*, *The Railway Record*, *The Railway Age* and *The Railway News*. We are also fortunate in being able to consult the published memoirs of a British engineer named T. C. Hanson, with his firsthand account that covers a period of thirty years from 1927, spanning the last decades of the Great Western company and the first years of the network following nationalisation in 1950.

I have also consulted important secondary sources, which include Estavão Pinto´s excellent *História de uma Estrada de Ferro do Nordeste*, published in 1949; Ademar Benévolo's *Introdução à História Ferroviária do Brasil: Estudo Social, Político e Histórico* (1953); Douglas Apratto Tenório's *Capitalismo e Ferrovias no Brasil* (1979); Richard Graham's *Britain and the Onset of Modernization in Brazil 1850-1914* (1968); Gilberto Freyre's *Ingleses no Brasil* (1948), and recent studies by Josemir Camilo de Melo, among many other works that are listed in the bibliography.

Furthermore, there is the industrial archaeology that still remains to be seen. I have walked along some of the Great Western railway lines, such as the tracks and viaducts of the Serra das Russas, and a memorable walk with members of the NGO *Amigos do Trem* in Pernambuco along the tracks of the original Great Western branch line from Carpina to Nazaré. I have visited many of the railway stations of the surprising number that have survived, in several cases metamorphosed into new uses - a car workshop, a restaurant, the offices of the local Secretariat for Education, a Town Hall, and even people's homes, when not abandoned to the elements or long since demolished leaving only the foundations. There is also the wonderful *Museu do Trem* in Recife within the original station (inaugurated in 1888) of the Pernambuco Central Railway, later assimilated into the Great Western network. This museum is the oldest in Brazil and reopened in 2014 after refurbishments that cost around half a million pounds. It houses several steam locomotives and much rolling stock, mostly British, as well as artefacts that help tell the history of the railway. Other steam engines redolent with the history of the Great Western have survived in the northeast of Brazil, mainly at *usinas* (sugar plantations), and are described in my internet catalogue 'Surviving steam locomotives in north east Brazil' (http://www.internationalsteam.co.uk/trains/brazil36.htm) and in my contributions as a collaborator for the project *Inventory of Steam Engines in Brazil*. On top of this, I have published extensively on surviving steam locomotives of the Great Western of Brazil Railway in the British magazine *Locomotives International*.

Chapter 1 of this book sets the scene by describing the special relationship that existed between Britain and Portugal, leading to the pivotal year of 1808 when Dom João Maria de Bragança fled the forces of Napoleon and, escorted by British naval ships, took up residence in Brazil. British businessmen soon began to arrive after Dom João ordered the opening of Brazilian ports to friendly nations. The history of the early development of railway building in Brazil is described in detail - following the first railway law of 1835 that granted concessions - as is the important role played by British railway companies in the later abolition of slavery within Brazil. Of great significance to the story of the Great Western is the account of the beginnings of The Recife and São Francisco Railway (a British company organised in London in 1853); the second railway to be built in Brazil chronologically but the first of true economic importance for the country, which was later assimilated by the Great Western of Brazil.

Chapter 2 focuses on the growth in importance of the British community in the city of Recife - the hub for the Great Western's extensive network covering four Provinces, later States, with their own cemetery, church, hospital, clubs, and their dominance of manufacturing, banking, urban transport, and public utilities in that city. The growth of British railways in Pernambuco until the year 1889, (encompassing the Recife and São Francisco Railway and the modest beginnings of the Great Western's original line from Recife to Limoeiro), as well as the inauguration of the initially state-operated Central de Pernambuco and Sul de Pernambuco lines, are the focus of Chapter 3. The key importance of the sugar industry and the central *usina* initiatives are also dealt with in this chapter. Chapter 4 deals with the growth of railways in Alagoas in the same period, up to the declaration of the republic, with histories of The Alagoas Brazilian Central Railway Company, The Alagoas Railway Company, and the ignominious Paulo Afonso Railway, all of which were similarly swallowed up later by the Great Western network. The following chapter, chapter 5, describes the history of railway construction to 1889 in Paraíba and Rio Grande do Norte, especially the British-owned railways with such picturesque names as The Conde d'Eu Railway Company and The Imperial Brazilian

Natal and Nova Cruz Railway, both later absorbed by the Great Western company.

Chapter 6 concentrates on the transitional period from 1889 to the outbreak of The First World War as both the federal and the state governments struggled with the legacies of the imperial period and attempted to impose a rational communications plan on republican Brazil. This chapter focuses on the circumstances surrounding the decision taken at federal level to expropriate the British railways in the northeast, excepting the Great Western, and then to lease them to the latter. Chapter 7 examines the affairs of the Great Western from the start of The First World War, through the acrimonious disputes surrounding tariff adjustment and the new contracts finally negotiated with the government, until nationalisation in 1950. This chapter takes in the skirmishes with the infamous bandit Lampião and his band of *cangaceiros* (outlaws) that so harried the railway administration. The final chapter, chapter 8, describes the manner in which the Great Western was nationalised, and the subsequent history of the lines that once carried passengers and cargo on Brazil's third most extensive railway network. There is also a general survey of what remains to be seen of this rich history.

I am grateful to the staff of the Arquivo Público de Pernambuco for their help in perusing their excellent Great Western of Brazil railway archives, as well as staff at the Fundação Joaquim Nabuco in Recife, especially for their help in accessing relevant photographs in their wonderful document centre. I also wish to thank André Cardoso of the NGO *Movimento Nacional Amigos do Trem* in Recife for his enthusiasm for this project and for showing me round the wonderfully restored Museu do Trem in Recife.

All translations from Portuguese into English are the work of the author, unless otherwise stated. I am grateful to my wife Verônica for her encouragement, and for her valuable comments on the first draft of this study. All errors are, naturally, my entire responsibility.

William (Eddie) Edmundson
João Pessoa, December 2015

The author beside the North British Company locomotive on display in the Railway Museum in Recife.

Marvellous Ineptitude
Early Railway
Construction to 1889

> The Empire is threatened with a railway system of marvellous ineptitude.
> Richard Burton, *The Highlands of the Brazil*.[9]

> This policy of guaranteeing interest [...] has created an insatiable army of parasites who have led the government into a labyrinth of unremunerative, unnecessary and costly enterprises, which have become fixed pensioners upon the revenues of the country. Then, in their turn, the 'professional directors' of the London market have not been altogether blameless. They have floated schemes which they must have known to be visionary and unpromising, and they have flattered and wheedled Brazilian officials into the belief that scores of these wretched enterprises could be made remunerative and that the 'natural resources' of the country are incalculably great, but can be developed properly only through these so-called improvements. In this they have quite made Brazil believe that building a railway into a desert would cause water to bubble forth in its waste places, and herbage to grow over its burning sands. Then they have turned to the confiding investor and have made him believe Brazil to be the long sought El Dorado, and that for every shilling planted there, nothing less than a sovereign could be produced. They have traded upon the amiability and rectitude of the Emperor, the peaceableness of the Brazilian people, the fertility of the soil, the wide expanse of territory, the product of a few gold and diamond mines, and the 'splendid future' in store for the country. They have baited their hooks with many a glittering generality and have never failed to catch their fish with them.
> *The Rio News*, Rio de Janeiro, 24 April 1887[10]

The correspondent of the English language *Rio News* was writing at a time when the Brazilian imperial government had been actively courting foreign investment since the decade of the 1850s, and this was particularly true of the development of railways. In fact, no other area of the Brazilian economy was subject to greater involvement by the imperial government than railways, nor to a greater influx of foreign investment. In essence, the government's policy was to fast-track the introduction of railway construction into Brazil through subsidies that guaranteed minimum dividends to investors - capital investments that carried no risk to shareholders. The first railway to benefit from the tempting offer was a British owned railway, the Recife and São Francisco Railway, which over time, along with other existing railway lines, became absorbed by the Great Western of Brazil Railway that practically monopolised rail transport in four States in the north east of Brazil.

Brazil started relatively late in railway building. In Latin America the first railway was constructed in Cuba, from Havana to Bejucal (inaugurated in 1837: length of 27.5

kilometres). This was followed by railways in British Guyana, linking Georgetown to Rosignol (1848: 97.4 kms.); Mexico, between Veracruz and El Molino (1850: 11.5 kms.); Peru, joining Lima to the port of Callao (April 1851: 13.7 kms.); and Chile, from Copiapó to Caldera (December 1851: 81 kms.). Brazil's first railway was opened in April 1854, without the benefit of government guarantees, and ran 16 kilometres from Mauá to Raiz da Serra in the then province of Rio de Janeiro. Argentina followed, with a 13 kilometre railway from Buenos Aires to Flores, inaugurated in 1857. Then, in February 1858, the first stretch of the British-owned Recife and São Francisco Railway was opened to traffic, running 31.5 kilometres from Recife to Cabo in the province of Pernambuco. This was the first railway of economic importance in Brazil - the line in Rio de Janeiro was built chiefly to impress the Brazilian Emperor Pedro II, and became essentially an attraction for tourists enjoying a day out. Many other British railway companies were established in Brazil, including the first line belonging outright to the Great Western of Brazil Railway, from Recife to Limoeiro in the interior of Pernambuco, which opened in 1882.

The immense British investment in railway construction in Brazil in the nineteenth century has to be understood in the context of close relations historically with Portugal, politically and economically; relations that carried over to the Portuguese colony of Brazil in 1808 and were later transferred to the independent Empire of Brazil from 1822. The special relationship between Britain and Portugal - the oldest European alliance - can be traced back to the times of the crusaders in the twelfth century.[11] Several agreements were reached over time, including the Anglo-Portuguese Treaty of 1373 signed between King Edward III of England and King Ferdinand and Queen Eleanor of Portugal that established a treaty of "perpetual friendships, unions [and] alliances" between the two seafaring nations. This relationship led to a treaty in 1642 that practically granted most-favoured nation status for England in Portuguese commerce, in return for English recognition of Portugal's independence and expressions of friendship. While nothing came of this, initially, this was the bedrock for all future treaties between the two nations. In 1654, a one-sided treaty was signed in the times of Oliver Cromwell that, according to the historian Alan K. Manchester, made Portugal "a virtual commercial vassal of England."[12]

Early in the following century, the Methuen treaty was concluded in December 1703 during the War of the Spanish Succession (1701-1714), and served to cement the close military and commercial relationships between England[13] and Portugal, although it was "signed only after the customary vacillation on the part of the king of Portugal and the usual trump card of the English fleet." (Alan Manchester). The treaty provided for the regulation of trade relations between the two nations. At the close of that century, war broke out between Britain and France and "Portugal was caught like a shellfish in a tempest between the waves of England's seapower and the rock of Napoleon's armies." (Alan Manchester).[14]

On 12 August 1807, Portugal received a note signed by both France and Spain, who were allies before Napoleon's army entered Spain later that year, declaring that if Dom João Maria de Bragança, Prince Regent of Portugal,[15] did not declare war against Britain by the first of September and send back the English minister, then war would be declared on Portugal. Napoleon also demanded that the Portuguese ambassador be recalled from London; that all the English residents in Portugal be seized and their property confiscated; that the ports of the kingdom be closed to the British; and that, without delay, his armies and fleets be united with those of the rest of the continent against Britain. Dom João froze, uncertain about how to respond, but fearful that the Portuguese monarchy would be swallowed by Napoleon. At the last moment, as the

French army entered Portugal, Dom João agreed to the British offer to convoy him and his mother Dona Maria I ("mad Maria") to the colony of Brazil, along with members of the royal family, the entire nobility of the court, and their servants and hangers-on - between 8,000 and 15,000 people in all - on thirty-six ships, hugging half the money then in circulation in Portugal.

The Prince Regent Dom João and his entourage arrived first in Salvador, in the captaincy of Bahia of All Saints,[16] on 22 January 1808. Within a few days of his arrival, Dom João was being pressed by the British for a *quid pro quo* for having escorted the royal household to Brazil, and by the colonists in Bahia who could now no longer trade with Portugal, and were anyway fed up of the current colonial pact of monopoly of trade with Portugal. Succumbing to being squeezed from both sides, Dom João issued a decree (known as a *Carta Regia*) entitled 'Opening of the Ports to Friendly Nations' on 28 January 1808 that opened Brazilian ports to direct commerce with "friendly nations," after three hundred years of colonialism that had suffocated Brazil and stifled trade. Britain had lobbied for just one port in Brazil to be opened exclusively to trade, but now became the main beneficiary of the decree. This deal was much more generous since there was now a *de facto* exclusive right to undertake commerce with all the ports of Brazil, at least while the war continued in Europe. Britain was the only 'friendly nation' with the wherewithal to conduct commerce on the scale suddenly offered by the colony of Brazil with all her potential. It is significant too that a later decree, emitted on 1 April 1808, permitted colonials for the first time to set up manufacturing industry in Brazil, and that this right was extended to foreigners. At the same time, as a favour to Portuguese shipping caught in Brazil, the Portuguese court decided to limit the Brazilian ports permitted to engage in foreign trade to Rio de Janeiro, Salvador, Maranhão (São Luis), Pará (Belém), and Pernambuco (Recife).

However, truly preferential rights for commerce with Brazil - rights which Britain had enjoyed hitherto with Portugal - actually came two years later. In April 1808, Viscount Strangford was named envoy extraordinary and minister plenipotentiary to the Portuguese court, now gathered at the capital of Brazil in Rio de Janeiro. He arrived in Brazil in July 1808. Britain's foreign secretary, George Canning, had given Strangford the task of negotiating a treaty of friendship and commerce, instructing him to base this on the existing preferential arrangements that Britain had enjoyed to this point with Portugal. Strangford was enormously successful in his mission, and on 19 February 1810 treaties were signed between Portugal and Britain that covered alliance and friendship, as well as commerce and navigation. These treaties in reality reflected Portuguese and British interests in opening up markets in Brazil, and no Brazilian colonist was party to the negotiations and final drafting of the agreements.

> In negotiating the treaties, the Portuguese court had in mind almost exclusively the necessities of Portugal itself. No Brazilian was in the ministry or in the prince regent's council of state to fight for the welfare of the colony and point out the stipulations which would be detrimental to its interests. (Alan K. Manchester).[17]

The Treaty of Friendship and Alliance guaranteed the perpetual alliance of Portugal and Britain, and a British undertaking never to recognise as sovereign of Portugal any prince who was not a legitimate heir of the House of Bragança. But the most momentous and enduring treaty, for both Britain and Brazil, was the Treaty of Commerce and Navigation that established a duty of only 16 percent on the importation of British goods. This compared with a tax of 24 percent on imports from other nations. Britain now virtually eliminated any competition in the Brazilian market. On top of this, British warships could now dock in Brazilian ports, and British citizens had the right of recourse to special tribunals in Brazil. Within two years, more than eighty percent of British exports to Latin America was arriving in Brazil. This trade dropped off with the end of the Napoleonic Wars in 1815, but the repercussions of the treaty set the scene for the rest of the century, with Brazil as a key market for British manufactured goods, but much less as a source of imports into Britain. Nevertheless, the northeast of Brazil did benefit; soon three-quarters of the cotton and half the sugar exported from Pernambuco was going to Britain.

Not surprisingly, the treaty was unpopular among Brazilians. Colonial relations with the court in Rio de Janeiro became increasingly fraught, and the British pressed Dom João to return to Portugal, now that Napoleon was defeated, where he could be more easily persuaded of the British point of view. The new British Foreign Secretary, Lord Castlereagh, sent out Rear Admiral Sir John Beresford in September 1814 with a British fleet to take him back to Lisbon. At the same time, and for the same reason, the Brazilians fought to keep Dom João in Brazil where they too had better chances of persuading him to the colony's point of view. For the time being their efforts paid off, and the fleet returned empty-handed to England.

In December 1815, The United Kingdom of Portugal, Brazil and the Algarves was formed, which raised Brazil from the status of colony to a kingdom on a par with the kingdoms of Portugal and the Algarves under the umbrella of the Portuguese empire. From this time on, the captaincies became provinces in Brazil, and Rio de Janeiro became the capital of the Portuguese empire, while Dom João and his court resided there. This was further encouragement to British merchants to settle in Brazil. This union of the three kingdoms gained extra force when, in 1818, the prince regent was crowned Dom João VI, King of the United Kingdom, two years after the death of his mother. It had now been ten years since Dom João had arrived in Brazil; the European War had finished in 1815, and yet he showed no inclination to return to Lisbon. Pressure built up in Portugal for him to return, backed by British insistence, and in 1820 he gave in to the stress. The immediate pretext was the Revolução Constitucionalista do Porto, a liberal revolt in Portugal in that year, and so, very reluctantly, Dom João set back across the Atlantic in April 1821 leaving his eldest son Dom Pedro behind as regent of Brazil.

Writing in her journal later that year, soon after arriving in Brazil, the diarist Maria Graham commented on the British she found settled there:[18]

> The English are [...] hospitable and sociable among each other. They often dine together: the ladies love music and dancing, and some of the men gamble as much as the Portuguese. Upon the whole, society is at a low, very low scale here among the English. Good eating and good drinking they contrive to have, for the flesh, fish, and fowl are good; fruits and vegetables various and excellent, and bread of the finest. Their slaves, for the English are all served by slaves, indeed, eat a sort of porridge of mandioc meal with small squares of jerked beef stirred into it. (28 October 1821).

Dom João's departure and the declaration of independence a year later concluded the first phase of tentative British steps to establish a foothold in Brazil.

> The commercial relations of England and Portugal from 1808 to 1821 constituted the intermediate step in the transfer of England's century-old preëminence in Portuguese economic life to the independent state of Brazil. (Alan K. Manchester).[19]

Independence from Portugal was declared by Dom Pedro on 7 September 1822, and he became Dom Pedro I, emperor of Brazil. But this was no *fait accompli*, especially given the length of Brazil's coast and the many ports that could harbour the Portuguese fleet, and victory at sea was needed. The Brazilians approached a Scottish admiral, Thomas Cochrane, whose mercenary services were available - he had recently led the Chilean navy to success against the Spanish in Chile - and he was offered command of the Brazilian Imperial fleet in March 1823. He accepted, and in so doing became Brazil's first admiral. Knowing of Cochrane's fame, the several troopships in Salvador left in a panic as he approached, and the Portuguese fleet made for the northern port of São Luis in Maranhão. Cochrane reached São Luis first, outflanking the Portuguese, and by a simple but ingenious deception persuaded the authorities there that the Portuguese fleet was defeated and Brazilians were arriving in ships to take revenge on the city. By this ruse he took São Luis, without firing a shot, and when the Portuguese flotilla then arrived, they were forced to turn away. Within three months of arriving in Brazil, Cochrane had won the northern territories for the empire of Brazil.

The attractions of newly independent Brazil proved irresistible to British traders.

> British commercial advantages increased after independence. British goods flooded the market and British merchant houses were set up in Brazil to handle them. Although this period of unencumbered action in the field of importation came to an end in 1844 when the old treaty expired, the British found that they continued to hold their own as a result of their enterprise, their entrenched position, the industrial superiority of their home country, and their control of Brazilian shipping. (Richard Graham).[20]

Political independence had been achieved, but Brazil was financially in crisis, and needed an injection of money to survive. In 1824, the Brazilian government approached Nathan Rothschild in London and took out a loan of 3.7 million pounds sterling, and so entered into a long period of indebtedness to Britain. This loan was known as the 'Portuguese loan' and the 'independence loan', and was destined to cover debts left over from the colonial period. In essence, this was a payment to Portugal in return for their recognition of Brazil's independence.[21]

Britain was keen now to see a binding treaty signed by Portugal and Brazil, and acted as an intermediary to achieve this goal. Britain's Envoy Extraordinary and Minister Plenipotentiary to Portugal and Brazil, Sir Charles Stuart, negotiated Portuguese recognition of Brazilian independence in the name of Dom João VI. Stuart was successful in his mission, and in August 1825 the Tratado de Paz e Aliança (Treaty of Peace and Alliance) was signed in Brazil and ratified in November that year by Portugal. The catch for Brazil was that, in return for this helping hand, Britain sought a commercial treaty with Brazil that would transfer all the commercial privileges obtained from Portugal in the period after 1808, including low import tariffs and an extraterritorial judicial status in Brazil exclusively for British subjects.

Two years later, in August 1827, a commercial treaty between Brazil and Britain was signed that reaffirmed the most-favoured status terms of the 1810 treaty - The Treaty of Friendship, Navigation and Commerce. This was the price Brazil had to pay for British recognition of her independence. Of lasting importance to Anglo-Brazilian relations through most of the nineteenth century, Brazil also committed in a separate treaty to abolishing the trade in slaves in 1830. The 1827 commercial treaty needed to be renewed after fifteen years, in 1842, but the British argued that time was needed for negotiation, and gained an extension of two years to 1844. Brazilian resentment at these treaties was a major contributing factor in Dom Pedro I's decision to abdicate the Brazilian throne in 1831 and leave immediately for Portugal. From the British perspective, the fact that the commercial treaty was not renewed mattered little, since by then Britain was the dominant presence in Brazilian commerce.

Meanwhile, the world was waking up to the exciting prospects of steam power and railway transport. The first railway had run in 1825, from Stockton to Darlington. Quick off the mark, in May 1827, an Englishman named Charles Grace, who lived in Vila de São Sebastião, São Paulo, requested authorisation from the central government to build a railway from Rio de Janeiro to Serra de Itaguaí, to the west of Rio de Janeiro. His venture was named the Companhia Brasileira de Estradas de Ferro (Brazilian Railways Company) with the intention of constructing an 'Iron Railway'. Nothing came of this project. Instead, the provinces concentrated on the building of roads. In 1831, for example, a resolution of the General Council of the Province of Pernambuco voted for the building of four roads: to the north (Recife to Igaraçu), to the south (Recife to Ponte dos Carvalhos, near Cabo de Santo Agostinho), and two roads into the interior (Recife to Pau d'Alho and Recife to Vitória). However, by the time railways were being built in this province, the paving of the road north was stopped and partly in ruins; the road to Pau d'Alho was in a dreadful state; the road to Vitória in a better state but not good; and the road to the south unusable during the winter months.

This stagnation in the development of transport communication away from the ports of Brazil was in part due to the period of turbulence in the provinces following Dom Pedro I's decision to abdicate on 7 April 1831. This ushered in a ten year period of regency - known as the *Menoridade* - until his son, also named Dom Pedro, was crowned Pedro II, Emperor of Brazil, in July 1841, at the age of fifteen. This period was marked by tension, agitation, and even local rebellions in the provinces. The central government spent scarce resources putting down uprisings, and little was left over to invest in transport infrastructure. And this state of affairs internally discouraged investment from outside. At the same time, landowners were pressing for improved and cheaper communications for their produce, and the government turned to subsidising railway construction by means of guaranteed minimum dividends on capital invested. "The subsidies implicit in the guarantee policy reduced the perceived risk and permitted the railway either to obtain capital that it would not have received, or to obtain it more cheaply than would have otherwise been possible."(William Summerhill).[22]

The first tentative step to promote railway construction in Brazil was taken on 31 October 1835, when the legislative passed Law no. 101 authorising the Regency to award railway concessions that came allied to certain privileges. This was during the Regency of Padre Diogo Antonio Feijó, who had assumed the reins of government earlier that same month. Feijó sent the Marquês de Barbacena to represent the Brazilian government in London, and this law was designed to give support to the marquis's diplomatic efforts on behalf of the imperial government. Regent Feijó's mandate was for four years, but opposition in the legislative assembly and rebellions in the provinces led him to resign in September 1837. This law authorised the concession of privileges for a period of forty years to companies organised to build railways linking the capital of Rio de Janeiro with Minas Gerais, with Rio Grande do Sul (over 1,000 kilometres to the south!), and with Bahia (about 1,200 kilometres to the north!). Clearly unrealistic and overambitious - this would have created a network of over 5,500 kilometres - the law nevertheless set down norms that could be studied and modified later in the century. These concessions included a subsidy for the agreed cost of every league of railway line constructed, exemption of duty on imported machinery, and the donation of state lands and authority to expropriate privately-owned land.

A Scotsman was inspired by this 'Feijó law' to organise a company that he named the 'Imperial Companhia de Estradas de Ferro' (Imperial Railways Company). This was Dr. Thomas Cochrane, a second cousin of the Scottish admiral, and a homeopathic doctor living in Rio de Janeiro from early in the 1830s decade. His proposal was to link Rio de Janeiro and São Paulo by 450 kilometres of railway, and to this end he signed a contract in 1839 with the Brazilian government. The project did not get off the ground, despite an extension granted in 1849, and in 1853 the contract was declared officially lapsed, despite continual complaints from Thomas Cochrane. The fact is that he had to abandon the initiative since his company did not have the financial resources to take on this enterprise, and historians generally see this protracted negotiation as holding back railway development in Brazil in this early period.[23]

There were no other takers for several years, until the law was changed in 1852. Douglas Apratto Tenório in his book *Capitalismo e Ferrovias no Brasil* (Capitalism and Railways in Brazil) describes how: "Brazil, recently born as an independent nation, was committed to consolidating her position as a national state, due to threats, external and internal; it was more profitable and secure to invest capital in the slave trade; [and] finally the period that marks the so-called Menoridade is one of great insecurity and turbulence, of socio-political convulsion".[24] On top of this, the national currency - the mil-réis - had depreciated in value during the first half of the nineteenth century, and this rendered the purchase of rolling stock, rails, and equipment from abroad very expensive.

There were also some special difficulties that affected railway construction in Brazil. In many parts of the country there is a steep ascent to be conquered from the coast to reach the interior. There was, anyway, only scant knowledge of the topography which necessitated expensive survey missions and led to frequent changes in the agreed route. Once started on the concession, there was the financial burden of building tunnels and viaducts, which was not only expensive but also stretched to the limit the available technology needed to carry out such engineering feats. This proved to be especially problematic in the provinces of São Paulo and Rio de Janeiro, but was also a major challenge in the north east of Brazil. In addition, the heavy downpours in the tropical climate hindered progress in construction; it was common for partly completed construction works to be carried away by floods, and funds were never enough to ensure adequate maintenance after the construction was completed. And disease was rife in this tropical country; as we shall see later in this book, yellow fever was endemic for many years in Brazil, notably in the north east, and was only brought under a degree of control in the early twentieth century. Finally, steam locomotives ran then on coal, and, while there is coal in the south of Brazil, it is of poor quality, and the Brazilian coal-mining industry did not take off until the time of The First World War.

The 1835 law, then, had no immediate practical effect, but it did point the way forward for the country's transport policy, in that the government admitted that future development depended on railway construction. Legislation to that date was totally inadequate and obsolete, but now the seeds were sown for government strategy over the next two decades - a strategy predicated on two key objectives: a national network that would link the coastal provincial capitals to the national capital in Rio de Janeiro, and the creation of pioneer railways to open up the interior. "Responsive to sectional economic interests and tempered by commercial considerations, the underlying thrust of the construction programme was essentially strategic." (Colin Lewis).[25] Above all, national integration was paramount in this strategy for a national imperial government threatened by calls for republicanism backed by major revolutions in Pernambuco and in the south of Brazil. The *Farroupilha* Revolt was the longest lasting; a conflict that

that took place between 1835 and 1845 and led the provinces of Rio Grande do Sul and Santa Catarina to proclaim themselves as two independent republics. The *Praieira Revolt* in Pernambuco raged from 1848 to 1850, influenced by the 'February Revolution' of 1848 in France which ended the Orleans dynasty, and the breaking out of liberal revolts against monarchies and conservatism in general elsewhere in Europe during the following two decades. There was also the worry that popular revolt and political turmoil would prove contagious and encourage insurrection among slaves on the plantations. For the government, railway construction promised the potential for integrating the country and ensuring stability and social order.

Before railways began to be built in Brazil, communications by land were rudimentary and precarious. "The roads, if we can call them that, those trails that were no more than narrow tracks, which offered no kind of comfort to travellers. There was no conservation. When it rained, they transformed into quagmires, making them impractical for months. [...] Cattle and slaves, valuable colonial merchandise, covered the routes on foot, and the cargo, transported by animals, or even on the heads of the men [was carried] on short journeys." "The longer journeys were truly a Via Crucis. They demanded special preparations, such as the choice of a guide, the purchase of animals, preparation of food, and provision of weapons as a precaution against robbers and wild animals. [...] For the transport of merchandise they used oxen, convoys of slaves and troops. The link between the centres of production in the interior with the embarkation ports on the Atlantic coast was frequently effected by means of river transport." (Douglas Apratto Tenório).[26] In short, colonial 'roads' were barely transitable.

While there was no response to the imperial decree in the short term, the 1835 law did alert the provinces of Rio de Janeiro, São Paulo, and Minas Gerais to the potential of building railways to improve land communications. In 1836, the province of São Paulo considered joining the port of Santos with the city of São Paulo and other towns in the hinterland by railway, and in March 1838 a provincial law was passed to build a railway from Santos to São Paulo. This concession was awarded to the firm of 'Aguiar, Viuva, Filhos & Companhia' and the English construction company of Platt & Reid, for the rights to construct a railway line from Santos to São Carlos (present-day Campinas), Constituição, Itu, and Porto Feliz. As with Thomas Cochrane's scheme in 1839 for a railway from Rio de Janeiro to São Paulo, this project too was not carried out; there were too many obstacles. The government reflected on the experience and concluded that no railway line would be constructed in Brazil without further government help, especially in the form of a guarantee for the interest on the capital invested. Thomas Cochrane insisted that the government would need to offer a guarantee of interest of 5% for approved railway construction projects, and this led to the provisions of the law of 1852.

But there was one other major obstacle to foreign (that is, British) investment in railways - the Atlantic slave trade and the continued existence of slavery within Brazil. It is important to understand this in some detail, since the 1852 law specifically addressed the issue of slavery, and the first British-owned railway, built in north east Brazil (and later part of the Great Western of Brazil Railway network), was the first foreign enterprise prohibited from using slaves, even while the rest of Brazil continued as a slave-based society. By the 1830s, slavery was a matter of considerable disgust among the people in Britain, and this was a feature of capital investment in Brazil that British companies could not afford to ignore. In her *Journal of a Voyage to Brazil* - a very popular read in Britain from 1824 - Maria Graham noted in her entry for 21 September 1821, after arriving in Pernambuco:

We had hardly gone fifty paces into Recife, when we were absolutely sickened by the first sight of a slave-market. It was the first time either the boys or I had been in a slave-country; and, however strong and poignant the feelings may be at home, when imagination pictures slavery, they are nothing compared to the staggering sight of a slave-market. It was thinly stocked, owing to the circumstances of the town; which cause most of the owners of new slaves to keep them closely shut up in the depôts. Yet about fifty young creatures, boys and girls, with all the appearance of disease and famine consequent upon scanty food and long confinement in unwholesome places, were sitting and lying about among the filthiest animals in the streets. The sight sent us home to the ship with the heart-ache: and resolution, 'not loud but deep,' that nothing in our power should be considered too little, or too great, that can tend to abolish or to alleviate slavery. [...] I saw a white woman, or rather fiend, beating a young negress, and twisting her arms cruelly while the poor creature screamed in agony, till our gentlemen interfered. Good God! that such a traffic, such a practice as that of slavery, should exist. Near the house there are two or three depôts of slaves, all young; in one, I saw an infant of about two years old, for sale.

Slavery remained a thorn in the side of British relations with Brazil for many years, both before and after independence, with Britain demanding that the trade in slaves be suppressed, in conformity with agreements reached with Portugal before Brazilian independence was won. Slavery had been abolished as trade for British subjects in 1807, and no slave was to be admitted to British colonies from 1808. As we have seen, the 1810 treaty of alliance included a clause prohibiting the slave trade to Brazil, to be achieved by 1830, but Dom João had simply outlawed the importing of slaves from any part of Africa which was not colonised by Portugal. In 1815, Portugal agreed to stop the slave trade north of the equator, which left much of the slave commerce from Africa to Brazil still open. An agreement with Portugal in 1817 - the Portuguese Convention - gave the right to the British navy to stop and search merchant ships for the presence of slaves. Tragically, this agreement stipulated that a merchant ship was engaged in unlawful activity only if slaves were actually found on board, which led to slaves being thrown overboard when a British cruiser approached. In any case, this measure was a failure; more slaves actually entered Brazil in 1821 than in 1808.

So powerful was the resistance in Brazil to abolition that when Britain offered to recognise Brazilian independence in November 1822, even without consulting with Portugal, with the proviso that Brazil committed to stopping the traffic, Dom Pedro was compelled to turn down this otherwise tempting offer, despite the huge gains Brazil would make politically and economically if this recognition were granted by Britain. There was a very real risk that Brazil would break up into independent regions, just as had happened in Spanish America, if the landowners were dissatisfied with the central government's policy on this issue. Britain was just as resistant to any notion of the trade in slaves continuing, and this led to an impasse - both sides had a lot to gain from recognition of Brazil's independence, but neither was willing to give way on the slavery question.

The 1810 treaty came up for revision in 1825, and the British hoped to use this as a means to lobby for the effective abolition of the Brazilian slave trade. Accordingly, the Anglo-Brazilian Abolition Treaty was signed on 23 November 1826 and ratified by Brazil in 1827. In essence, Brazil agreed to assume the commitments made by the Portuguese Convention in 1817, and to end the slave trade within three years of ratification; that is, by March 1830. This did not happen, and the British exerted as much pressure as they could, with the result that Padre Feijó, the Minister of Justice, passed a law (known now as the 'Lei Feijó') in November 1831 that, with certain exceptions, abolished the slave trade. Article 1 begins "All slaves that enter by land or through the ports of Brazil, coming from outside, are free." The law was worthy, but it made no difference. "Para inglês ver" is a common expression in Brazilian Portuguese, and translates literally as 'for the Englishman to see' but actually means 'nothing you need to worry about; only an Englishman would bother about this'. Many explanations are offered for the origin of this expression, but one of the most convincing is the Brazilian response to the statutes of the Lei Feijó.[27] Although nominally illegal, the trade in slaves to Brazil actually rose, despite the efforts of the British Navy to stop it, until a peak of 60,000 was reached in 1848.[28]

On 1 January 1844 the British Consul in Recife, H. Augustus Cowper, (Consul at Pernambuco from 1841 to 1861), wrote to the Earl of Aberdeen (British Foreign Secretary between 1841 and 1846) to relate how 1,115 slaves had been landed in Pernambuco during the previous year, a number which represented a decrease. He put this down to the attractions of the slave market in Rio de Janeiro while the British squadron was away further south, in the River Plate, and to the fact that slave-owners paid in cash in Rio de Janeiro but not in Recife. "It is this which makes Rio de Janeiro the desired resort, the *el dorado* of the slave-trader; he lands his slaves, receives his dollars, and returns to the African coast for more victims." This was also the year that Britain and Brazil failed to renew the terms of the 1810 treaty. Instead, Brazil introduced legislation in August 1844 that became known as the Alves Branco Tariff, after the Minister of the Treasury. Import duties were introduced on around 3,000 products, ranging from 20 percent to 60 percent.

In March 1845, Brazil informed Britain that the conventions regarding slavery signed in 1817 and 1826 were no longer applicable. Britain's response was the Slave Trade Suppression Act of 1845 (commonly known as the Aberdeen Act); a response both to the Brazilian stance on slavery and to the protectionist nature of the Alves Branco Tariff. This Act gave the Royal Navy authority to stop and search any Brazilian ship suspected of being a slave ship on the high seas, and to arrest slave traders caught on these ships. The Act also stipulated that arrested slave traders could be tried in British courts. The Aberdeen Bill served to exacerbate the problem - Brazil was embittered by Britain's attempts to abolish the transatlantic trade in slaves, given that the 1817 and 1826 conventions had lapsed, and were particularly chagrined by the right to stop and seize Brazilian ships; actions which they argued were now illegal between nations at peace with each other. Undeterred, British cruisers began to seize ships carrying the Brazilian flag.

The Act had little effect, and in exasperation, in June 1850, the British government authorised its cruisers to enter Brazilian ports to seize any ship that was being prepared for the slave trade. This pressure finally paid off, and by Lei no. 581 of 4 September 1850, Brazil finally determined that slaves would no longer be imported into Brazil. This is known as the Eusébio de Queirós Law, and Article 3 stipulated that the owner, the captain or master, and the pilot and the quartermaster of the ship could be prosecuted for illegally importing slaves, and the crew and those helping disembark slaves on Brazilian territory were guilty as accomplices. This had an immediate effect; only around 3,000 slaves were imported into Brazil in 1851. While there was sporadic contraband in slaves, often to bays and inlets away from the main ports of Brazil, the main consequence was an increase in the internal traffic in slaves, mainly shipped from the northeast to the southern provinces, but this too led to strong objections by the British government. Consul Cowper in Pernambuco wrote to the Foreign Office on 9 April 1860 to report that: "Coasting Slave Trade from the north to the south of this empire greatly increased with the cessation of the foreign trade," and that the cost of labour had risen as a result.

Slave labour continued within Brazil, quite legally, but the writing was on the wall and the first abolitionist law was passed in September 1871. This Lei no. 2040, known as the *Lei do Ventre Livre* (the Free Womb Law), was signed by Princesa Isabel in the name of the Emperor Dom Pedro II, and legislated that all babies born of slaves from that date onwards were considered to be born free. The fight to end slavery in Brazil continued into the 1880s, and key to understanding how the battle was finally won is the relationship between Joaquim Nabuco, the leading Brazilian abolitionist, and the Anti-Slavery Society in London. Joaquim Nabuco was born in Recife and he founded the Brazilian Anti-Slavery Society, and contributed a great deal to the final abolition passed in 1888.[29]

The dramatic reduction in the number of slaves arriving on Brazilian shores after 1850 had the effect of injecting capital into the internal market; the money tied up hitherto in the lucrative slave trade was now available to support productive activity within the country, and to invest in railway construction. At the same time, the abolition of the Atlantic slave trade also posed two urgent questions for sugar and coffee planters in Brazil - where to find alternative sources of labour when the export of agricultural products was growing, and how to respond to the now anticipated abolition of slavery within Brazil. However, the immediate worry for planters was the exponential rise in the price charged for slaves in Brazil.

Undoubtedly, the measure brought about significant changes that were beneficial to Brazil's economy.

> To the extent that the area worked by slaves was reduced, this freed up the use of a free labour force, including the foreign hands who came, let's say, to make up for the burden of slave work and the deficiency of free labour at the national level. This transition from servile work to free labour had a very sensible repercussion on our economy because, with this, we had the introduction and development of capitalism in Brazil, inasmuch as hitherto our economic, political and social landscape was one that came from the colonial period." (Apratto Tenório).[30]

Machinery began to be introduced to work the land, especially for the cultivation of coffee; urban centres expanded; and a stream of immigrants began to arrive in Brazil - although these changes were felt less intensely in the north east of Brazil, where the rural aristocracy, principally the sugar cane landowners, held the power. Nevertheless, even these sugar estate barons realised that change was in the air and regarded investment in railway building as a means to counteract the negative consequences, for them, of the curtailing of the overseas slave trade. In her working paper on *The 'labour question' in nineteenth century Brazil: Railways, export agriculture and labour scarcity*, Lucia Lamounier emphasises the significant roles played by the new railways:

> Firstly, railways eased the pressures of increasing labour demand. They permitted the re-location of thousands of workers, previously engaged in backward systems of transport, to other activities within the export agriculture sector. Secondly, by promoting the development of capitalism, railways aided directly and indirectly the formation of free labour relations.[31]

And slavery was incompatible with capitalism. Nevertheless, it must be borne in mind that until the final abolition of slavery inside Brazil in 1888, the opening of railways into the sugar-producing regions of the interior actually helped maintain slavery as an institution, since slaves could still work legally on the plantations.

Brazil badly wanted to modernise but did not have the capital, nor the know-how. The equation was now established: Brazil needed foreign capital and the fruits of the industrial revolution, and Britain led the world at that time in investment overseas and industrialisation. At this time, in the middle of the nineteenth century, annual imports into Brazil from Britain already accounted for roughly 50 percent of imports from all countries together, and Britain was the third export market for Brazilian produce, losing only to the United States and Germany. By 1860, around one third of British exports to Latin America were arriving in Brazil - a share that rose to over 37 percent in 1880.[32] Regarding foreign investment in Brazil, nearly 94 percent of the capital came from Britain in the period 1860 to 1875, and by the end of 1880 British investment in Brazil totalled nearly 39 million pounds sterling, massively more than any other country.[33] Of a total of forty-six foreign companies in Brazil in the period 1876 to 1885, thirty-five were British, and accounted for nearly 86 percent of the total foreign investment in the country. Investment in railways alone in Brazil made up 60 percent of the capital invested in the period 1876 to 1885. The British stake in Brazil continued strong into the next century, although it tapered off to around 73 percent of total foreign investment by 1905, and 53 percent just prior to the start of The First World War (with The United States beginning to make an appearance at 20 percent of the total).

British investments in Brazil were of two kinds: loans to the government, and the founding of joint-stock companies; that is, business entities with shareholders. The bank of N. M. Rothschild & Son in London was the major player in finance, and organised no fewer than twenty-eight bond issues on behalf of the Brazilian government in the period to 1914. In fact, in recognition of this bank's early confidence in Brazil, the bank was appointed the sole agent and banker for the Brazilian government in the United Kingdom in 1855. Many of these loans provided the finance to build the country's developing railway network. Such was the near stranglehold on foreign commerce in Brazil that in 1859 the Brazilian Minister in London wrote:

> The commerce between the two countries is driven by English capital, in English ships and by English employees, in English firms. The profits [...], the interest paid on capital [...], the payment of insurance premiums, the commissions and the dividends derived from the financial operations, everything is adduced to the pocket of the English.[34]

It was in this economic climate, following the abolition of the transatlantic slave trade, that the next major legislation affecting railway investment was passed in June 1852. This was Lei no. 641, and was specifically inspired by a desire to attract capital from Britain. The imperial government maintained features of the 1835 law, and, while less absurdly ambitious, it expanded on the offer, with the aim of jump-starting railway construction as the means to achieving national integration. In general terms, the law offered privileges, exemptions, and guarantees to attract capitalists, giving priority to lines that would link the Court in Rio de Janeiro with the provinces of São Paulo and Minas Gerais. It is important to point out that government subsidies for railway building were common in many countries in the nineteenth century and the guarantee of minimum dividend returns on the capital invested was not unique to Brazil. What was unique in the case of Brazil was the promise of a generous privilege zone - no other railway line would be permitted within five leagues (approximately thirty kilometres) on either side of the railway.

A key difference for investors, when compared with the *Lei Feijó* of 1835, was that the period during which the government guarantee of privilege applied was extended from forty to ninety years. The clauses relating to the rights to import matériel; to the handover for free of state-owned land; to the expropriation of privately-owned land "that is necessary for the bed of the railway, stations, warehouses and other adjacent works"— all of this was kept and amplified. The tariffs charged would be decided by the government in consultation with the concessionaires. However, the really crucial point that excited the capitalists in Britain was the guarantee of 5 percent in interest (the dividend) on the capital invested, paid in gold in London. Since Russia and Italy at that time offered the same 5 percent it was necessary for the Province of Pernambuco - the first province to actively pursue railway investment under this new law - to offer an additional 2 percent. This quota was never in fact paid by the province; Pernambuco defaulted and the imperial Ministry of Finance had to assume the full 7 percent. This initiative was followed by the provinces of Bahia, Rio de Janeiro, and São Paulo, and 7 percent became the norm in the late 1850s and 1860s. The prospect of earning dividends at this level on investment proved sufficient in attracting foreign investors. This law "threw open the doors to foreign investors, offering them the lion's share in these undertakings, with irresistible favours",[35] although it should be borne in mind that Brazilian capitalists were also attracted by this safe return on capital invested.

In general terms, this is how it worked:

> The guarantee arrangement with each railway set a minimum dividend rate on an agreed value of the firm's capital. When the railway's net earnings failed to attain the prescribed level, the government aided the company by paying to it the difference between its profits and the legislated rate of return. When the company achieved net earnings in excess of the prescribed dividend level by a sufficient margin, the additional profits were divided with the government in order to reimburse any guarantee payments. (William Summerhill).[36]

This proved to be polemical at the time, and it still is the subject of debate among historians and economists. For example, the historian Rory Miller points out that:

> There were several disadvantages in the guarantee system. It promoted careless and wasteful construction and management, especially as few governments had the expertise to control the companies firmly. Moreover, the combination of political pressure and investor mania in a boom meant that governments frequently approved guarantees without considering the financial consequences.[37]

Nevertheless, the fact remains that this policy did attract investment in railway construction that the country had failed to obtain previously; there really was only one choice - railways could only be built in this early period with foreign capital and foreign expertise, or they would not be built at all. The Pernambuco Provincial President, in his annual report for 1855, saw only a gain, in mitigating against: "the great danger that has always threatened the [Brazilian] Empire [that] was the spirit of separation of its provinces that are not linked by very strong commercial relations and consequently by frequency of communications and solidarity of interests".

And there was more to the law to catch the eye of British investors; the question of slavery was deliberately addressed, which was still legal within Brazil at that time, and remained so during the following four decades. Article 1 paragraph 9 was almost certainly drawn up to make railway concessions more attractive to the British, although it also had effect of appeasing the sugar planters who would not have to compete with the railway companies for increasingly scarce and expensive slave labour. The law stated that "The company will be obliged not to possess slaves, [and] not to employ in the business of construction and funding of the railway other than free people." This led to the most significant social contribution of the construction by the British of railways in Brazil, and the effect was especially felt in the slave-dependent sugar producing regions of the north east of the country. But this effect was not immediate, since there was no restriction on the employment of slaves in agriculture - the sugar oligarchs needed to be placated - and slavery continued despite the abolition of the international trade and the moratorium on slave use on the railways.

Josemir Camilo de Melo estimates that in 1850 there were 154,000 slaves in the province of Pernambuco, representing 21 percent of the total population, and he shows that slave numbers in Pernambuco actually increased to 250,000 in 1867, representing 25 percent of the population.[38] Significantly, this number had fallen to 41,000 slaves by 1887. There was a similar rise and fall in numbers in the neighbouring province of Paraíba. While it is true that this fall-off in numbers derived from the many slaves who were sold to work on the coffee plantations in the south of Brazil, and it is also true that maintaining a large number of slaves on the sugar plantations was becoming progressively more expensive, it is also beyond dispute that this railway law of 1852 set the new trend, of a free and salaried work market, with foreign workers and engineers leading by example. Before slavery was finally abolished within Brazil, in 1888, there were four railways operating in just the province of Pernambuco - all destined in time to form part of the Great Western of Brazil railway network.

Not that the British contractors were always conscientious on this matter, since it appears that they were willing to turn a blind eye to slaves being used on the railway. The *Diário de Pernambuco* carried this announcement on 6 July of 1857, when the British owned Recife and São Francisco Railway was being built:

> Anyone who may have slaves and wishes to rent them to work on the railway, paying [one] mil-réis per day, or even free men who wish to submit, direct themselves to Rua Estreita do Rosário, n° 25. (translation).[39]

The explanation may be that there was a loophole in the law, in that those sub-contracted by the main contractor were not obliged to adhere to the prohibition. H. Augustus Cowper, British Consul in Pernambuco, made sure that this news got back to Britain. On 15 April 1856, Cowper wrote to George Villiers, 4th Earl of Clarendon and Secretary of State for Foreign Affairs in the government of Lord Aberdeen, to complain that:

> One of the conditions of the Imperial concession [for the Recife and São Francisco Railway] was that none but free people should be employed by the Company, and the prospectus [...] holds this fact out as an inducement to the people of England to embark their capital in the undertaking. I find, however, that the contractors do not intend to carry out this arrangement, and contend that they may employ slaves indirectly, without infringing it; thus, if they employ a sub-contractor, being a free man, to construct any portion of the road, and he does so by slave labour, no breach of engagement can be charged against them. This course of argument appears to me to be an evasion of their contract with the Imperial and Provincial Governments upon the one hand, and with the British public upon the other, and is not supported, as they contend, by Article 12 [of the concession] or even by the plea of necessity, for his Excellency the President [of the province of Pernambuco] informed me yesterday that he had offered and could obtain for them 1,000 Indians whenever they required them.[40]

Villiers forwarded this letter to the directors of the Recife and São Francisco Railway, and the company secretary, W. H. Bellamy, responded on 17 June 1856:

> I am desired by the Board [of RSF directors] to state that they not heard of, nor do they believe the existence of, any such intention on the part of the contractor [George Furness], who is an Englishman of undoubted character as well as respectability. [...] The directors would respectfully and earnestly request of Lord Clarendon not to give encouragement or credence to every rumour that may reach the Foreign Office from Pernambuco [against an enterprise which promotes] a field opened for the employment of free labour in lieu of that until recently supplied by the Slave Trade.

W. H. Bellamy enclosed an extract from a speech made by the chairman of the Recife and São Francisco Railway on 2 April 1856, which (haughtily):

> [...] explains our motives for having become connected with a railway in a country where slavery exists, believing that the introduction of railways is one of the best and most efficient means that can be employed, not only for developing the resources and capabilities of a country, but for promoting civilization and ameliorating and improving the condition of the people.

This was clearly a tricky and sensitive issue for the company, especially when some of the firm's own directors were supporters of the anti-slavery movement, and the exchange occurred at a time when Consul Cowper reported on 30 June 1856 that African slaves were being sold in Pernambuco for between 700$000 réis and 800$000 réis, a price that Cowper calculated at between around £80 and £91 each. The internal trade in slaves was still buoyant. Henry Krause, the acting vice consul in Paraíba, noted that in that month: "A number of slaves of all descriptions have been purchased by agents from Rio de Janeiro and sent coastways in the Brazilian steamers, paying a provincial tax of 100$000 réis a head."

Consul Cowper was far from satisfied with Bellamy's explanations and wrote to Villiers on 16 August 1856 to say that "The tenour of this letter greatly surprised me" since the railway concession given to the de Mornay brothers clearly stated that slaves were not to be employed. But when two men arrived from England to start work on the line, "Messrs. Gardner and Lowden", Cowper had asked them on whose authority slaves were being used, "and they replied, by Mr Furniss [sic], who had the right of doing so if the slaves were indirectly engaged." Following this reported conversation, Alfred de Mornay (one of the concessionaires) and George Furness arrived in Recife and "upon speaking to these gentlemen respecting the employment of slaves, the question assumed a more decided and, I may say, conflicting character, by Mr. de Mornay declaring that the contractor had the right of employing slaves directly or indirectly." Cowper's letter ended emphatically with his statement that "It is very far from my intention to prejudice Her Majesty's Government against the undertaking; on the contrary, it has my best wishes for its success, and, whenever it may require it, shall have my hearty co-operation."

The letter was accompanied by a copy of Cowper's letter dated 1 August to Mr. Lowden asking him bluntly if "during the period of your administration of the railway works here, you employed slaves, directly or indirectly, upon them; and, if so, whether you did so upon your own responsibility, or in consequence of orders received from Mr. Furniss." Mr Lowden's reply (copied with this letter) was dramatic: "It was in consequence of instructions I received from Mr. G. Furniss that I employed slaves in the construction of the railway. The letters containing such instructions I am unable to produce, owing to Mr. G. Furniss having surreptitiously obtained possession of them, but in one the words were these, 'Tell Lowden to go down with De Mornay and make arrangements at Villa de Cabo with the slave-owners for the employment of a thousand of their slaves, for De Mornay tells me that there are plenty to be got there'." Lowden explained that this letter was from George Furness to his agent in Recife, R. B. Gardner, and dated 8 March 1853.

This led the Earl of Shelburne (Under-Secretary of State for Foreign Affairs) to write to Bellamy on 7 November reminding him of the responsibilities of the Recife and São Francisco Railway in not using slaves. Mr Bellamy's response dated 12 November summarised the company directors' discussion with George Furness, who happened to be in England, and the latter "informs the Board that the statement is not true; he denies ever having given any authority, either in writing or by word of mouth, for the engagement or employment of slaves upon the works. That Mr. Gardner and Mr. Lowden went out to the Brazils in his employ, but left it in May last, having acted for him for three months only." The letter then swings a punch at consul Cowper: "The Board learn with some surprise, from Mr. Furness, that a heavy Consular tax, per head, is levied [...] by Mr. Cowper upon the introduction of labourers from this country [from Britain]." Bellamy then closed by saying that the board: "trust that Lord Clarendon will give direction that this impost shall be abandoned; and will point out to Mr. Cowper the inadvertence into which he has been led in communicating to his Lordship information so erroneous, and so calculated to leave upon his mind impressions unfavourable to this Company."

The Earl of Shelburne then wrote to Bellamy on behalf of Lord Clarendon on 18 November to draw attention to Lowden's allegations and give the Foreign Office view that "it would appear that the charge against the agents of the Company of having employed slave-labour is not without foundation." Shelburne added that Cowper would be asked to explain why a consular tax was being levied on labourers coming into Brazil from Britain. In his response, of 2 December, Bellamy softened his tone - "The Board of Directors have not failed to give to this communication all the attention that it deserves" - and offered explanations "which the Board are of opinion will completely dispose of the case." Bellamy continued by citing the 'tone and spirit' of Lowden's letter which "indicate the existence of unfriendly, if not vindictive, feelings towards his late employer;" dismissed the allegations as untruths; and pointed out that taking possession of the correspondence between Furness and Lowden was a matter of company policy. Shelburne replied (on 5 December) to say, sweetly, that "the production of the letter in question would be the most satisfactory mode of attesting the accuracy of Mr. Lowden's statement."

This infuriated the company, and Bellamy wrote back immediately (on 6 December 1856) to say: "The result of [the board's] inquiries was communicated to your Lordship in my last letter. They decline further to pursue that part of the subject to which your Lordship's letter of to-day refers," claiming that the company had no right to demand personal papers from their contractor, and that even if they had the right the company would do nothing "which might have the effect of bringing [Furness] into collision with a person who is no longer in his service, and who is evidently influenced by no friendly feelings towards him."

The consul was equally incensed and wrote to the Foreign Office on 6 January the following year to say that "This correspondence is very little creditable either to the company or to the contractor." Consul Cowper thought that the suggestion that the letter from Furness to Lowden be produced was a reasonable request, and that the company's refusal led him to the obvious conclusion "that Mr. Lowden's statement would have been confirmed, and not refuted, by the production." In a more conciliatory tone,

Cowper continued: "I must, nevertheless, in justice to the contractor repeat that I believe no slaves to have been employed upon the works since May last, when Mr. Bayliss took charge of them; and, moreover, that it is his desire to finish the whole undertaking, if possible, by free labour."

> It is, however, my duty to state to your Lordship my fear that the Article no. 12, obtained by Mr. De Mornay subsequent to the original Concession, does give the Company (strictly speaking, the contractor) the right of employing slaves; and that, consequently, it would be no breach of their engagements to the Imperial Government, or any infraction of the laws of England, were they to do so: but that which astonishes me is that a Company possessing a privilege of this sort should have recommended itself to the notice of the British public by an assertion at variance with this fact.

Cowper then closed by suggesting that the Foreign Office might approach the imperial government for their views on the matter. In the meantime, not content with letting the matter rest, Cowper then recounted this exchange of views to the President of the Province of Pernambuco, who "appeared to be much surprised at this statement: he assured me that nothing could be further from the intention of the Imperial Government than to permit the employment of slaves even in the most indirect manner," and asked Cowper to take up any new allegation relating to the employment of slaves directly with him. This seemed to satisfy Cowper, and Clarendon at the Foreign Office, and there the matter rested.

A few years later, the American Civil War (1861-1865) showed the plantation oligarchy that there was no long-term future in slavery, and by 1870 the economic centre of gravity had anyway shifted from the north-east to the south and south-east of Brazil, along with the use of slaves - at that time around two-thirds of all the slaves in Brazil were concentrated in the provinces of Minas, São Paulo, Rio de Janeiro, and Rio Grande do Sul, and the economic importance of slavery in the north-east was diminished. The north-east was in a period of transition.

Returning to the 26 June 1852 law, the third article stipulated that 'Thomaz Cocharane' [sic] would be reimbursed for the fine he had apparently paid, together with interest at 6 percent per year, for failing to build his railway line from Rio de Janeiro to São Paulo. Another visionary, but with a greater grasp of business dealings and, most importantly, independent access to investment funds, was the Brazilian Irineu Evangelista de Souza, who later became Baron (in April 1854) and then Viscount of Mauá (1874) in recognition of his railway initiative and other business investments. He managed to build a short railway - the first railway to operate in Brazil - without benefit of the 1852 law. On 27 April 1852, two months before the new imperial legislation was passed, Mauá negotiated a contract with the Provincial Assembly of Rio de Janeiro, which was subsequently approved by the Assembly by Provincial Law no. 602 on 23 September 1852, and work soon started on a sixteen kilometre line from port of Mauá on the Bay of Guanabara to Raiz da Serra of Petrópolis. All he asked for was a privilege zone that prohibited the construction of any parallel railway; he did not request a guarantee of interest on the capital expended. Quite possibly this was due to Mauá's friendship with Thomas Cochrane, and a desire not to disturb the still ongoing negotiations over a guarantee of interest for Cochrane's project, but more probably this derived from his great self-confidence in getting the job done without any outside favours. After all, "Mauá was pioneering on a vast scale. He was the greatest single entrepreneur on the Atlantic coast of South America for a quarter of a century."[41]

SUPPLEMENT, JUNE 24, 1854.] THE ILLUSTRATED LONDON NEWS 595

OPENING OF THE IMPERIAL PETROPOLIS RAILWAY, BRAZIL.—BENEDICTION OF THE LOCOMOTIVES.

"Opening of The Imperial Petropolis Railway, Brazil — Benediction of the locomotives", *The Illustrated London News*, **24 June 1854.**

Author's Collection

To carry out his project for the railway, which was complemented by a steamship line from the port of Estrela to the city of Rio de Janeiro, Mauá founded the Imperial Company of Steam Navigation and Railway of Petrópolis, which enjoyed a ten year period of privilege for the steamship arm of his company, conditional on the railway being built. Mauá knew that there was little economic importance to the project - receipts were low, and the railway actually proved popular as a kind of tourist outing. But he expected that the Emperor would look favourably on the idea, since Petrópolis was a favourite place for the Emperor, and currying favour with the court could only help with Mauá's many other commercial interests, which included his very own bank. Dom Pedro II had decreed the construction of a summer palace in Petrópolis, which was finished in 1847, and still stands today. The sixteen kilometre railway was opened to traffic on 30 April 1854, with the first steam locomotive to run on rails in Brazil - the BARONESA, in homage to his wife - and, naturally, the inauguration was blessed with the attendance of Emperor Dom Pedro II.[42]

The second railway to be constructed in Brazil was the Recife and São Francisco Railway Company, in Pernambuco in the north east of Brazil - the first to be backed by the articles of concession in the 1852 law; the first undertaken by a British company; and the first railway in Brazil of economic importance. Mauá invested money in this project, but British investors owned the greater part of the shares. This company was organised in London in 1853, but only started operating in February 1858, in part delayed by the effect of the Crimean War of 1854 to 1856, which made capital difficult to access in the London money market.

This railway was clearly influenced by the imperial dream of integrating the provinces by means of railway communications. In this case, this resulted from an obsession in the

"Commencement of the Pernambuco Railway, on the Island of Nogueira," *Illustrated London News*, 3 November 1855. Inauguration of the Recife and São Francisco Railway. *Author's Collection*

1850s to link the middle reaches of the great São Francisco River, above the impassable cataracts of Paulo Afonso, with the coast. There was rivalry between the provinces of Bahia and Pernambuco to reach this goal first, with the result that two railways started out with this objective in mind: the Recife and São Francisco Railway in Pernambuco, and the Bahia and São Francisco Railway in Bahia (the fourth railway to be built in Brazil). Neither company ever reached the river. The third railway to be constructed in Brazil was the Dom Pedro II Railway, renamed the Central Railway of Brazil after the fall of the monarchy, the first section of which opened on 29 March 1858.

Railway building in the following decade was hindered by the government's massive debts, mainly due to Brazil entering the war against Paraguay from December 1864 to March 1870 as a member of the triple alliance of Brazil, Argentina, and Uruguay. Debts accumulated, exacerbated by the government's efforts to build its own railways and the need to cover the guaranteed interest payments on the foreign-owned lines, most of which never made profits sufficient to meet the guaranteed 7 percent dividend on capital expenditure. Brazil only began to recover financially in 1873, although the country remained in deficit until 1880.

At the same time, the war in Paraguay did have a salutary effect; it served to demonstrate just how vulnerable the Empire was in the south - Paraguay had invaded the province of Mato Grosso in December 1864 and Rio Grande do Sul in early 1865, and initial attempts to dislodge the Paraguayan army were dogged by disorganization and communication difficulties. Realising that there was a pressing need for a cogent national transport policy, and perceiving that railways - the new wonder of the age - could have a significant role to play, the Brazilian government began to take on a larger presence in the management of railways in the 1870s decade. This expressed itself through imperial government pressure on the existing railway companies to build faster - inducements were offered for those who completed before the agreed inauguration date - and lobbying for branches to be opened leading from the initially contracted main lines. Throughout this period, to the end of the Empire in 1889, the commercial and financial relations that held between Brazil and Britain were consolidated, and Britain continued to be the main commercial partner for Brazil.

The next important piece of legislation affecting railway construction was passed on 24 September 1873, when the government felt that financial recovery after the war with Paraguay was imminent, and decided to take on an even greater burden of debt to pursue its policy of national development based on railway construction. This new law altered certain features of the 1852 law, which had in fact achieved remarkably little in these two decades. Only five companies had been established and only around 750 kilometres of track had been laid. This contrasted unfavourably with railway investment elsewhere in Latin America. "It was recognized that a fundamental liberalization of guarantee arrangements was necessary if the 1852 decree was to fulfil initial expectations and draw private capital into the sector." (Colin Lewis).[43]

The 1873 law (imperial decree no. 2,450) was aimed specifically at railways in the provinces that could improve communications between the centres of agricultural production in the interior and the exporting ports, and now included provision for central government finance for top-up provincial guarantees. The imperial government was also authorised to offer a subsidy for each kilometre constructed and an annual guarantee of interest (not to exceed 7 percent of the agreed capital expenditure) for a period of thirty years. However, prospective candidates now needed to demonstrate by means of a detailed business plan that their company could achieve a net return of at least 4 percent. At times this had the effect of companies making the line as long as possible, avoiding even the slightest gradients. Nevertheless, this law was an important watershed: 90 percent of railway expansion in the imperial period occurred during the railway boom of 1874 to 1889, with 9,583 kilometres constructed in Brazil in this period - a yearly average of 553 kilometres compared to just 63 kilometres in the years 1854 to 1874.[44]

But first the demarcation between the jurisdictions of national (imperial) and local (provincial) initiatives needed to be attended to, and by decree no. 5,561 of 28 February 1874, the imperial government sought to regulate the laws of 1852 and 1873. Article 1 ascribed to the central government the authority to award concessions for railway construction where the line would link two or more provinces, or the court (in Rio de Janeiro) with the provinces, or the Brazilian Empire with adjoining countries. This also applied in those cases where the proposed railway was an extension of a line already belonging to, or already sanctioned by, the state. In addition, the state could grant a concession where the line was in the national interest, even if lying within the confines of a province. This provision was used for the central government's construction of the Sobral Railway of 129 kilometres and the taking over by the state of the Baturité Railway of 110 kilometres, both sited in the northern province of Ceará. The main justification in this case was the welfare of the population severely affected by a prolonged drought. Article 2 stated that the provincial governments could give concessions for railway construction where the line in question did not go beyond the borders of the given province, unless the line intruded into the zone of thirty kilometres on either side of a line belonging to the central government which had already been established or started.

Among the main beneficiaries of this law were railways in the north-east of Brazil that later amalgamated to form the Great Western of Brazil network, and will be described in detail in the following chapters. By imperial decree no. 5,608 of 25 April 1874, the government authorised the construction of the Conde d'Eu Railway in the province of Paraíba (then spelt Parahyba, and also known as Parahyba do Norte). This was a sop to the Brazilian emperor, since the reference would have meant little to investors in Britain. The French-born Gastão de Orléans, Conde d'Eu, had become imperial prince consort on marrying Dom Pedro II's daughter, D. Isabel Cristina Leopoldina de Bragança, in 1864. This railway set out to link the provincial capital city of Paraíba (which changed its name to João Pessoa in 1930) with Mulunga in the interior, and enjoyed the backing of 7 percent annual interest over a period of thirty years. On 20 February 1875, decree no. 5,877 authorised the construction of the grandly named Imperial Brazilian Natal

The second locomotive to operate in Brazil, on the Recife and São Francisco Railway, photographed in 1858.
*Augusto Stahl,
Author's Collection*

and Nova Cruz Railway in the province of Rio Grande do Norte, which was completed in 1882. Of great importance to this history, decree no. 6,746 of 17 November 1877 gave a concession for the construction of a 92 kilometre line baptised deliberately with the grandiose name of the Great Western of Brazil Railway, from Recife to Limoeiro in the province of Pernambuco. Another railway destined to become part of the Great Western's network was the Paulo Afonso Railway (often spelt Paulo Affonso in older documents) constructed in response to the great drought of 1877 to 1879, which was started in 1881 and completed two years later.

Still intent on promoting railway building in the shortest possible time, and following advice from the Brazilian Embassy in London, the imperial government passed further legislation on 10 August 1878 (decree no. 6,995). This law answered a key concern of foreign investors - security against currency exchange depreciation - by instituting a special exchange rate of 27d (pence) per 1$000 (one mil-réis) for guarantee payments. This decree made it easier for railway companies to expropriate private land, and offered too the right to "the wood and other materials existing" and to mining within the privilege zone. This zone, however, was now limited to twenty kilometres on either side of the line. This led to the issuing of imperial decree no. 7,517 on 18 October 1879 that authorised two Brazilian businessmen to undertake surveys for railway of one metre gauge from Maceió to Vila da Imperatriz in the province of Alagoas. This concession was acquired in August 1881 (decree no. 8,223) by The Alagoas Railway Company Limited, organised in London for this express purpose, and destined too to be swallowed early in the next century by the Great Western of Brazil Railway.

These railways in the four north-eastern provinces were predicated especially on the sugar plantations, and this poses an interesting question - why would British capital flow into railway building in this region when sugar from this region was no longer the profitable activity of older times. The answer seems to be that British capital responded to the generous terms offered by the imperial and provincial governments - the opportunity to make money at no risk was too tempting - and it was not an altruistic gesture to help with Brazilian agricultural development, nor even to benefit British companies in the international sugar trade. In order to understand this, and the importance of the railway lines on sugar plantations that interfaced with the Great Western of Brazil Railway and its ancestors, we need to appreciate just how important the sugar industry was to the economy of north-east Brazil.

Sugar planting was introduced into Brazil in the early sixteenth century, and over time many *engenhos de açucar* were established. The *engenho* consisted of a rudimentary sugar producing plant typically worked by slaves and surrounded by sugar plantations. The first kind of *engenho* was known as an *engenho banguê*, which used a pre-industrial process that produced dark brown sugar, known as *mascavo* in Brazil. Little changed over several centuries, but the sugar industry in Brazil faced a crisis in the second half of the nineteenth century, threatened by the challenge of Europe turning towards beet sugar - by 1880 sugar beet had replaced sugar cane as the main source of sugar on continental Europe. Companies in Europe also offered a better product to the consumer, and there was increasing competition too from sugar produced in the Caribbean. The immediate answer for the sugar-based economy of the north-east of Brazil was to mechanise production at the *engenhos*, often introducing machinery to produce crystal sugar, and to promote railway construction to ease transport to the coast. In the decade of the 1870s, a transformation took place in sugar production at the national level, but especially affecting Pernambuco, which at that time was the main provincial producer of sugar. The *engenhos banguês* were increasingly obsolete, and in time were driven out of business, to be replaced by *usinas* from around 1875 - larger scale enterprises that had more capital and land, and fused agricultural and industrial activity by milling sugar cane from their own supply and other nearby producers. The crisis was fuelled too by the siphoning away of slave labour to the more profitable coffee sector in the south.

Under pressure from the provincial assemblies in the north-east, the government became convinced that the only way forward was to promote larger and more efficient *usinas*, known as *usinas centrais*. With this in mind, decree no. 2,687 was passed on 6 November 1875 that "authorised the Government to guarantee interest of 7% per annum, up to a capital invested of thirty thousand contos de réis[45] to Companies that come forward to establish central *usinas* to manufacture sugar cane, by means of the employment of modern or improved machines and processes" (translation). Perhaps with an eye on British investors, these concessions came with the proviso that slave labour was not to be used in the construction or operation of the factory. A central *usina* generally did not possess its own lands; the idea was to erect a processing factory that would take in the sugar production of several *engenhos* and *usinas* in the neighbouring district. A later decree (no. 8,357, of 24 December 1881) set out, belatedly, to tie the guarantee payments to actual production, and to allow the guarantee to cover the costs of building railway systems. The decree was shortly afterwards modified to build in safeguards that allowed the government to suspend guarantee interest payments permanently, or to suspend them temporarily, when a company failed to meet its commitments.

The first *usinas centrais* began to emerge in Pernambuco in 1884, and in fact this province received over one quarter of the government finance available under this scheme, which never worked properly, and guarantees were removed from 1891 and the central *usinas* began to disappear. Nevertheless, the greater concentration of land ownership that resulted from this transformation led the owners to invest in railway transport as a means of getting their product to the factories. Tagore Siqueira's study of the first railways in the north-east of Brazil shows that "The introduction of the *usinas* in the last decades of the nineteenth century led to a significant expansion of privately-owned railways, which came to represent, in certain periods, more than 50 percent of the railway network in Pernambuco." Siqueira shows that by 1899, sixteen *usinas* possessed 222 kilometres of railway, which represented 44 percent of the state's network.

The picture of railway construction in north-eastern Brazil in 1883, covering lines that either belonged to or would be run by the Great Western of Brazil Railway from early in the next century, can be summarised as follows:[46]

1	2	3	4	5	6	7	8	9
Recife & São Francisco	London	7 Aug 1852	13 Oct 1853	13 Oct 1853	124	---	7 Sept 1855	8 Feb 1858
Great Western	London	5 Jun 1868	30 Oct 1875	30 Oct 1875	96.300	46	25 Mar 1879	24 Oct 1881
Conde d'Eu	London	15 Dec 1871	12 July 1876	12 Sept 1877	99.784	22.500	9 Aug 1880	7 Sept 1883
Imp. Braz. Natal & Nova Cruz	London	2 Jul 1874	6 Apr 1878	---	121	---	1 Oct 1878	28 Sept 1881
Alagoas Rly. Company	London	12 Nov 1880	12 Nov 1880	12 Nov 1880	---	88	25 Mar 1882	---
Recife to Caruaru	State owned	19 Oct 1978	28 Feb 1880	---	---	83.128	26 Oct 1881	---

Headings: (1) Name of the company. (2) Headquarters. (3) Date of the concession or of the authorisation to begin construction. (4) Date of the approval of plans. (5) Date of the approval of the budget. (6) Total length in kilometres. (7) Total length under construction. (8) inauguration of the line (construction). (9) inauguration of the line to traffic. (*Quadro estatístico da viação fórrea do Imperio do Brasil: Anno de 1883*, 10 May 1884).

This was not a very encouraging state of affairs, and in 1886 (still in imperial times) the interim secretary for state for Agricultural Business, Commerce, and Public Works presented a 'general transport plan' to the General Legislative Assembly.[47] The minister, Rodrigo Augusto da Silva, described the picture of Brazil's railway system when drawn on the map of the Empire as bleak. One of his conclusions related to the north-east:

> If we study [...] the relative positions of the railways of Alagoas, Pernambuco, Parahyba, and Rio Grande do Norte, we see immediately that, since the distances separating one from the other are short, the linking together of all of them will be easy, leading in this way to an improved and very important transport network, covering the four provinces, [which] will generally serve the richest and most productive valleys, and at the same time the [provincial] capitals. (translation).

The minister had consulted with an engineer, and had concluded that in all only around 110 kilometres of additional railway would be needed to connect together the several lines, and with this "relatively small sacrifice" the state would gain a network of 1,023 kilometres, covering the four provinces and their capital cities. He was particularly anxious to fuse the companies operating in Paraíba and Rio Grande do Norte by means of the "suppression of one of the administrations," which would result in "an immediate and appreciable economy," and he also advocated the amalgamation of the Conde d'Eu railway with the Great Western of Brazil line from Recife to Limoeiro. Having made these points, the minister realised that what he was really saying was that all the railways from Alagoas to Rio Grande do Norte needed to be amalgamated.

This analysis was to set the scene for the Great Western of Brazil Railway to take over management from the beginning of the twentieth century of the entire railway network in the north-east of Brazil.

The Great Stronghold Of British Interests In Pernambuco
The British Community In Recife

> In political consequence, with reference to the Portuguese government, Pernambuco holds the third rank amongst the provinces of Brazil; with reference to Great Britain, I know not whether it should not be named first. Its chief exports are cotton and sugar; the former mostly comes to England.
>
> Henry Koster, *Travels in Brazil*[48]

One early British visitor to Recife (also known then as the city of Pernambuco) was Henry Koster, who arrived there in December 1809, having been recommended a stay in the tropics on account of his poor health. Henry Koster published a book in 1816 entitled *Travels in Brazil*, and in his closely observed account of his experiences he describes Recife as "a thriving place, increasing daily in opulence and importance."

The British were quick to respond to the opening of Brazilian ports to British trade in January 1808. Just four months later, the first foreign ship to enter the port of Recife in the then captaincy of Pernambuco arrived on 11 May 1808. This was the ALEXANDER from London, captained by Walter Atkins, and this event heralded the start of a huge and very influential British presence being established in Recife, and further afield in the interior of Pernambuco. This special interest derived in large part from Recife's situation: it has an excellent natural harbour sheltered by the reef from which it takes its name; it is close to the most easterly point of the Americas - Cabo Branco, just to the north of Recife and close to João Pessoa, the capital of Paraíba; and it benefits from the predominantly south-easterly trade winds. All of this made Recife the natural stopping-off port for traffic crossing the Atlantic, including ships making for the Magellan Strait and the western seaboard of the Americas until the opening of the Panama Canal in 1914. The resulting influx of British commercial interests made Recife the natural hub for the railway system run by the Great Western of Brazil Railway Company, and it is crucial for this history to sketch out just how important the British presence was in this captaincy, later a province in imperial Brazil.

As we have seen, the treaties signed in February 1810 between Britain and Portugal, soon after Dom João's ignominious flight to Brazil escorted by the British navy, granted British subjects in Brazil very special rights. Britain could nominate special magistrates to act as 'judges conservators' in Brazil, following the practice that had been adopted in Portugal. British citizens were also granted religious toleration, and the privilege to worship as they pleased at home or in churches and chapels, as long as the latter were constructed to resemble private houses on the outside and no bells were rung. Also, Article XII of the Treaty of Commerce and Navigation sanctioned the British to "bury in places designed for this purpose the subjects of His British Majesty [George III] who should die in territories of His Royal Highness the Prince Regent of Portugal [Dom João]"

Accordingly, negotiations soon took place for the setting up of a British Cemetery in Recife, which was inaugurated in 1814. The land chosen was on the Luis do Rêgo road that linked the cities of Recife and Olinda. The cemetery was extended in 1852, and again in 1873. The gates at the entrance still stand today, manufactured by the Fundição d'Aurora foundry in 1852, and are emblazoned with the words 'BRITISH CEMETERY' and the years '1814' and '1852'. Incidentally, this same British-run foundry also made the gates for the Municipal Cemetery in nearby Olinda, in the same style. Despite the well-meaning promises of the 1810 treaty, in 1813 Viscount Strangford, British minister in Rio de Janeiro from 1808 to 1815, was complaining to the Prince Regent Dom João of the "inconvenience and indecency" of British citizens being buried in the captaincy of Pernambuco on the beaches, along with unbaptised slaves, in contravention of the treaty. Dom João, in turn, instructed Caetano Pinto de Miranda Montenegro, the governor and *capitão general* of Pernambuco to demarcate land for this cemetery, and not only for British subjects who died there, but also for foreigners of other countries who were 'dissidents' - that is, not Catholics. Among the British citizens buried there are Henry Koster, who returned to Recife in 1819 and died there in early 1820, although the exact location of his tomb is unknown, and the first chief engineer to work on the Recife and São Francisco Railway, Michael Borthwick. Previously the resident engineer on the

Gateway to the British Cemetery in Recife.

Author

North and Eastern Railway in Britain, and a friend and colleague of the eminent railway engineer Robert Stephenson, only son of George Stephenson, Michael Borthwick arrived in Recife in 1853, but died there of typhoid fever in 1856.

The British community in Recife then set about building a church, with a special fund started in 1811 destined towards this objective. A chaplain was appointed in 1822, and for the time being services were conducted in a rented building. By 1839 they had finished building the Holy Trinity Church on Rua da Aurora at the side of the Fundição d'Aurora, which was owned by Christopher Starr. This venture was not without its problems. The community was very much aware of the potential hostile response of the authorities and the general public in Recife, and their plan initially was to combine the building of a hospital with a church in order to attract less unwelcome attention. In the event, these concerns had largely evaporated by 1829, and exceptional permission was given in 1835 for the church to be built on a separate site, provided that its design would discretely hide its use behind a faceless façade - the plans described the construction as "a plain Edifice". The foundation stone was laid on 6 March 1838, and building started with the subscription of forty-five British companies and individuals. Oddly enough, the authorities attempted to tax the building because it was not a church, and therefore not exempt, but the community was able to resist this initiative.[49] The church stood on this site for nearly one hundred years, until being demolished in 1938 and making way for the buildings that are found there today, the Edifício Duarte Coelho and the São Luiz cinema. The original iron gate, also manufactured by the Aurora foundry, was re-installed at the entrance of the modern day Anglican Church in Recife.

The community wanted its own hospital, and in 1818 the British Hospital opened in Recife on the Aterro da Boa Vista, which today is the Rua da Imperatriz. This was a four storey house, backed by a pier on the River Capibaribe. On account of the outbreak of yellow fever and the resulting prohibition for hospitals to function in the centre of Recife, the British Hospital moved to a house in the district of Santo Amaro, where it functioned until being closed in 1878. A tombstone in The British Cemetery in Recife reads: "In affectionate remembrance of John Loudon M. D. surgeon R. N. and 16 years surgeon to the British Hospital in Pernambuco who died 23rd. May 1843 aged 49 years."

A soon-to-be-distinguished British visitor to Recife in these early years of the growth of the British community in Recife was Charles Darwin - albeit a very reluctant visitor, since he would have much preferred to be making for home at the close of the five-year-long second voyage of the BEAGLE. Perhaps his bad mood at Captain Fitzroy's unexpected turn to the north-eastern seaboard of Brazil in 1836, and his general homesickness, coloured Darwin's comments on Recife:

> The town is in all parts disgusting, the streets narrow, ill-paved, filthy, the houses very tall & gloomy. There was nothing in the sight, smell or sounds within this large town, which conveyed to me any pleasing impressions. (*Beagle Diary*, 12 August 1836).

But the British had arrived, were determined to stay, and had already established a strong presence by this time. So much so that when the Commercial Association (Chamber of Commerce) of Pernambuco[50] was founded three years after Darwin's visit, in 1839, many British names appeared among the list of the founders and collaborators. These British names included Comber, Hibbert, Saunders (of Saunders Brothers & Company, who prepared an unsuccessful proposal to construct the Conde d'Eu railway in Paraíba in the 1870s), William Smith, and Philip Frith Needham, one of the first presidents of the association, who was elected to this position three times in the years 1865 to 1868 and again in 1872. Philip Needham was also a subscriber to railway companies that later formed part of the Great Western of Brazil network - the Conde d'Eu, for which he became a director, and the Alagoas Railway Company. In fact, this association played an important role in encouraging railway construction in the province - the captaincies became provinces from 1821 - since the members were more inclined to collaborate in these ventures than the sugar plantation owners.

In his book *Ingleses no Brasil* (English in Brazil), the Brazilian sociologist Gilberto Freyre lists twenty important British businesses in Recife that appeared in the *Almanak de Pernambuco* in 1845; names such as Fox Brothers, G. Kenworthy & Company, Wm. E. Smith, and Henry Gibson, at a time when there were just twenty-seven Brazilian businesses, and many fewer commercial enterprises belonging to other nationalities.[51]

Of particular importance to this history of the Great Western of Brazil Railway, the British came to dominate the export of sugar and cotton, the principle agricultural products of Pernambuco and of the adjacent provinces. The firm of Saunders Brothers & Company was prominent in this business, having been established by Charles and Frederick Saunders, "merchants of Liverpool," in association with Philip Frith Needham, their local representative; a partnership that was dissolved in November 1873. Another important sugar exporter was John Harvey Boxwell, who established his company J. H. Boxwell & Company to trade in sugar and cotton. He became the main exporter of cotton and established the first hydraulic baling press in Pernambuco. Boxwell was joined by his cousin Arthur Llewellyn Williams, and from 1892 the company became Boxwell Williams & Company. By the beginning of the twentieth century the firm had become the largest cotton baling company in Brazil. The present-day Williams Shipping Agency traces its history back to this company and has a head office in Recife. Sugar imports into Britain were especially high in the period 1855 to 1889, peaking at £9,152,871 in 1875-1879, but began to decline from 1895 onwards.[52] Not surprisingly, the British stake in the cotton industry led to the import of machinery from Britain, such as the standing steam engines used in the cotton fields manufactured by Rushton & Hornsby in Lincoln.

The British also invested in public utilities in Recife. The Beberibe Water Company caused a sensation when it brought the first piped water to Recife in 1838. The firm lasted until 1912, when it was taken over by the local government, citing the company's poor standards of service, and is the ancestor of the present-day Pernambuco State water company, COMPESA. Important renovations were carried out in the period 1884 to 1887, with major reforms overseen by Oswald Brown, an engineer brought out from London, that substituted the water taken from *açudes* (ponds/lakes) for water taken through underground galleries. In neighbouring Paraíba, the Parahyba Water Company was founded in Manchester in 1898, and lasted under this name until 1906.

The Recife Drainage Company, organised in London in 1868, had the inglorious task of treating sewage for thirty-five years, working in tandem with the water company, and subsidised by the provincial government. This British firm lasted until 1908 when the local government took it over, alleging the poor service offered by the company. One of the managers was John Frazel Mackintoch. "The company encountered special difficulties because Recife was a more traditional city than Rio de Janeiro or São Paulo and it was only the elite who there shared the foreigners' belief in plumbing" (Richard Graham).[53] This firm ended in bankruptcy, according to Alfredo Watts' study of *A Colônia Inglesa em Pernambuco*, due to losses made in currency exchange.[54] At an Extraordinary General Meeting held in December 1908 the shareholders decided "that the company be wound up voluntarily."

A British company, *Feilden Brothers*, was awarded a concession in 1859 to install facilities for the gas illumination of the streets and buildings of Recife, and this ushered in a British firm, the Pernambuco Gas Company, that provided gas until 1895, when the city decided to change to electric lighting. Among the managers of this company were James Craven, Thomas Jones, and Edward Lee.

We have mentioned already the British foundry on Rua da Aurora. This was started by a mechanical engineer named Christopher Starr, who arrived in Recife in 1819 and established a foundry in 1829 in partnership with an Englishman called Harrington. This firm was known as Harrington Starr & Company, and it set out to serve, especially, the sugar and cotton industries. Harrington died in Recife, and Christopher Starr married his widow. The foundry now became known as the Fundição Starr, and later the business was carried on by his sons George and Henry Starr. The success of this company stimulated others to invest in foundries. The main competitor was David William Bowman who established the Fundição Bowman on Rua da Brum in Recife in around 1844. This firm also provided machinery and ironwork for the sugar and cotton industries throughout the northeast of Brazil, and took on other assignments, such as the gates for the central prison in Recife, still visible in what is now the Casa da Cultura. British workers became so numerous that a British Mechanics' Library was opened on Rua da Aurora in 1847 and lasted until at least 1860.

The British were, naturally, also dominant in Recife in the financial sector. The first bank to open its doors to the public, in 1863, was the London & Brazilian Bank. In his study of *A Century of Banking in Latin America*, David Joslin describes how "The office at Recife do Pernambuco was well placed to benefit from British connexions, as British mercantile houses were prominent in exporting sugar and cotton, and an English railway had been built to join the plantations of the interior to the port."[55] This was the Recife and São Francisco Railway. Four years later, in 1867, The English Bank of Rio de Janeiro opened its second branch in Brazil in Recife - "the great stronghold of British interests in Pernambuco"[56] - and in 1894 a branch of the London and River Plate Bank was opened in Recife.

Another sector where the British held sway for many years in Recife related to communications by telegraph. The Barão de Mauá was awarded a concession, and by imperial decree of 18 June 1873 he was permitted to transfer these rights to a firm specially organised for this purpose in London - the Brazilian Submarine Telegraph Company Limited. Cables were laid on the ocean floor from Lisbon to Recife in 1874. Another British company, the Western and Brazilian Telegraph Company, founded by John Pender, the British pioneer in submarine communications, held the concession from 1873 for establishing telegraphic links between the coastal cities of Brazil. In 1899, the two companies were amalgamated to form The Western Telegraph Company, the precursor of the modern-day Cable & Wireless Company. The building that once housed the head office of the Western Telegraph has been refurbished in the Praça do Arsenal da Marinha in the port area of Recife. The letters WTCL, standing for 'Western Telegraph Company Limited', can still be seen in the lintel over the main entrance. The port facilities were also dominated by British companies, notably Cory Brothers, and by Wilson, Sons & Company, who built the original line of the Great Western of Brazil Railway in Pernambuco and the Conde d'Eu Railway line in Paraíba.

Public transport in the nineteenth century within Recife and its environs was in the hands of British individuals and companies from the beginning. While the actual date is uncertain, we know that before 1839 Thomas Sayle from Cheshire was running an omnibus service within Recife, and from Recife to nearby Olinda. These stagecoaches were pulled by four horses, and were sometimes double-deckers. It seems that Thomas

Sayle abandoned the service for some time, until he placed a notice in the *Diário de Pernambuco*, Recife, on 13 November 1843 that reads (in translation): "Thomas Sayle wishes the respectable public and other customers of this city to know that he has once again established his well-known omnibus, with the best cleanliness possible. [...] The diminutive cost is one mil-réis for each person." Thomas Sayle died soon afterwards, in 1845, and he is buried in the British Cemetery in Recife.

Of more lasting significance for the future of public transport in Recife were the British companies established to provide communications using steam power and rails set in the roads. The Brazilian Street Railway Company started to operate from 5 January 1866, backed by a provincial law passed in June 1861 that guaranteed exclusive rights for thirty years of operation.

William Rawlinson was the general manager and head engineer in the early years. As we shall see later, Rawlinson came up with a proposal to build a railway in the province of Paraíba. From 1872, Ranson Colecome Batterbee became general manager of the company, following a career with the Great Eastern Company in England, and he operated the tramway from Recife to Caxangá. Apparently, Batterbee arrived at a time when the company was in the doldrums:

> This undertaking, which was of a peculiar nature, had fallen into disrepute, and it required considerable tact and firmness to reinstate it. Mr. Batterbee gave great satisfaction in a very difficult position, his management being distinguished by sound good sense, attention to the interests both of the Company and the public, and strict integrity. (*Minutes of Proceedings*, Institution of Civil Engineers, XCV, 1889: 383.)

Ranson Batterbee remained in Recife until around 1876, when he returned to England, and did not take up professional employment again until 1883, when he went to Paraíba as resident engineer on the Conde d'Eu Railway. Another general manager of the Brazilian Street Company was Henry Fletcher, long remembered afterwards in Recife.

According to Allen Morrison, in his study of *The tramways of Brazil: Recife, Pernambuco State, Brazil*,[57] the first two street-running locomotives for the company were manufactured in 1866 by Manning Wardle & Company in Leeds, and five similar units arrived over the next four years, as well as passenger cars built by George Starbuck in Birkenhead. The company had working lines that reached Caxangá and Várzea in 1866 and, later on, branches were inaugurated to the districts of Dois Irmãos (1867) and Arraial (1871). The gauge used was four feet, equivalent to 1.219 metres. There was another tramway using steam power - the Trilhos Urbanos do Recife a Olinda e Beberibe, established with Brazilian capital - that opened a service from Rua da Aurora in Recife to Olinda in 1870, using a different gauge of 1.400 metres. Allen Morrison mentions that this company also purchased locomotives built by Manning Wardle.

The locomotives became known locally as *maxambombas*, and it is commonly believed that this term owes its origins to the English word 'machine' and the Portuguese word for 'pump' - bomba. In other words, a corruption of the phrase 'machine pump'. There exists an alternative explanation for the derivation, which perhaps seems more likely. A *maxambomba* was the name given in colonial Brazil by the sugar plantation owners to a traction mechanism operated on one or two rails, that was used to take the sugar cargo safely onto a boat. It may be relevant, too, to point out that there was an *engenho* with the name of Maxambomba in Nova Iguaçu, in the captaincy/province of Rio de Janeiro, where sugar was embarked on boats that followed the River Maxambomba.

The Brazilian Street Company faced many difficulties in the 1890s, and after concluding that "the Company cannot, by reason of its liabilities, continue its business, and that it is advisable to wind up the same," the shareholders decided to liquidate the company at a special general meeting held in April 1899.

One of the reasons for this company's demise was the founding in 1871 of the Pernambuco Tramways Company, which ran trams in Recife and was much more successful. It is a curiosity that in Brazil trams are known to this day as *bondes*, and, once again, there are various explanations for this usage. One version traces the derivation back to the introduction of electric trams financed by The Electric Bond and Share Company; originally a holding company created by General Electric in 1892 that sold the securities of electric utilities.

However, it is certain that the word *bonde* was used earlier, and the several versions most widely accepted trace the usage back to the late 1860s, and appear to be variations on the same theme. Douglas Apratto Tenório, for example, refers to the bonds sold in Rio de Janeiro when an American, Charles B. Greenough, bought the concession for the Botanical Railroad Company in 1866 from the Visconde de Mauá.[59] This railway began to operate in Rio de Janeiro in 1868, and another version holds that the company issued tickets to passengers that included the word 'bond' in the wording, in the sense of a promise to pay or to provide a product or service. The word 'bond' apparently appeared at the side of a drawing of a donkey-drawn carriage on rails, and the general public began to call the trams *bondes*, even after the lines were electrified. There is yet another version, perhaps related, that at the time trams were being introduced, the general public in Rio de Janeiro was debating the issuing of bonds by the imperial government backed by interest payments in gold; a decision taken in August 1868 by the then Minister of the Treasury, the Visconde de Itaboraí.[60] Yet another probably related version traces the usage back to 1879, when a tram ticket cost 200 réis, but there were no coins or notes of this value in circulation. As a result, a tramway company - which may have been the Botanical Garden Railroad - hit on the idea of issuing tickets in packs of five units that cost one mil-réis. These tickets were printed in the United States and had the word 'bond' printed on the ticket, in the sense of an obligation assumed by the company to accept these tickets as payment, and soon the tickets and then the trams themselves became known as '*bondes*' (the Portuguese pronunciation of 'bonds') by the local population. The tickets could also be exchanged for cash at the company's offices.

The Pernambuco Tramways Company prospered in Recife, using *maxambombas* until the advent of electric trams in 1914. Surprisingly, Recife was probably the last major city in Brazil to undertake this conversion. Allen Morrison writes in his history of the tramways in Brazil that The Great Western of Brazil Railway proposed an electric line in 1899 that would have run from its station at Brum in Recife to Olinda, but it seems that the Western Telegraph Company protested that electricity would interfere with its underwater cables, and this plan was never carried out. To achieve this goal of introducing electric trams, the Pernambuco Tramways Company had to invest in the provision of sufficient electricity, a move that necessitated a change in its name - the words 'and Power Company' were added. The new company was registered in London in January 1913 and the contract for the building of this electric tramway in Recife was awarded to J. G. White and Company of London.

The Tramways and Power Company now had new responsibilities for providing electric light to the streets and homes of Recife, according to an agreement signed in October 1913 with the state government. The first electric tram service was inaugurated in May 1914, and gradually extended on the tramways network, until the last *maxambomba* ran in 1922. The American & Foreign Power Company (AMFORP) acquired the company in 1928, which continued to operate under its original name. Electric trams continued to run until the decade of the 1950s, but in increasingly precarious conditions, until the company decided to operate the last trams in March 1954. According to Allen Morrison, local politicians accused Pernambuco Tramways of breaking its contract with the government and started legal action. The result was that the tram service was restored, but at minimal level, with just one four-wheel open car that ran once a day from Parque 13 de Maio to Fundão, until late 1960! The present-day electricity company in the State of Pernambuco - known as CELPE (Companhia de Eletricidade de Pernambuco), and founded in 1965 - traces its history back to this British company.

One of the electric trams has survived, and can be seen on display in the grounds of the Museu do Homem do Nordeste in Recife. This thirty-six-seater tram once ran along Rua da Aurora bearing the number 104. And one tram passenger station remains, at Ponte d'Uchoa on Avenida Rui Barbosa, lovingly restored after being partially destroyed in 2013 by a late night speeding driver. Other vestiges of this period when trams rattled along rails, and left an indelible memory among older members of the population in Recife, are the several tramlines that are still visible embedded in the cobblestoned roads of Old Recife, such as along Rua do Bom Jesus.

There were so many British residents in Recife in the nineteenth century and the first half of the twentieth century that, naturally, several amenities were founded for their recreation. Many clubs catered for the British. In the port area of Recife, The Town British Club functioned on Rua Bom Jesus, and there was The Pernambuco British Club, founded in1906, as well as The British Country Club on Rua Rosa e Silva (founded in April 1920). The latter still exists, and was established with the aim of promoting athletic sports and social meetings. The original statutes stated that those members who were not British did not have the right to vote in the general assemblies. One of the signatories to the club's charter was J.G. Castles, the then general manager of the Great Western of Brazil Railway, and the first president of the club was William Ewart Gladstone Boxwell. Until 1958, the club's board of directors was always made up of British-born residents or their descendants.

Other clubs sprang up that focused on the British passion for sports. In 1928, an employee of The Great Western of Brazil Railway named George Little, joined with a group of his friends to found The Pernambuco Golf Club, with G. G. Griffith-Williams as the first president. The club changed its name in 1944, to become The Caxangá Golf & Country Club, which still exists under this name on the outskirts of Recife. There were also The Pernambuco Cricket Club, and The Lawn Tennis Club, but of course the sport that the British encouraged and that has left a lasting impression on Pernambuco was football.

Lúcia Gaspar, a librarian at the Fundação Joaquim Nabuco in Recife, tells the following fascinating story about the introduction of football in Recife, in an account that involves The Great Western of Brazil Railway.[61] The first person to introduce football was a young man from Pernambuco named Guilherme de Aquino Fonseca who had studied in Europe, and had brought back a love of football. Guilherme approached a club called Náutico, which at that time was devoted exclusively to water sports, but he came up against the view of several club members who regarded football as less than a real sport, just a matter of passing a ball around. In some exasperation, Guilherme turned to employees of the Great Western, who played football at weekends at home and even on an improvised pitch in the Derby district of Recife, and with a scratch team of his friends a game was played in 1904 against a Great Western side. Such was his

Maxambomba, Pernambuco postcard.
Author's Collection

Tram pulled by horses on Rua Victória, Recife, postcard.
Author's Collection

Trams of the Pernambuco Tramways and Power Company, postcard.
Author's Collection

"Time de Futebol de Pernambuco Tramways & Power Company" (Pernambuco Tramways & Power football team).
Courtesy Biblioteca Central Blanche Knopf, photograph library, Fundação Joaquim Nabuco, Recife. Ref. F.R. 15.975

commitment to football that in May of the following year, Guilherme founded the Sport Club do Recife, and in June a match was held between this club and the English Eleven - a team consisting of employees of several of the British companies in Recife.

> In the first ten years of football in Pernambuco, the press reported the games calling the players "senhor" (sir) or "doutor" (doctor), using various English words, for example team, goal, goal-keeper, match, referee, foul, centre-forward, dribbling, corner, off-side, penalty, full-back. Some of these words were intentionally corrupted, like quipa (keeper), centrefó (centre-forward), dribe (dribble), córne (corner), while others were incorporated into football vocabulary in Brazil, like off-side and penalty. (Lúcia Gaspar, *Football in Pernambuco*).

One event involving a British club is considered today of great importance in the history of football in Pernambuco: the Pernambuco British Club hosted in 1909 a football game between Club Náutico (which had been won over to the beautiful game) and Sport Club do Recife, and both clubs still play professional football in Recife at the top level nationally. Náutico won on this occasion by three goals to one. Over time, both the Great Western and the Pernambuco Tramways companies came to have their own football teams, initially composed of players who worked for the two firms. The Associação Atlética Great Western was founded in March 1928 when a wealthy landowner sold his assets to the Great Western, and the company decided to cede this property to the athletics association that carried its name. In 1936, the Great Western side played in the Pernambuco State first division championship. Later, the club's name changed to Ferroviário Esporte Clube do Recife, and in 1955, the name changed yet again, to Clube Ferroviário do Recife, which still exists today in Recife.

This, then, is the backcloth to the story of the Recife and São Francisco Railway, the first British railway to be built in Brazil, that went south-west; the Central de Pernambuco Railway that went west; and the original Great Western of Brazil Railway that went north-west - all railways that ran out of Recife; that were later amalgamated under the umbrella of the Great Western; and whose stories will be told in the following chapter.

Guaranteed Against All Risk
Railways in Pernambuco to 1889

The Emperor himself has expressed the most lively interest in the success of this undertaking. A monarch as noted for his enlightened views as he is solicitous for the welfare of his subjects throughout his vast dominions, he is most desirous to secure for them the inestimable advantages to be derived by opening up, by means of the railway, the teeming regions of the interior, which, from the want of any roads at all, are at present a sealed book to the rest of the world (cheers).

Edward de Mornay:
Address to the half-yearly shareholders' meeting of
the Recife and São Francisco Railway, 11 April 1857

Central Railway Station, Pernambuco. Postcard, RMSP & PSNC series no. 4, Raphael Tuck & Sons Ltd., London.

Author's Collection

The first railway in Brazil to take advantage of the concessions enshrined in the imperial law of June 1852 was built by The Recife and São Francisco Railway Company Limited. Chronologically speaking, this was the second railway to be constructed in Brazil, after the Mauá Railway in Rio de Janeiro, but it was the first of real economic importance in the country. At that time the province of Pernambuco was responsible for almost 50% of Brazilian sugar exports.

While this was a British company, with mostly British shareholders, it enjoyed the support of Barão Mauá, and there was local investment too.

> It was the Recife to São Francisco railway that brought together an amount of local capital, giving a start to a process of economic growth, that would stretch out in provincial and interprovincial time and space, causing economic and social changes. [This was] the only large business capable of assigning the capital hitherto invested in the slave trade. The Recife and São Francisco Railway opened up routes for local investment, reinforcing the bourgeoisie, [and] attracting both the rural oligarchies (thirty-eight *engenho* owners with 1,491 shares) as well as established businessmen, founders of the Commercial Association. (Josemir Camilo de Melo, *Ferrovias Inglesas e Mobilidade Social no Nordeste (1850-1900)*, translation).[62]

This initiative was kick-started by two Anglo-Brazilian brothers, of French lineage, but perhaps descended from a branch of the family that may have passed through Portugal - Edward and Alfred de Mornay, whose names usually appear in Portuguese as Eduardo and Alfredo. Their father, Aristides Franklin de Mornay, was an engineer and seems to have passed on his enthusiasm for engineering to his four sons, Charles, Edward, Alfred, and Frederick.

This enterprising family moved between Pernambuco and Alagoas, specialising in survey work and engineering projects. Aristides was for some time the *engenheiro fiscal* (supervising engineer) of Public Works in Alagoas, where it seems that Edward and Alfred also found work soon after their arrival. Between 1835 and 1838, Aristides and his eldest son Charles (born in London in 1818) journeyed from Ouro Preto in the province of Minas Gerais to the mouth of the River São Francisco to report on the potential for steam-driven navigation on that river, which may help account for the brothers' later interest in constructing a railway to this river. Aristides is mentioned in the *Diario de Pernambuco* in Recife of 5 February 1840 as "Engenheiro Aristides Franklin de Mornay."[63]

In the same year, 1840, the president of Alagoas asked Charles de Mornay to carry out a topographical survey of the province. Soon afterwards, Charles installed a water-driven wheel at the Jenipapo *engenho* in Coruripe, Alagoas, and apparently fell in love with Isabel Carolina de Carvalho, the daughter of the owner. They eloped, since her mother was of the opinion that she had not raised a daughter merely to marry a carpenter. In 1856, Charles became the owner of the Jenipapo *engenho* on the death of his mother-in-law. Like his brothers, Charles adopted a Portuguese form of his name, as Carlos de Mornay. In 1862, in recognition of his contributions as an engineer, the president of Alagoas province wrote to the Imperial Government requesting an honorific title for Charles, praising "the same engineer [who] has rendered great services to the industry of this Province, where he has resided for many years, improving the condition of our factories, to the extent that one can say that to him are owed the progresses that here we note in the sugar *engenhos*."[64] In 1866, he submitted to the Ministry of Public Works a report on the navigability of the River São Francisco. In 1868, he was appointed supervisor of public works in Alagoas. Charles died in October 1883.

But it was Edward and Alfred who were destined to more lasting fame. They are often referred to as twins, but the historian Josemir Camilo de Melo notes that their death records show that Edward was born in 1819 and Alfred in 1820.[65] What is certain is that Edward and Alfred became known as designers of machinery for the sugar cane industry. "Alfredo de Mornay" appears in newspaper announcements in 1844 describing himself as a "surveyor and civil engineer" willing to take on work at an *engenho*.[66] The brothers introduced iron ploughs for use in the sugar cane fields; they improved the efficiency of the water wheels used in the *engenhos*; and they invented 'Mornay's Patent Sugar Cane Mill'. This mill had four forty-inch diameter rollers, and was patented in 1851, with a fifteen year privilege of use by imperial decree. This machinery promised at least 15% more cane juice, and it was first introduced in the Caraúna *engenho* in Pernambuco in 1851, and then went on to revolutionise sugar processing in the north-east of Brazil. In the following year, 1852, the two brothers turned their attention to the project linking Recife to the São Francisco river by railway.

An English traveller named Charles Mansfield met one of the de Mornay brothers, either Edward or Alfred (he does not give the first name), on a voyage to Pernambuco in 1852 and left this account of their meeting:

> My great ally is a young Englishman named De Mornay, of French lineage, who has lived in Brazil for thirteen years; an engineer by profession, and a very gentlemanlike fellow, acute, clever, and very observing, and who seems to know the interior of some parts of Brazil very well. [...] He has just been over to England about a patent which he has lately taken out for some improvement in the sugar machinery.[67]

Charles Mansfield must have been invited by this de Mornay to meet him and his brother after arriving in Pernambuco, and subsequently he met up with Edward and Alfred. They explained that they were "getting up a project for a railway to Rio de Janeiro, and they require to ascertain which is the best line to take, at a point some thirty or forty miles from this place," and they invited him to accompany them on horseback on this survey. He offers this description of the two brothers: "These two gentlemen are engineers, twin-brothers, exactly of my age and so exactly alike that many people do not know them apart,"[68] which may explain why they are so often referred to as twins.

The survey work paid off, for on 7 August 1852 they were granted by Imperial Decree no. 1,030 the following concession to "Eduardo de Mornay and Alfredo de Mornay [for an] exclusive privilege for the time of 90 years for the construction of a railway in the Province of Pernambuco, between the city of Recife and the township called Água Preta," which is just short of present-day Palmares. As prescribed in the 1852 law, the government guaranteed 5% interest per year over the agreed capital investment, which in 1853 was fixed at £875,123 in conformity with studies carried out by Michael Borthwick. On top of this, there was a privilege zone of five leagues on either side of the track. The decree also stated that the longer term objective was to continue the line from Água Preta to Garanhuns, and then "terminate in one of the points of the extensive navigation of the river São Francisco." Presumably this was vaguely worded because so little was known with any accuracy about the terrain the company would meet in this extension. As we have seen, this was the first railway in Brazil obliged not to use slaves, neither in the construction nor in the operation.

Edward and Alfred wasted no time in seeking local investment capital. They placed several advertisements in the local press, such as this announcement that appeared in *O Liberal Pernambucano* on 13 October 1852 (page 4):

> Alfredo de Mornay, businessman of the railway that will be constructed in the province of Pernambuco invites those who by chance wish to obtain shares in the respective company to direct themselves to the referred businessman up to the 18th day of the month of October. (translation).

It is interesting to note that in the column beside this advertisement that are several items offered for sale, including lime from Lisbon, a donkey, and "a pretty creole slave, with some abilities, and of very good behaviour; the reason as to why she is being sold will be given in person to the buyers."[69]

Their brother Charles also played an important role in the enterprise. According to the historian Moacir Medeiros de Santana, Charles was paid one thousand pounds plus expenses for the survey for the best line to be taken by the railway between Recife and Una, which in 1873 was renamed Palmares.[70] Apparently, he spent ten and a half months in this work. Charles continued afterwards to carry out work for the company, receiving "fifty pounds a month and forty mil-réis for my beast of burden." The younger brother, Frederick, also worked on the construction as an engineer, and like his brothers he bought shares in the railway. In order to launch the company in Britain, Edward and Albert decided to forgo their rights to the ninety year privilege, and instead received 500 shares of 20 pounds each, apart from other advantages.

There followed a flurry of decrees that led to the Recife and São Francisco Railway Company being organised in London in 1853: no. 725 of 3 October 1853; nos. 1,245 and 1,246 of 13 October 1853, (the latter approved the statutes for the new company, and gave permission for the company to operate in the Brazilian empire); and no. 1,629 of 11 August 1855.[71] 48,000 shares were issued, of which 12,000 were reserved to be sold in Pernambuco and Rio de Janeiro in the hands of Alfred de Mornay, and supervised by a commission led by the president of the province of Pernambuco. Of these, according to the Pernambuco provincial president (his report on the year 1855, published on 21 April 1856), 4,000 were taken up by investors in Pernambuco "despite being offered during the deplorable state which the epidemic [of yellow fever] has dragged us through." Of great significance, in 1855, the provincial assembly in Pernambuco raised the agreed capital outlay to £1,200,000, and conceded a guarantee of a minimum of 2% on top of the 5% offered by the central government. In May 1857, a company meeting in London sanctioned this increase in capital from £900,000 to £1,200,000.

Nevertheless, the project took a long time to get off the ground; the necessary capital was not forthcoming at first, and the brothers' partners in England began to complain at the delay. Barão Mauá came to the rescue, and his support together with his partner in England, Reynell de Castro, was decisive. They acquired 7,000 shares, supported by Mauá's bank. In his biography of Mauá, Jorge Caldeira writes that "For many years, the attempts to get money for the works had stalled, until Mauá got interested in the railway; managed to raise resources in London; sent his engineers to check and correct the projects; put people on the works; [and] bought shares."[72] This was not without a cost to Mauá; he had little cash left on hand to pursue other business interests. Mauá soon sold these shares, but remained interested in the progress of the company.

The first stretch of the railway was authorised to reach the confluence of the rivers Una and its tributary Pirangi (or Piranji) at Una (later called Palmares), with the concessionaires permitted to prolong the railway to a point *above* the Paulo Afonso falls on the river São Francisco, according to a plan prepared by a British engineer named Michael Andrews Borthwick. This engineer's background is interesting; he was born in 1810 in Dunbar, Scotland, and had worked closely with Robert Stephenson. Borthwick was the resident engineer on the Northern and Eastern Railway with Stephenson as engineer-in-chief, and later they cooperated closely on a railway in Egypt. Cristiano Ottoni, a member of the Imperial Council, mentions him in his 1859 study of *O Futuro das Estradas de Ferro no Brasil* (The future of the railways in Brazil): "The English engineer Borthwick, who came especially from England to survey and budget that railway," and quotes from Borthwick's report to the company in London. In this report, Borthwick touches on the issue of the rivalry between the provinces of Bahia and Pernambuco to be the first to reach the river São Francisco:

> There can be no motive for rivalry between the two Provinces. It would really be convenient if they could work in common agreement, so that other Provinces do not prematurely claim their rights, hindering in this way projects already advanced and of general interest. And that this could happen was proven by the Alagoas Deputation requesting the construction of a railway from Maceió to Garanhuns [i.e. crossing from Alagoas into Pernambuco] that certainly no-one would consider as an integral part of the great communication link from Rio de Janeiro to the North of the Empire. This Alagoas railway will serve no other purpose than the development of some local resources.[73]

The rival railway in the province of Bahia was the Bahia and São Francisco Railway, and while the Recife and São Francisco never actually reached the river, this company in Bahia was in fact successful, but only by an extension opened late in the century. Joaquim Francisco Alves Branco Muniz Barreto was granted a concession by Imperial Decree nº 1,299, of 19 December 1853, to build a railway that would leave Salvador and continue to Juazeiro (facing modern-day Petrolina) or some other township on the southern bank of the river São Francisco, passing through Alagoinhas. In 1855, Joaquim Barreto sold the rights to his concession to a company in London specially formed for this purpose - the Bahia and São Francisco Railway, with a declared capital of £1,800,000. The concession was for ninety years, and construction work started in 1859. Alagoinhas, around 123 kilometres from Salvador, was reached in 1863. The contractor in charge of the works was an Englishman named James Watson. As with the competing São Francisco railway in Pernambuco, the gauge chosen was 1.60 metres.

One of the Waring Brothers who completed the construction of the Recife and São Francisco Railway, Charles Waring, published a paper on *Brazil and her railways* in 1883 in which he refers to the two railways, and comments: "It was the intention that both these lines should, as may be inferred by the names, be continued to the river São Francisco, making a junction above the falls, and tapping the immense inland district served by that waterway. Any extension, however, is likely to be a work of the distant future."[74] He was correct in his assessment; there was some doubt regarding the availability of a 7% guarantee for the stretch between Alagoinhas and Juazeiro, and the shareholders in Britain gave up on this extension, which became the subject of a separate concession and opened to traffic only in the 1890s.

Returning to the Recife and São Francisco Railway, on 27 August 1855, the *Diário de Pernambuco* reported that Sr. E. Mornay, "one of the agents of the Railway that will be made in this province, had arrived in Recife from Rio de Janeiro on the steamship GREAT WESTERN, on his way to England."[75] The newspaper added that "During the time that he was at the Court [that is, in Rio de Janeiro], Sr. E. Mornay received from the imperial government the concessions that he sought as indispensible to carry out the grandiose enterprise that promises such fruitful results to this province." In the following month, on the anniversary of independence and the start of the Brazilian Empire - 7 September 1855 - the foundation stone was laid on the island of Nogueira, which is now part of reclaimed land in the district of Pina in Recife. The provincial president of Pernambuco commented enthusiastically in his annual report for 1855 (page 64) on the event, which took place "at four in the afternoon, on the Ilha do Nogueira, in the fervour of the most complete rejoicing, with the attendance of the first Authorities and high-ranking people."

The first contractor for the railway was Thomas Brassey, who is considered to be the first great railway engineer in the world. By the time of his death in 1870 he had been responsible for building about one-third of the railways in Britain, three-quarters of those in France, and major lines in many countries throughout Europe, and in Canada, Australia, South America and India, together with their associated docks, bridges and viaducts, stations, tunnels and drainage works. He constructed the Central Argentine Railway in 1864 at a time when British investors were beginning to focus on railway investment in Argentina in the 1860s. The Pernambuco President's Report for 1855 explains that the imperial government had accepted the plans and budgets prepared by Michael Borthwick for the "eminent contractor Mr. Brassey," but had not been able to raise the necessary capital. The provincial assembly had made the investment more attractive by offering an additional 2% over the 5% from central funds "following the example of Bahia" - money was tight in the capital markets of London on account of the Crimean War (October 1853 to February 1856). But there was a more pressing problem with the chief engineer, according to the provincial president. "The contractor existed, [...] it was Mr. Brassey, a man sufficiently qualified and powerful, capable of inspiring the shareholders with complete confidence. But at the moment when I called him to comply with his word, his clear and positive commitments, he refuses, he disappears." It seems that Thomas Brassey felt overwhelmed by the project at that juncture: Borthwick had left for Egypt taking the plans with him; new studies had shown that the budget was really insufficient; and he had anyway too many commitments in Europe. The project was now at an impasse.

The Provincial President's report sent to the Pernambuco Legislative Assembly in its opening session of April 1856 (page 62 ff.) mentions the difficulties the company was facing. A contract had been signed in London on 29 March 1855, but it had proved impossible to issue shares without the recruitment of a contractor committed to the construction:

> It is true that Mr. Brassey had already given his word, but when he was called on to fulfill it, he refused to do so, alleging sometimes the complications he found himself facing with other works, [and] sometimes that Mr. Borthwick's budget was low. In the light of this, it was necessary that our Ministry already on 7 June find a way to put the concessionaires in communication with another very capable contractor, recognising too that it was indispensible to alter Mr. Borthwick's budget. (translation).

Notwithstanding the company's initial opinion to the contrary, believing that the estimates of the costs of construction were in fact sufficient, the contract was altered by the imperial government, and then by the provincial government in August 1855, including the extension of the guarantee to 90 years' privilege, as the imperial government had stipulated. The provincial president's report for 1855 concluded effusively:

> A thousand thanks to the Imperial Government, a thousand thanks to the General and Provincial Legislative Bodies, and much applause to all those who rendered their patriotic contribution, the railway of Pernambuco is no longer a problem. I see with the greatest satisfaction many pounds sterling employed in the material improvement of my country. My most ardent wishes have been met: the rest belongs to the future, which cannot but be prosperous, if we continue to have good sense, and perseverance.

This early confidence was reciprocated in London, and while Edward de Mornay was travelling on the GREAT WESTERN steamship to London to discuss the latest adjustments to the contract, a new chief engineer arrived in Pernambuco in September 1855. This was George Furness (1820-1900), who now took over the construction from Thomas Brassey. The two engineers knew each other, and were friends; George Furness had been engaged for four years on the construction of the railway line between Paris and Rouen under Thomas Brassey. Work started immediately on the line, with around 2,000 unskilled workers and some 200 specialised foreigners, mostly British. It should be borne in mind that at that time railway construction was a very labour-intensive matter. There was in fact no problem as regards recruiting the labour force he needed. At the start of the construction work, George Furness reported to the company directors that labour was found to be abundant and that the general condition of the men employed was very healthy.

Nevertheless, there were delays, and the first stretch opened to traffic only on 8 February 1858, along a line from Recife (Cinco Pontas) through Afogados, Boa Viagem, Prazeres, Ilha, arriving at Cabo, 31.511 kilometres in all. J. T. Wood, the manager of the Recife and São Francisco Railway, gave a speech after the train arrived in Cabo in which he praised the Emperor of Brazil for backing the undertaking. In response, the provincial president raised a toast to Queen Victoria. The party that followed lasted the whole day. More than 400 passengers had been carried on this first journey; this rose to more than 30,000 in the first year, and nearly 115,000 by 1860.

Within a few months of George Furness's arrival, newspapers in England, such as the *Daily News* on 12 January 1856, were carrying advertisements for the company:

> This company is established for the purpose of constructing, maintaining, and working a Railroad, traversing the sugar district in the province of Pernambuco, commencing at the port of Recife (Pernambuco), and terminating at the junction of the rivers Una and near the town of Agua Preta. The line has been carefully surveyed, and estimates have been made by Mr. M. A. Borthwick, assisted by other English engineers of local experience.

The Railway Record on 26 April 1856 reported on the Extraordinary General Meeting of the Recife and São Francisco Railway held four days earlier to approve the appointment of directors and to receive the board's report. Robert Benson presided over the meeting, and remarked on the company's prospectus which had been circulated, and emphasised that "since the issue of the report they had received replies to their first despatches addressed to the Brazils and they were of the most satisfactory character. The whole of the 12,000 shares reserved for the Brazils had been subscribed for." Benson then turned to address the issue of the estimates for construction - "the subject of discussion out of doors.[...] It had been said that the estimates were not sufficient for the completion of the line. There was no ground whatever for that assertion. The directors had the most perfect reliance and confidence that the estimates were sufficient." He hoped that the fact that Alfred de Mornay "one of the concessionaires, an engineer, and fully acquainted with the country by personal experience" had surveyed the line, as well as Mr. Johnson, "an eminent engineer," and Mr. Borthwick, "the able engineer of the company," would ensure confidence among the shareholders. The expected earthworks would cost less than the average in England, and "they had nothing like viaducts of any kind, and only one tunnel of a quarter of a mile long, which they hoped to avoid by deviation." This was wishful thinking. Branner (1887) gives the cost per mile of construction as US$ 92,432, much the same as the Bahia and São Francisco (at US$ 91,343), but much higher per mile than the Natal and Nova Cruz (US$ 31,982), the Conde d'Eu (US$ 34,915), the Great Western to Limoeiro (US$ 33,343), and even the Paulo Afonso Railway (US$ 31,686).

For the moment, according to the chairman, the prospects looked excellent - "There was no doubt [...] that the traffic would be large and remunerative, and there being no roads, all the merchandise being now carried from one place to another on the backs of mules, it would be more rapidly developed by the facilities which railway communication offered than it was in England." Shareholders need not only rely on this factor, he added, there was also the guarantee of interest of 7% offered by the imperial government and the provincial government, 5% and 2% respectively. "The shareholders were consequently guaranteed against all risk, and were certain of the 7 per cent, whatever might be the traffic of the Pernambuco." Finally, Benson appealed to "the probable effect of railways in the Brazils in ameliorating the condition of the black population, and, by encouraging the immigration of free labour, for which the Brazilian government was most anxious, abolishing slavery." The Brazilian minister in London, Francisco Inácio de Carvalho Moreira, is listed in the company report as an *ex officio* director of the company, (he was a close confidant of Mauá), who "assures [the directors] that the undertaking is regarded with peculiar favour by the imperial and provincial governments." As for George Furness, the report noted that "every reliance may be placed upon the contractor for his faithful and effectual fulfilment." Michael Borthwick died later that year, in June 1856, of typhus contracted on a voyage to Pernambuco, and was replaced by William Michael Peniston as engineer-in-chief, with Edward de Mornay acting as the resident manager.

Regarding the labour force, company secretary Bellamy's explanations to the Earl of Sherburne on the subject of whether slaves were employed by the Recife and São Francisco Railway in his letter of 2 December 1856 offer an insight (somewhat rose-tinted) into how labourers were contracted in the early period of construction, and is worth quoting at some length.

> Mr. Furness affirms positively that since the commencement of the works the labourers employed consist indifferently of mulattoes, blacks, Indians, and Portuguese, and are worked in gangs as in England, under the direction of skilled labourers as foremen or superintendents. That they are, and have been from the first, engaged individually, at daily wages which are paid to them individually, in money, either weekly or in the course of the week, as wished by themselves. That each man finds his own victuals, is subject to no punishment at the hands of any one; is in no way, so far as Mr. Furness knows, under the control or authority of any one while engaged in his service, except that of himself or his staff; and is employed or discharged, at any time, at pleasure. That in fact the whole of the men employed upon the works are engaged, paid, treated, worked, and discharged in all respects as they would be in England . [...] Scattered through the Province of Pernambuco there exists a large body of free labourers of the races already referred to. The ordinary rate of wages paid in the interior for their labour averages from 1s. 6d. to 2s. a day in English money. Mr Furness, however, informs the Board that the rate of wages that he pays for unskilled labour on his works is 2s. 3d. a day. This increased rate of payment is [...] calculated to draw to his works all the able-bodied free labourers in the district; and another inducement to obtain employment under him is the exemption of all native free labourers so engaged from liability to military recruitment and active service in the National Guard, which otherwise press heavily on free labourers.[76]

We have already seen that, at least in the early period of the construction, this was not quite the dreamland painted by this account. Nevertheless, the building work seems to have got off to a good start. *The Railway Record* reported in the following year on the half-yearly shareholders' meeting held on 11 April 1857 in a mood of great confidence that:

> The works have proceeded with very slight interruptions; free native labour continues

abundant, and the natives employed are becoming daily more skilled and efficient. With one slight exception, the engineer reports that all his staff are in very good health. The directors have the gratification of stating that they have the cordial co-operation of his Excellency the Commandeur F. I. de Carvalho Moreira, the Brazilian Minister in this country, from whom they have received assurances that the warmest interest continues to be evinced towards this undertaking by the Imperial and provincial governments.

The report mentioned that Mr Rendel, yet another consulting engineer, had died and Charles Hutton Gregory had been appointed in his place. The company chairman, Robert Benson, then rose to give his views, and to do his best to paper over the cracks that were beginning to appear: "With the exception of those minor difficulties which are inseparable from such works, we have had what I may venture to describe as an unexampled success (hear, hear)." There were now around 2,000 men working on the line. The chairman reported that "There has been a little sickness among the [British] staff, but I am happy to say that we have lost only about seven men altogether of those sent out from this side." There was also a suggestion of difficulty at management level; in response to a question, the chairman explained that Edward de Mornay "had suggested some alterations in the details of management and the construction of the executive abroad," but the board "did not quite agree, considering it upon the whole better that they should adhere to their original plan, whereupon Mr de Mornay expressed a wish to resign his post [as resident manager]." Edward was present at the meeting and explained his decision: "I did not think the resolutions of the board were in accordance with the statutes of the company; or that a representative of the company, acting 4,000 miles away from the seat of the board, could undertake the responsibility attached to the proper management of their affairs in Brazil, when the departmental officers corresponded directly with the board, and received instructions unknown to him."

Nevertheless, it seems that the board came round to his point of view, and soon began to delegate more to local management. The following half-yearly shareholders' meeting, summarised in *The Railway Record*, (the edition of 17 October 1857), was told that a "consultative committee" was now operating in Pernambuco working within a remit handed down by the board. The chairman reported that "many unavoidable delays have occurred." Putting a brave face on the situation, he added that "Whilst the shareholders will regret, with the directors, that the perhaps too sanguine expectations of the progress to be made with a railway in a new country have not been fully realised," the opening was confidently expected to take place in December that year of 1857. This too was wishful thinking, and the first short stretch was ready only in February 1858. And it seems that Edward de Mornay voiced his criticism of the board again at this meeting.

Edward and his brother Alfred had sold their belongings at auction in Recife and were now living in England in 1857, the same year that their father Aristides probably died.[77] Edward's criticism of the company management was echoed by the author of a letter to the editor published in the *Daily News* on 15 April 1858, and signed "A Shareholder", who begins his diatribe:

> The shareholders of this grievously mismanaged undertaking owe Mr. Edward de Mornay a great obligation. [...] I for one, who am seriously prejudged in pocket by the depreciation and disrepute of the property, feel that he has done his duty in thus fearlessly and frankly giving publicity to facts as they are, and in throwing light on at least some of the causes which have reduced this originally fine enterprise to its present unprofitable level.

The author questioned "the fitness of the existing executive to bring it to successful completion," given that, among other worries, only twenty miles had been opened to traffic out of the planned total of seventy-seven, with one half of the earmarked capital already spent. On top of that, "The contractor and engineer are at war, and the general advancement of the enterprise is retarded by their disputes." The shareholder concluded: "We have an executive which no longer inspires public confidence, and a local management which, judging by events, is seriously defective." The chairman of the board, Robert Benson, answered these criticisms with expressions of hurt pride in the next meeting, held on 20 April 1858, in a report carried in the *Daily News* on 21 April 1858: the board "had laboured with zeal and earnestness for the company, and felt that in every way they had done their duty."

However, the project continued to be beset by delays, and the construction programme was unfortunate in coinciding with a period of disease in Pernambuco. Yellow fever arrived in Pernambuco in a ship from Bahia in December 1849, and spread rapidly, although the worst of this outbreak was over by May 1850. An isolation hospital was established on the Ilha do Nogueira, and victims were also taken to the British Hospital. So many died that the local authorities forbade the ringing of church bells to accompany funeral processions, so as not to frighten those who were in good health and those who showed symptoms of the disease. Deaths recorded in the Register of Burials show a sudden increase in deaths of foreigners from seventeen in 1849 to sixty-five in 1850. The half-yearly report submitted to shareholders by the chairman, Robert Benson, on 8 April 1861 noted that progress on construction was proceeding satisfactorily, despite delays caused by sickness, "the past month having been the most unhealthy yet experienced by the European staff; many members of which, including the contractor's agent [...], had been attacked by yellow-fever, and the brother of the traffic manager and several of the English workmen having died of it." Yellow fever returned to Pernambuco with great force in the years 1871 to 1873, and intermittently thereafter. A tombstone in the British Cemetery reads: "In affectionate remembrance of Mary, the beloved wife of Frederic Joseph Kenworthy, born at Braudon, Warwickshire, April 9, 1851, died March 24, 1875, of yellow fever."

This experience moved the local government to establish quarantine facilities for passengers arriving at the port of Recife, especially when news of cholera in Europe began to reach Brazil in 1854. It was now only a matter of time, and on 28 January 1856 the first case was reported in Recife, having come overland from Bahia. In the following three months, cholera killed 3,338 residents of Recife, the equivalent of 5% of the city's population. The outbreak only began to cease in 1857, when the *Diário de Pernambuco* reported on 3 February 1857 that Recife was now free of cholera, but that 'vômito preto' (black vomit) – a symptom of yellow fever – had returned, with already more than seventy victims. "The English workers on the railway have been very afflicted, and among the number of deaths already we find almost all the foremen and one engineer;" a fact that the newspaper blamed on the "intemperance of the foreigners" in their abuse of alcoholic drinks and their love of eating fruit! In fact, the situation was much worse - seven British engineers lost their lives in just one month, January 1857, as recorded in the British Cemetery's Register of Burials. And more engineers died later: C. Wilks in September 1857, and H. C. Tarring "Chief Engineer to the Railway" in May 1858, apart from several foremen. As a result, the company had to contract specialised workers from abroad, and around two hundred Belgians and some Germans arrived to fill the ranks and give an impetus to the works, adding to the costs of the construction.

These two diseases decimated the ranks of the British engineers, but there were other problems too. Foreign workers on the construction were sometimes attacked and robbed. Under the headline 'Murder of two Englishmen, in Brazil', *The Manchester Guardian*: 24 September 1861 (page 3) reported on "a very sad affair [that had] occurred on the works of the Pernambuco Railway" in August that year. Tracks had been laid as far as the town of Escada, and it was necessary to send the wages, paid fortnightly, on horseback to workers further inland in the charge of two Englishmen, who were joined by an English carpenter who expected to leave Brazil shortly, after completing his two year contract. Money had been left at several stations, but on passing through a wood at a place called Aramaragi, still carrying the equivalent of around £2,800, they were attacked by five men armed with sticks, knives, and one gun, who killed two of the Englishmen, including the poor carpenter, and wounded the third. According to this account, within an hour up to one thousand workers from the line were scouring the countryside for the thieves. "The authorities also acted with great energy, a considerable force of cavalry and police being at once despatched to the scene of the murder," with the result that the thieves were eventually found, still with about £2,500 in their possession.

To add to the company's trials and tribulations, there were also strikes - the first railway strikes in Brazil took place on the Recife and São Francisco Railway, led by Belgian workers. This was the first challenge to established order in a still slave-owning but slowly industrialising society. The first strike took place in 1858 when the Belgian workers complained that their wages were less than had been promised to them, and to protest at working ten hours a day, six days a week, even in the pouring rain. According to Josemir Camilo de Melo, in 1854, Thomas Brassey was paying his specialised workers 7 shillings 6 pence a day, the equivalent of 3$420 réis, and 6 shillings 5 pence (2$926 réis) to non-specialised foreign workers.[78] The non-specialised Brazilian labour force received much less, just 1 shilling 3 pence (0$570 réis) per day.

The Belgian workers, who were seen in Britain as model workers, were brought to Brazil in 1858 in a group of 238 Europeans, but soon realised that they were earning about 30% less than the other foreign workers. The company rejected their request for an increase, saying that such wages were for specialised workers, so the Belgians formed a committee of thirty men who went to talk with the Belgian consul in Recife, a businessman named Luiz A. Sequeira, a Brazilian who was also a shareholder in the railway company. The consul sided with the company and called the police. But the men were adamant, and the contractor's agent in Recife, John Bayliss, noted that "It was easier for them to go to prison than to work for less than 2 shillings 7 pence (1$178 réis) a day." There was an improved offer from the company, but in the end the police were called in to send the men back to work. Fourteen of them fled; some became drunkards and beggars, while others found work in *engenhos* in the neighbouring provinces.

And as if that was not enough, the company's high hopes for the new engineer-in-chief, George Furness, ended in acrimony. The report on the half-yearly meeting held on 13 April 1860 tells the story. Furness had been replaced in February that year, but there were outstanding "claims to a considerable amount against the late contractor in respect of loans and advances made to him, and for damages for breach of contract, as well as for large sums of money expended by the company in perfecting and completing his unfinished and defective works." Furness had responded by starting legal proceedings against the company, but he was not successful. *The Railway Times* on 17 December 1864 (page 613) reported that George Furness had lost his action against the Recife and São Francisco company, in which he claimed £500,000 in damages. The company was awarded £15,000 in costs and 300 of the railway contractor's shares.

By the time he left in early 1860, George Furness had completed only the first section of the railway, and the company turned to Waring Brothers, an English company specialising in railway structures, to complete the remaining three sections of the line. Interestingly, this new contract provided for the company and Waring to share in any loss on construction costs for the completion of the line, based on Borthwick's original estimates, with Waring Brothers earning a bonus if they finished by the deadline of 2 December 1861. Fortunately, Waring Brothers worked harmoniously with William Peniston, the engineer. At the half-yearly meeting held on 12 April 1860, the chairman, Robert Benson, told shareholders that "The arrangement with Messrs. Waring was upon the give and take principle; and, indeed, from the state in which the works were left by the former contractor they could not well have entered upon any other."[79] The deadline was in fact extended by two years by the provincial government of Pernambuco later that year.

The inauguration of the third and fourth sections of the line expected in late 1861 (actually opened, respectively, in September and December 1862) was delayed due to torrential rains, a factor which plagued the construction from start to finish. The company chairman reported in the half-yearly meeting held on 14 October 1861 that "The large amount of rain had led to an extraordinary amount of sickness, and no less than thirty-eight deaths, and this was an important cause of delay."[80]

And then there was another strike, in 1862, which was triggered when an engine driver accidentally killed a woman on the tracks and was immediately taken prisoner. Josemir Camilo de Melo describes how six English engine drivers and eight firemen, of whom seven were Brazilian, refused to take the trains out unless their companion was set free.[81] The strike spread, with workers complaining about low wages and poor working conditions, and, to complicate matters, it seems that seventeen specialised British workers demanded the right to be heard in a British court. The two sides negotiated during a week, and then the company took a decisive stand; the striking workers would be sent to prison and dismissed unless they returned to work at once.

But the strikers had the upper hand since all the workers had joined the protest, and anyway they knew that the engine drivers could not be sacked - there were no others available to replace them. The imperial government was shaken by these events; the Minister of Agriculture commented: "This affair, which was not the first to take place on our railways, deserves serious considerations." Two months later, the government passed decree nº 2,913 of 23 April 1862, under which any locomotive driver or stoker who refused to work "deliberately or through negligence" was subject to imprisonment for fifteen days to two months as well as stiff fines. In the case of two or more drivers or firemen joining together to start a strike, the penalties were even higher: one to three months in prison and fines. In both cases, the company enjoyed the right to dismiss the workers. A clause in this decree exempted the workers from punishment if it was a matter of payment owed by the company or a contract that had been broken.

Despite the extravagant enthusiasm of the provincial president and certain other Brazilian authorities early on in the enterprise, there was criticism of the undertaking, and from a very influential and knowledgeable source. Cristiano Ottoni is considered to be the 'father of railways in Brazil', since he was the first manager of the Dom Pedro II Railway, and the force behind the initiative to push a railway up the escarpment from the port of Santos to São Paulo, and onwards to Minas Gerais. He was also a senator in the imperial government, and as a member of the Imperial Council he published a treatise entitled 'The Future of the Railways in Brazil' in 1859 outlining his vision for the future of railway construction in Brazil, and criticising the founding of companies in London:

In my opinion this is the worst of all the means of organising our railway companies: the

"Primeira locomotiva de Pernambuco" (The first locomotive in Pernambuco), on the Recife and São Francisco Railway. Photograph by Theóphile Auguste Stahl (known as Augusto Stahl in Brazil), 1858.   http://enciclopedia.itaucultural.org.br/en/pessoa21612/auguste-stahl, accessed 16 December 2015.

Augusto Stahl / Author's Collection

The railway station at Vila do Cabo on the Recife and São Francisco Railway. The British engineers' residence can be seen on the right of this 1858 photo.

Augusto Stahl / Author's Collection

results must naturally be ruinous: and from the little that has been published about the Pernambuco Railway, it seems there that my sad prediction has already started to come about. [...] May God allow me to be deceived. [...] In the first place the project [...] does not inspire any confidence regarding its being carried out; it is almost always the result of a slight reconnaissance of the land. [...] Add to this the ignorance of the costs of the materials and of the labour force, and even the fear that the yellow fever will affect ominously in the work. [...] Add to this the imperfection or lack of commercial and statistical data, and you will see that the English shareholder hands over his money completely in the dark about the products it will produce.[82]

Cristiano Ottoni foresaw the problems that came into prominence over the second half of the nineteenth century:

But if we have to put into the balance the future interests of the country, what can we reasonably expect of an English board of directors, resident in London, and almost indifferent to our prosperity? It is in their interest, they will say, to increase the income of the railway: yes, but this interest is limited to the period of the concession, and they do not care about the future; but this interest comes from the pockets of the shareholders, and is not always identical to that of the country; and finally the real needs of our commerce, the best way of reconciling the good of the country with the profit of the company, these cannot be well appreciated by foreigners at a distance of 2,000 leagues.[83]

Ottoni concluded that "It is for me a well demonstrated truth that the management of the railways in Brazil should be Brazilian," and that the foreign companies then existing in Brazil should revert to state ownership. He noted errors in construction that had come to his attention that "do nothing more than confirm my conviction that an English board of an English company cannot conveniently contract and manage a railway on the other side of the Atlantic."[84] Writing in 1949, and somewhat biased towards the company, Estevão Pinto noted that the enterprise was nearly abandoned when the first survey was shown to be deficient, and naturally this badly affected the company's reputation, "until some more reflective spirits understood that this was a means of closing the doors of English capital to the national markets" by means of decrees emitted in August 1857, June 1858, November 1860, and September 1867.[85]

Notwithstanding this disquiet and Ottoni's grave presentiments, in the same year of 1859 the emperor Dom Pedro II gave his personal stamp of approval. Accompanied by his consort Teresa Cristina, he visited Recife from 22 November to 24 December (when he left for Paraíba), and he rode on the Recife and São Francisco railway. A special commemorative publication entitled *O Monitor das Familias* recorded with fawning adulation their every move. On December 1, the imperial party took the train from the Cinco Pontas station to Cabo de Santo Agostinho, on a journey that lasted thirty-seven minutes. At Cabo, the emperor rode out on horseback to inspect the extension of the railway that was under construction. Lunch was served at the station in Cabo, at the expense of the railway company, after which the party returned to Recife, taking thirty-six minutes on the journey. There was a second journey to Cabo by train on 10 December, to visit sugar *engenhos* in the region.

More than 30,000 passengers were transported in first year of operation, a figure that rose to nearly 115,000 in 1860 when the second stretch of the line was opened to Escada. At first two trains ran every day from Recife to Cabo, at 09:00 and 17:00, and it became quite fashionable to make this journey as a tourist excursion. When the final stretch reaching Una (later named Palmares) was inaugurated at the end of 1862, the total length of the railway was nearly 125 kilometres. The station at Una was opened on 30 November 1862, and this building still stands today. The undertaking had cost £1,842,202 and involved ten bridges, and the building of a tunnel of 145 metres in length with a diameter of nearly four metres near Cabo between 1858 and 1859 - the first railway tunnel to be constructed in Brazil, which still stands today.

The company was the first in Brazil to adopt the gauge of 1 metre 60 centimetres; a gauge that was abandoned in Brazil in 1905. As elsewhere in the world in the early period of railway construction, different track gauges existed simultaneously in Brazil, with a one metre gauge the most popular. Writing in 1887, John Casper Branner noted in his study of *The railways of Brazil* that "It is very unfortunate that there should be several railway gauges on the Brazilian roads. The most common one is that of one metre, forty-four out of the sixty-one roads in the empire having this gauge." The rails were imported from England, starting with the Barlow rail, patented in 1849, which could be laid on the ballast without sleepers, although this proved inadequate, and was replaced by double-headed rails. Not surprisingly, most of the locomotives also came from England. According to Benício Guimarães,[86] the initial rolling stock consisted of twenty-three locomotives manufactured by Avonside Engine Company and Fox Walker & Company, both in Bristol, but that must have been after 1864 when these companies were formed. By the mid 1860s, 40% of Fox Walker's production was destined for narrow gauge railways in Europe and South America. Two Manchester-based manufacturers also exported locomotives for this railway: Beyer, Peacock & Company (manufacturing from 1854), and William Fairbairn & Sons, which manufactured the first locomotive to run in Brazil; the 'Baronesa' on the Mauá line. Benício Guimarães writes that in 1884 there were also twenty-five Fives Lille locomotives on this line.[87] According to Cyro Pessôa, in 1886 there were thirty-three locomotives, ten first class carriages, six second class, eleven third class, six carriages for baggage and mail, 200 covered wagons, sixty-seven open wagons, and seven wagons for the transport of animals in operation on the line.[88]

The company headquarters were of course in London, and there was a general manager resident in Recife. James Templeton Wood arrived in Brazil in February 1857, and he was the general manager in 1858 when the first train ran. The company chairman described him as "a gentleman in every way qualified for the duties required of him, which involved legal rather more than financial and commercial questions."[89] The company resolved to build the railway station at Recife beside the old Dutch fort of Cinco Pontas; sadly, a building that was demolished in modern times to make room for a road viaduct.

We have seen how in 1853 the agreed capital expenditure was fixed at £875,123 in conformity with studies carried out by Michael Borthwick. This proved to be insufficient when confronted with the real costs of construction, and the guaranteed capital was increased in incremental steps, first of all in 1855, when the provincial assembly in Pernambuco offered to raise the agreed capital outlay to £1,200,000. This too was not enough to cover the difference between the budget and the actual expenses. Barão Mauá supported the company in its efforts to convince the imperial government to increase the guarantee. In 1861, the company requested a further increase, but this was at first rejected by the government. The chairman explained at a special meeting of shareholders held on 20 December 1861 (see report carried in the *Daily News* 21 December 1861) that one of the directors, Major Vereker, had been sent to Brazil to ask the government in Rio de Janeiro for: "a guarantee to cover all the money honestly expended upon the railway, and as a return for that boon [sic] the company offered to concede to the ministers the right of inspecting the company's capital account, and that privilege the government had accepted [despite] a great many differences between the company and the government arising out of misunderstandings connected with the manner of their keeping accounts."[90]

Essentially this was an increase on the amount of guaranteed capital invested, an extra £485,660 over the present guaranteed share capital of £1,200,000,[91] for which the shareholders would have to provide funds. But this needed the approval of the Brazilian government, which was reluctant to once again raise the total outlay and face the consequent increase in the guaranteed interest payments to the company. Negotiations continued over the following years from 1861, with the government insisting that the maximum of the capital guaranteed not exceed that for the Bahia and São Francisco Railway, and on an audit of the books. A government-appointed commission in Brazil and another group of auditors in London pored over the company's accounts with

> access to every book and document belonging to the company, and the fullest information afforded to them by any and every official or servant of the company whom they have thought proper to examine, all of whom were placed by the directors unreservedly at their command. The directors are not aware of any complaint or dissatisfaction whatever, either with the expenditure or accounts, having been expressed by the commissioners in Brazil.[92]

This protracted delay, and the suspicion of poor management and questionable accounting practices, provoked criticism of the company, both in Brazil and in Britain. The company chairman, Robert Benson, reported to shareholders in the half-yearly general meeting held on 8 April 1861 that while relations with the Brazilian Minister in London "were those of harmony and respect."

> The cold shoulder had been shown in some quarters, but whether it came through the interference of the concessionaires [the de Mornay borthers], or of people in a higher position - whether it arose from the fact that the company did not keeping its banking account with an eminent member of the Hebrew faith who possessed great influence with the daily press [i.e. Rothschild] - he was not aware; but it was undoubtedly true that the mind of the Brazilian government had been poisoned against the company.[93]

The de Mornay brothers had recently sold their shares, and no longer attended meetings of the board.

Over this period, relations with the imperial government continued to be fraught, especially over the issue of increasing the capital guarantee. Probably in some exasperation, and presumably fearful of what they might be committing themselves to, the government told the company in 1865 that instead of increasing the guaranteed capital they now wished to purchase the railway, which came as an unwelcome shock to the board. Robert Benson reported to shareholders in the half-yearly meeting held on 24 October 1865 that:

> The change in policy on the part of the government which had occurred took him, as no doubt it did the shareholders by surprise. He heard of it at first with extreme regret, as it was calculated to cause the public to think that there was uncertainty in the movements of the government, and that they were playing fast and loose with the company.[94]

Time passed, and there was still no resolution in 1866, in part because the government was much more preoccupied with the war with Paraguay, which raged from 1864 to 1870. The chairman reported to shareholders in October 1866 his great disappointment at having to meet shareholders still "without a settlement having been come to by the imperial government of the just and admitted claims of the company to an extension of the guarantee," despite the board having sent a director, Mr. Bramah, to Rio de Janeiro to negotiate with the government there.[95] He had "proceeded to press resolutely [...] for a settlement in some shape, but without effect; the government appearing to be altogether absorbed in, and embarrassed by, the war and its consequences [the Paraguayan War], and to be fixed in their determination not to assist the company by an appeal to the legislature," which their representative had pushed for. As a result, Mr. Bramah returned to London empty-handed.

Manoel da Cunha Galvão, an imperial councillor, remembered in 1869 that:

> M. Bramah, superintendent of the Pernambuco railway came to the Court to request a new increase in the guaranteed capital, justifying his request from the inequality [of the agreed capital vis-à-vis actual costs], and with the lack of the necessary elements to organise from the beginning an approximate budget, given that the company to which I refer has been the first to be organised in Europe for works of such magnitude in Brazil. [...] I added that not having entire confidence in the good employment of the guaranteed capital in the Pernambuco railway, I would not take into consideration any request for new favours without the most thorough verification of the expenditure of that capital.[96]

If this audit should show "severe economy and zeal" in the running of the company, he would look again into this request, although irritated by "the British tenacity in asking for favours" and inclined to giving a "a resounding no, which is always the safest way, although not so gracious, to turn away troublesome aspirants, and to kill at birth bothersome pretensions."[97]

Nevertheless, the chairman in 1866 was able to report that traffic on the line "is in a very flourishing and healthy condition, increasing year by year in a ratio which bids fair in a comparatively short space of time to supersede the guarantee." Gross profit for the first six months of 1866 was equal to that of the previous year, despite flooding which had damaged the line, and "the entire staff are happily free from sickness, notwithstanding the severity of the labour during the wet season caused by the incessant floods." The government did grant a loan of £16,000 for the purchase of additional rolling stock in 1868, which the company would have preferred covered by the extended guarantee; the impasse over this issue continued into 1870, and no more rolling stock was acquired. The company concluded that

> as things now stood, [we] had no interest in increasing the traffic. All the advantage would be in favour of the Government. [...] So long as the extended guarantee was withheld he could not see how they were to co-operate to any great extent for the development of the traffic or provide additional rolling stock." (Robert Benson, half-yearly meeting held on 26 April 1870).[98]

Negotiations had been so fractious, with both sides stubbornly taking opposing positions, that it comes as a surprise to learn that relations with the government did actually improve, to the point that in April 1872 the chairman was able to report that "the Government had paid the guarantee, and they were on good terms with them."[99]

However, there was still another bone of contention with the government. Having completed the line as far as the terminus at Una (Palmares) by December 1862, the Recife and São Francisco company was required by contract to submit studies within six years for an extension of the railway to the river São Francisco, which, after all, was the stated objective of the line, as enshrined in its name. It is not entirely clear why the

Recife and São Francisco company did not submit plans. They were invited to do so, but the problems over the guarantee increase presumably convinced the company that there was little profit to be made in this extension, or perhaps it failed to secure the capital that would be needed. Six years passed, and still there was no proposal from the company. The imperial government tired of waiting and decided by Law n° 1,953 of 17 July 1871 to authorise a survey and begin the necessary construction; "When the Bahia and Pernambuco railway companies proved impervious to official exhortations to extend their respective main lines, an exasperated government assumed this charge." (Colin Lewis).[100]

In October 1872, the survey work was handed to the engineer J. M. da Silva Coutinho, whose project was ready by 1874, and a contract was agreed in June 1876 with F. J. de Castro Rebelo for the building of an extension from Una through Garanhuns to Águas Belas, about 130 kilometres from the river, then on along the northern bank of the São Francisco river to Boa Vista bypassing the rapids, along the route taken later by the Paulo Afonso Railway. The extension would amount to 256 kilometres in all. Payment was by units of work with a monthly assessment of the services carried out. The French Fives Lille company was contracted to provide the rolling stock and the rails, and this would be one metre gauge, and therefore different from the Recife and São Francisco railway. This was the beginning of what later became the state-run Sul de Pernambuco railway, and subsequently part of the Great Western of Brazil network. There were delays, in part caused by labour disputes. Josemir Camilo de Melo tells the story of how, in around 1879, the labourers working on the construction complained about errors in their salaries and went on strike.[101] Several of these workers were men employed by the state who had fled from the effects of the great drought in the north east of Brazil at that time.[102] The strike was violently broken up by the police, who arrested four of the men, one of whom was beaten so badly that he would never work again. It was shown that the labourers were justified in their complaint, and the contractor paid the full amounts, and then immediately dismissed them all from the works.

The first stretch of eighteen kilometres from Una to Catende was opened to traffic only in December 1882. In the end, the line arrived at Garanhuns in September 1887 - at an altitude of 866 metres, 146 kilometres from Una - travelling through a zone with many sugar *usinas*. A branch line from Glicério to União (today named União dos Palmares) was inaugurated in May 1894. However, this railway was a financial failure and proved to be a constant drain on the government treasury. And the river São Francisco was never reached.

The operation of the Recife and São Francisco Railway proved to be costly, and this led to disagreements between the company and the government in the late 1880s. The directors' report on the second half of 1886 was described by the chairman as "distinctly favourable;" however:

> Among the items of expenditure we notice the sum of £595 paid as taxes to the provincial government of Pernambuco this half year. It appears the imperial government will not allow this as part of working expenses, although such claims were formerly admitted without question. Since the June half of 1883, however, these items have been disallowed, with the result that there is about £4,000 now owing by the imperial government on this account.[103]

Nevertheless, from the company's perspective, the financial situation continued to be good. For example, for the period June 1887 to June 1888 the board reported net earnings of £68,617, against an expenditure of £62,312, "consequently the Imperial

Government of Brazil has been called upon only for £11,666 to make up £80,283, which is the annual income guaranteed to the company," leading the directors to recommend an annual dividend of 5%.[104] But this topping up added to the general strain on government finances. The 1852 decree awarding the concession to the de Mornay brothers had stipulated that the government had the option of buying back the Recife and São Francisco Railway after thirty years, with proper indemnity. The government's budget in 1900 authorised the government to redeem the railway, at a cost of £1,637,200.[105] As we shall see in detail later in this book, this expropriation was part of the government's plan to take over several railways in the north east of Brazil in the first decade of the twentieth century. "The railways, that had been conceded with a guarantee of interest paid in gold, had become, in general [...] very onerous for the country, for several reasons, including the low exchange rate and insufficient income."[106] (Estevão Pinto).

The Recife and São Francisco and the Sul de Pernambuco, along with all the other railways in four states, were then rented out to the Great Western of Brazil Railway Company Limited. Curiously, while this company came to practically monopolise railway transport in the north-east of Brazil, it had actually started in Brazil in a very modest way, with a short line from Recife to Limoeiro in the interior, and a branch line to Nazaré - just ninety-five kilometres in all. Plantation owners had petitioned the provincial government of Pernambuco from the 1850s for this outlet to the coast for their produce, chiefly sugar and cotton. Several of the 'nobles' of Pernambuco saw an opportunity for investment, and came up with proposals. It is important to understand that Dom João VI had started the custom of distributing titles in Brazil after his arrival in 1808; a fashion that his son Dom Pedro II, Emperor of Brazil, was happy to continue with - conferring titles on the heads of rural oligarchies and urban families involved in agribusiness had the benefit of bringing them to his side as he consolidated his position in Brazil. These were the titles of *marquês*, *conde* (count), *visconde* (viscount), and *barão*, with the result that the 'coffee barons' held sway in the south-east, and the 'sugar barons' prospered in the north-east. In around the year of 1883 the province of Pernambuco had forty-five nobles, made up of one *conde*, four *viscondes*, with the rest as *barões*.[107] And if you were a *barão* or a *visconde*, this conferred a certain local legitimacy.

The province of Pernambuco passed law n° 856 on 5 June 1868 in which the government was authorised to aid in and subsidise the construction of this line, offering an exclusive privilege of ninety years for the concession and an exemption of taxes on the material used; an exemption confirmed by imperial decree n° 2,144 of 8 March 1873. The first to step forward was the Visconde de Camaragibe, who requested an exclusive privilege for the construction of this railway. The Barão do Livramento was similarly interested; he was one of the founding partners of the Brazilian Street Railway. The first to enjoy success, however, was the second Barão da Soledade (a baron since 1867) whose name was José Pereira Viana - a rich businessman in Recife, who had studied in England. Viana was awarded the concession in a contract awarded by the province of Pernambuco dated 16 July 1870.

Nothing more happened until a group of English capitalists met in London on 21 December 1872 to incorporate a company expressly founded to exploit this concession. The company was called The Great Western of Brazil Railway, a name justified by the generally western direction taken by the proposed line, (actually to the north-west), but clearly also intended to benefit from the fame of the 'Great Western' name in Britain. The first map published by the company to drum up interest among potential shareholders stressed the potential for linking together the sugar plantations. At that time there were many *engenhos* along the proposed route: twenty-three in São Lourenço, forty in Pau-d'Alho, seventy-three in Nazaré, and thirteen in Limoeiro. But these sugar industries were not in a position to develop any significant railway network on their own because of a crisis in cane production, especially between 1860 and 1880, that compelled the planters to divert their available capital into the modernisation of their sugar-mills.

Now that a company had been established which promised to find the necessary capital, Brazil took the steps needed to confirm the arrangement. Provincial law n° 1,115 of 17 June 1873 conceded a guarantee of interest of 7% over thirty years for a maximum capital investment of 50:000$000 per kilometre constructed, to be paid twice a year in February and August. Imperial decree n° 5,704 of 5 August 1874 confirmed this interest payment for the concession on a line to be built from Recife to Limoeiro, with a branch line to Nazareth (Nazaré today). On top of this, state-owned and unoccupied land would be given at no cost, along with the right to exploit the wood within the zone of privilege, and an exemption of import duty on the importing of rails, machinery, and all instruments destined to the construction of the railway. As with the previous railway concessions, no slaves were to be used in the construction and operation of this railway.

Satisfied with these developments, the Great Western company in London sent a 'petition' dated 15 March 1875 to the provincial president of Pernambuco in which they named the Barão da Soledade "their true and legal procurator."[108] Soledade then transferred this concession to the company. There were modifications made to the original contract: the gauge was fixed at one metre; the maximum capital per kilometre reduced to 46:000$000; and the final total cost was not to exceed 5,000:000$000. In addition, the concession would run for ninety years; the government would not to allow any other railway within twenty kilometres on either side of the line; the line had to be built within three years (not including any branch); and the company needed to provide a minimum rolling stock of ten locomotives, twenty first class carriages, fifty second class carriages, and two hundred goods wagons, using Vignolles rails for the tracks.

Now that a bona fide concession existed and a company had been organised in London, the time had come to amass the capital needed to carry out the enterprise. Announcements appeared in newspapers in Britain in 1878, such as this one published in November in *The Graphic* in London:

> This Company is formed to carry out a concession granted by the Provincial Government of Pernambuco confirmed by Decree of the Imperial Government of Brazil, for constructing and working a Railway from the Sea-port City of Pernambuco to Limoeiro, a distance of about fifty miles, with a branch to Nazareth, in all about sixty miles. [...] The railway will traverse the rich and productive Capibaribe valley, embracing the best cultivated and most prolific Districts of the Province, and convey to Pernambuco [i.e., Recife] for shipment a large proportion of what forms the total exports of the Province, such as sugar, cotton and other valuable products. [...] There being no navigable rivers, the bulk of this valuable traffic, now carried chiefly by pack horses, will be conveyed by the Railway.[109]

The first president of the company was Sir James Fergusson, who left this post in 1880 to become governor of Bombay. 15,000 shares were on offer, with a face value of £20 each, but of the 2,000 shares reserved for subscribers in Brazil only 698 were purchased. Work started on the line with great festivity, accompanied by the provincial president, in the following year of 1879, in the district of Santo Amaro in the northern outskirts of Recife. The company contracted the firm of Wilson, Sons & Company in Recife to construct the railway; a firm that had been authorised to do business in imperial Brazil in 1878.[110] The first stretch of the line, from Recife to Pau-d'Alho, was opened to traffic on 24 October 1881. The *Diário de Pernambuco* in Recife carried the news the following day: "Along all the route of the trains there was a constant acclamation of the masses stationed on the borders of the line. Everywhere could be seen flags, arches of leaves, and wreaths of flowers."[111] The newspaper reproduced a telegram from Ailsa Janson, the company's general manager since 1879, congratulating the newspaper and the province on this momentous step forward, to which the *Diário* responded by thanking the company for bringing to conclusion a project that Pernambuco had dreamed of for a long time "as a necessary element for its progress, its happiness, [and] for its material and moral enhancement."

In 1882, the line from Pau d'Alho to Limoeiro was opened, as well as the twelve kilometre branch line from Carpina to Nazaré. According to the Brazilian economist Tagore de Siqueira, the initial rolling stock consisted of ten locomotives, six tenders, seven first class carriages, seventeen second class, and three third class. For cargo transport, there were four baggage cars, fourteen wagons for animals, 109 covered wagons, twenty-three open wagons, six wagons for wood, an inspection carriage, twenty wagons for ballast, and one tanker wagon.[112] Four years later, in 1886, these numbers had risen; there were now fourteen locomotives, 148 covered wagons, and four tanker wagons. Numbers grew over the following years, so that by 1893 there were nineteen locomotives in use on the railway.

As with the Recife and São Francisco railway, the Great Western started in Recife from a station built beside a Dutch fort, in this case the Forte Brum. The line to Limoeiro crossed seven bridges and seventy-two *pontilões* (small bridges), and climbed from sea

The wheel arrangement of a locomotive that ran on the Recife and São Francisco Railway, on display in the Museu do Trem, Recife, Pernambuco. This set of wheels may have belonged to the first locomotive to run on this line.

Author

level to nearly 184 metres altitude at Carpina and then descended to Limoeiro at just over 133 metres. Construction costs averaged 51:978$660 per kilometre, exceeding the maximum declared in the concession. The company's head office was established at 6, Great Winchester Street, London. The company directors were listed in the report submitted to shareholders at the Annual General Meeting held in London in 1879: Sir James Fergusson (president), David Davies (involved in the construction of several railway lines in Britain), Hugh Robert Baines (superintendent of the 'São Paulo Gas Company'; he left the board in the same year of 1879 and was replaced by Frank Parrish), Alfred Phillips Youle (involved in the Conde d'Eu Railway), Edward Keir Hett (a director until 1911), and Spencer Herapath (who had experience with railways in northern England and Argentina). Frank Parrish succeeded James Fergusson as president. Parrish was born in Buenos Aires, was president of the 'Buenos Ayres Great Southern Railway', and had managed several other railways in Argentina and Uruguay. The company secretary was Frederick Ward, and the superintendent for the construction of the railway was Ailsa Janson. Oliver Robert Hawke Bury was the resident engineer of the Great Western of Brazil Railway under Ailsa Janson, becoming locomotive superintendent in 1885. His appointment as Chief Engineer and Manager of the Great Western Railway of Brazil followed in 1892.

Compared to the Recife and São Francisco railway, the Great Western passed through a richer economic zone, and, while the company could not have survived without government support, this railway proved to be more profitable and better managed. The line was also completed in time to take advantage of the first '*usinas centrais*' (central sugar mills) for sugar production established in the early 1880s, in which British business interests had a commanding stake. The imperial government sought to increase the efficiency and quality of sugar production by means of switching management to central factories that each served several outlying *engenhos*, and actively courted foreign capital investment along the same lines as with the railways - concessions with a guarantee of interest corresponding to the amount of approved capital invested. British capital had hitherto favoured investment in railways and services in urban centres, but was drawn into *usinas centrais* where, once again, a minimum annual dividend was guaranteed. This was significant for the Great Western since the central mills were dependent on good railway services, given the increase in sugar production that they made possible.

However, generally speaking, these initiatives were financial failures and regarded by investors as providing little return on investment, despite accounting for nearly 11% of total British investments in Brazil in the period 1876 to 1885.[113] The British imported used machinery (in contravention to the spirit of the decree) for some of these *usinas*, as well as machinery produced for factories to be established in Egypt in others, and they did not have sufficient railway spurs, nor did they build the railways with sufficient care to ensure that the cane was taken efficiently and promptly to the factories. No mill extracted more sugar syrup than the traditional *engenhos*, and all ran deficits in the early years of operation. They were more interested in short-term profits, backed by the guarantee, than in longer term investment. On top of that, the British managers did not understand well the conditions to be faced in a tropical climate and, according to Manuel Andrade in his history of the sugar mills in Pernambuco, they did not maintain good relations with the providers of the cane sugar, and earned salaries that were incompatible with the profits to be made by the company.[114] This led the suppliers to keep back the cane they were contracted to provide and even return to milling cane with the traditional *engenhos banguês*. It is noteworthy that slave labour was also prohibited at the *centrais*.

The first important *usina central* in north-east Brazil was the Central Sugar Factories of Brazil Company Limited. Decree nº 8,627 of 28 July 1882 granted the company permission to function in Brazil, and offered a guarantee of interest at 7% annually. This British company acquired a concession that had been given to Anfrísio Fialho, who had the right to set up six *usinas centrais* in the municipalities of Cabo, Escada, Água Preta, Palmares, Jaboatão, and Goiana. Anfrísio Fialho was joined in this venture by Theodore Christiansen, an Englishman who was married to a wealthy planter. In actual fact, only four factories worked for the Central Sugar; Santo Inácio in Cabo, the Firmesa in Escada (worked from 1884 to 1888), the Cuiambuca (or Cuyambuca) in Água Preta (worked from 1884 to 1888) and the Bom Gosto in Palmares, which started working from the 1884 harvest. The company started liquidation proceedings in 1886. As a result, the Firmesa closed down, and the Cuyambuca, Bom Gosto and Santo Inácio factories were rented to the cane producers and transformed into traditional *usinas*, with only the latter enjoying any success.

A second central mill initiative, the North Brazilian Sugar Factories Company Limited, was authorised to function in the Brazilian empire by decree nº 8,882 of 17 February 1883. Advertisements appeared in Britain in July 1883,[115] describing the aim of the company as: "to collect the sugar canes produced on several plantations at given points, and there treat it by the best known appliances. WASTE OF EXISTING SYSTEM. By the present system employed in Brazil the canes are treated on each plantation by inferior machinery of imperfect design, and in consequence a large percentage of the sugar contained in the canes is wasted." The prospectus cited the "great success of the Central Sugar Factories [that] has been demonstrated by the large amount of their net earnings" and their expectation that they would process 3,550 tons of sugar cane "per day of 24 hours."

The North Brazilian was organised in London in 1882 by Reed, Bowen and Company - a company that was involved in railway construction in north-eastern Brazil - and a group of civil engineers in London. Reed Bowen had started the construction of the Natal and Nova Cruz railway in Rio Grande do Norte in 1878, and later they were involved in building the Great Northern of Brazil Railway. This company was more successful, and remained under British control until 1927. Initially, the firm secured fourteen concessions to build *usinas centrais* with a guarantee of 6% on the agreed capital outlay over twenty years. But there were delays, and government decree 9,564 of 6 March 1886 declared as "lapsed the concession of the *engenhos* of Serinhaem, Ipojuca, Pilar, Maroim, and Camaragibe, given to the North Brazilian Sugar Factories Company Limited." This measure left the company with just three concessions. Still the company dragged its feet, no factory was yet milling cane, and in November 1886, the government decreed a deadline of end January 1887 for the company to complete work on the *usina central* of São Lourenço da Mata in Pernambuco, and end of September 1887 to complete work on the factories of São José do Mipibú in Rio Grande do Norte, and Pau d'Alho in the province of Pernambuco. In the meantime, all guarantee payments were suspended until this work was finished.

In the end, only two central mills worked for the North Brazilian; Usina Tiúma in the municipality of São Lourenço da Mata (Pernambuco) and Usina Cansanção de Sinimbu (Alagoas). The Tiúma mill started operations in 1887, in the same year that Reed Bowen was facing bankruptcy.[116] The company was reconstituted in 1888 with help from Barings Bank. The Tiúma *usina* actually survived and did reasonably well, despite polluting local waters and killing the fish that local people depended on, and having to send home the English manager who had become a drunkard, among other problems that convinced the government in 1895 to again suspend the guarantee of interest. In 1927, Tiúma was acquired by the Fileno de Miranda group, and in 1929, this *usina* owned eight sugar properties, sixty-one kilometres of railway, seven locomotives, and 339 wagons.

The Brazilian economist Marcelo de Paiva Abreu summarises the reasons behind the failure of these initiatives:

> The most important sectoral failure of British investment in Brazil occurred in sugar milling, namely the central mills installed in the North-East of the country in the 1880s. They were depicted as a revolutionary advance that would fully exploit the advantages of large-scale production and as intrinsically more efficient than traditional, estate-based *engenhos*. But most central mills went bankrupt for reasons which ranged from fraud and gross mismanagement to technical problems and difficulty in obtaining access to supplies of low-cost sugar-cane. (Marcelo de Paiva Abreu: 2000)

In 1882, the imperial government decided that it would make sense to link the Great Western branch line to Nazaré in Pernambuco with the Conde d'Eu Railway in the adjoining province of Paraíba at Timbaúba, and approached the Great Western with an offer. The concession for this undertaking included the usual clauses, but there was no guarantee of interest, and after a period of seventy years this line would revert to the state with no indemnity, including all the works and buildings and materials used to build the extension. Work started on this connecting line in June 1886, when Jason Rigby was general manager, and two years later the two sections were inaugurated, Nazaré to Aliança and Aliança to Timbaúba.[117]

While the Great Western was happy to build this extension to their network, the company may have been motivated by the threat of initiatives on the horizon that might compete with their business. In May 1881, the company had petitioned the provincial president of Pernambuco to suspend the tender that had been announced for a railway linking Goyanna (today Goiana) with Timbaúba.[118] A later petition, also addressed to the president, and dated 13 April 1882, was heavy-handed; the company "demands the non approval of the surveys that were presented by the concessionaires of the provincial railway from Goanna to Timbaúba."[119] The provincial authorities paid no attention, and granted Henrique (Henry) Snell of the Reed Bowen Company his request to the inspector of the provincial treasury for acknowledgement of his contract of 16 June 1882, an agreement that referred to the building of a railway from Goyanna to Timbaúba. The Great Western was horrified, and on 19 July they sent an official petition to the provincial president demanding that their protest against the Goyanna-Timbaúba project be forwarded at once to the imperial government - "an act that [the company] considers offensive to its contract," citing Article 38 that provided for a privilege zone of twenty kilometres on either side of their line. This petition concluded: "The violation of its contract is aggravated in consideration of the undeniable right that the Great Western has to the natural extension of its branch to Nazaré."[120] The province was unmoved, and on 8 August 1882 a contract was signed with representatives of the Reed Bowen Company for the construction of a railway between Olinda and Itambé, uncomfortably close to Timbaúba, from the Great Western's perspective.

The imperial government came to the rescue, with decree n° 8,822 of 30 December 1882, which declared: "the Recife to Limoeiro railway and the Nazaré branch with its extension as far as the junction with the Conde d'Eu railway in the province of Paraíba to be of general interest to the state." This was in effect an embargo against Reed Bowen's project, and authorised the Great Western to construct this line. Henrique (Henry) Snell and Francisco (Francis) Arthur Bowen of the Reed Bowen Company appealed against this decision, "considering that this act of the imperial government is offensive to the concession for the railway between Goyanna and Timbaúba awarded by the presidency of the Province of Pernambuco." To no avail. The central government enjoyed the 'constitutional attribution' to make this decision; the judges hearing the case ruled that it had acted "within the plenitude of its rights when it decided on the issue of general interest, on which it is the supreme judge," backed by the 1874 decree that ascribed to the central government authority to award concessions for railway construction where the line would link two or more provinces.

But this was not the end of the matter. The provincial president did abide by the ruling, but it seems that Reed Bowen proceeded with their construction work, so that on 3 February 1883 the Great Western felt obliged to petition the president again, complaining that the company "was prejudiced in its acquired rights, given that the Great Western Railway Company also has a contract agreed for the same stretch of the railway on which they are working,"[121] and they asked for the necessary steps to be taken. Perhaps irritated by this complaint, or perhaps playing along with both companies to see which would have the best proposal, on 10 March 1883 the province authorised the transfer of the contracts held by Henry Snell and Francis Arthur Bowen, representing the concessionaire Reed, Bowen & Company, to James Strick, a director of the Great Northern of Brazil Railway in London (expressly founded to take over the concession), and Edgar Norris Brandon, secretary to the new company.[122] Then a new president took over in the province in April, and Francis Bowen went on the offensive. On 20 July 1883 he sent a petition to the provincial president: "to complain against the act of the predecessor presidency in the ruling where he denied the approval of the respective railway for being in the privilege zone of the Great Western Company, contrary to article 04 of the contract made with the appellant."[123]

The imperial government also dithered over the matter; imperial decree n° 9,089 of 15 December 1883 conceded "permission for the Great Northern of Brazil Railway to function in the Empire." The wording is explicit: the central government "conceded the right to construct, maintain, administer and operate a railway between the cities of Olinda and Itambé, and also [...] the right to construct, maintain, administer and operate a railway from the city of Goyanna to the villa of Timbaúba." The Great Northern was invited to present a detailed proposal, and in January 1884 they were given an extension of nine months for these studies to be presented. The Great Western was furious, and on 20 February they sent an official note to the provincial president to complain "against the second extension of the deadline conceded to Henrique Snell and another as legal representatives of the Great Northern Railway Company Limited for the studies of the line taken by the first section of the Olinda to Itambé Railway, asking for its revocation, given that it was requested by a procurator without power of attorney."[124] William Hughes, "representative of the Great Northern of Brazil Limited," duly requested permission to register the power of attorney for him to act on behalf of the Great Northern, as reported in the *Jornal do Recife* on 19 June 1884, and to ask for the 1882 imperial decree to be shelved.

In October 1884, two more years were given for the plans to be submitted,[125] but in the end the provincial government did not approve the studies. The conflict over this line rumbled on for many years. Reed Brown & Company petitioned the provincial president on 27 July 1889:

> The concessionaires of the Timbaúba-Goyanna Railway request measures to be taken against the claim of the Limoeiro Railway Company [that is, the Great Western] to build a

branch from Nazaré to Timbaúba that does not have the approval of the presidency [of the province], since it infringes the rights acquired by the plaintiffs.[126]

notwithstanding the fact that this line had apparently already been completed the previous year. There was litigation, pitting the Great Northern against the Great Western, which the latter won. The Great Northern also asked the central government for £297,100 as compensation, which they never received. The dogged persistence of the Great Northern in arguing its rights elicited this caustic response from *The Brazilian Review* in 1901:

> The Great Northern of Brazil Railway. If they have nothing else to boast of, at least the syndicate, or concessionaires, or whatever they call themselves, of this ghostly railway, cannot be accused of lack of patience or tenacity. In season and out of season they peg away at the Brazilian Government and drag in this Great Northern Myth into every discussion of things Brazilian like another King Charles' head. The letter we transcribe in another column, however, shows that even in London, people are not quite idiots and are able to read between the lines as well as anyone else. Still, holdfast is a good dog and if the Great Brazilian Northerners peg away long enough, we should not be surprised if some day they get something for their trouble after all. The ablest negotiator and diplomatist we ever knew owed his success chiefly to his inimitable faculty of making himself an unmitigated nuisance, so that people had to give in self defence. [...] If the Great Northern of Brazil Railway, in addition to their own capacities in this direction, could secure his services, their business would be as good as done![127]

In the Great Western's first year of full operation - the financial year 1882-1883 - 2,061 first class passengers were carried on the railway and 33,377 second class.[128] In the following financial year, third class carriages were introduced, and the total number of passengers rose to over 60,000, of whom around 4% were travelling first class. This figure rose over the next decades, so that in 1900, 361,650 passengers were travelling on the railway. Dübs & Company in Glasgow provided ten locomotives in 1884 for the railway.[129] The main products carried from the interior of Pernambuco to Recife were (in approximate order of importance): sugar, cotton, cottonseed, wood, and rum from sugar cane. On the outward journey into the interior, merchandise included jerked beef, cod, machinery, ironmongery, flour, salt, spices, kerosene, and wine. In the period to the end of the century the volumes carried of cotton and wood carried were relatively stable.[130]

This was less true of sugar, a business that was more volatile, subject to fluctuations, and harvests were a constant source of worry to the company. The volume of sacks of sugar carried to Recife (one sack of sugar weighed 75 kilograms) in financial year 1892-1893 amounted to 1,700,000 sacks, rising two years later to 2,800,000 sacks. But the volume during the two crises for sugar, in 1885-1886 and 1889-1890, came respectively to 99,000 sacks and 178,600 sacks. And there was competition. The Great Western had no monopoly in the early years: in 1884-1885, only 19% of the sugar transported in Pernambuco was carried by this railway, (compared to 37% on the Recife and São Francisco railway), while 32% was carried by water and 12% still on horseback[131]. However, the Great Western's share had grown from 8% when it opened two years previously.

In the period to 1889, when Brazil changed from empire to republic, there were only two periods of deficit: the second year of operation (1883-1884), and during the financial crisis of 1885 to 1886.[132] In his annual report for the year of 1890, the chairman Frank Parrish was able to report: "There is no doubt that our little railway, with its pretentious title, for which I bear no responsibility, has been creeping ahead and has been making steady progress for some time past."[133] But the line was not without its problems. The Great Western was often the target of cartoons and criticism in newspapers in this period. There were frequent complaints of the high tariffs charged, and the precedence given to British residents. The Brazilian historian Estevão Pinto quotes a certain Van Ufel who complained that:

> Entire English families travelled for months successively in first class carriages between Pau d'Alho and Recife without at least using the respective passes, as if the railway was a private property of these families. Not only that, the trains stopped at the doors of the houses where the British subjects lived, in flagrant abuse of the regulations. Or it happened that the line was obstructed by some special train destined to transport the English notables.[134]

Soon after the Great Western inaugurated the Recife to Limoeiro line, another railway started operation in Pernambuco, this time going truly west from Recife, to Caruaru in the interior - the Central de Pernambuco railway. As with the Sul de Pernambuco (the extension to the Recife and São Francisco Railway), this railway was built by the state, and in time was also taken over by the Great Western. Farmers wanted an outlet to the coast for their growing agricultural produce, and petitioned the provincial and imperial governments to invest in this initiative instead of building the proposed extension of the Sul de Pernambuco from Garanhuns to Águas Bellas, in the direction of the São Francisco river, and in fact this was never built.

Provincial Law n° 649 of 20 March 1866 (two years before the similar provincial law for the Great Western) authorised the Pernambuco government to contract the building of a railway that would link "centres of population in the interior of the Province (a) with the stations of the Recife to São Francisco Railway, (b) with the roads of communication of the capital [Recife], (c) with the points on the coast of easy access to navigation." (translation). A concession for the first stretch from Recife to Jaboatão was awarded to José da Costa Júnior, but this lapsed and the imperial government declared its interest, not only in the short railway to Jaboatão, but in an extension onwards to Caruaru. As a result, imperial decree n° 7,055 of 26 October 1878 authorised studies to be carried out for this line, and the same contractor who had expected to build the railway from Garanhuns to Águas Bellas was contracted. Construction started in 1881, fifteen years after the provincial law was passed. It seems that the management at the Recife and São Francisco Railway complained to the imperial court in 1884 that this line would invade its privilege zone, but this got nowhere.

A short seventeen kilometre section from Recife to Jaboatão was opened to traffic in 1885, and other sections were inaugurated successively until Caruaru was reached in 1895; the inaugural train ran on this 180 kilometre track from Recife on 1 December 1895. The line ran from a station (which still stands) besides the prison on the banks of the Rio Capibaribe, and climbed from near sea level to Vitória at 146 metres. The railway then faced a stiff climb to Bezerros at 459 metres, before reaching Caruaru at 554 metres altitude. The Serra das Russas was a formidable obstacle between Vitória and Bezerros, and the constructor had to build twenty-one tunnels, one of which 259 mts long, and nine bridges, including the Grota Funda bridge with a span of 180 metres. The route taken to climb the granite mass of the Serra das Russas escarpment was much criticised. Estevão Pinto believes that this was the product of "A hurried study, or bad administrative management, [which] diverted the true path of the route between kilometres 54 to 88, taking it in the direction of the Serra das Russas" over ground that was rocky, unproductive and excessively hilly.[135] There was also no water along this

"Pessoas da sociedade Pernambucana. Piquenique em um dos engenhos de São Lourenço" (People of high society in Pernambuco. Picnic at one of the sugar engenhos in São Lourenço)
Courtesy of Biblioteca Central Blanche Knopf, photograph library, Fundação Joaquim Nabuco, Recife. Ref. F.R. 3.010.

track, and this had to be carried to the works by train. In the event, the worst stretch, from Russinha to Gravatá, took seven years of intensive labour to construct, while it took the company only one year to reach Caruaru from Gravatá. Before the Central de Pernambuco railway was opened, the interior to the west of Recife only exported cotton, tobacco twist, and hides. Sugar now became an important item of cargo on the new railway.

There was one other and quite incredible railway initiative in Pernambuco; a concession awarded to the Visconde de Figueiredo to build a railway from the terminus of the Recife and São Francisco railway across Argentina to Valparaíso in Chile authorised by imperial decree n° 10,069 of 27 October 1888. Not surprisingly, this project never got off the ground.

In the closing years of the Brazilian Empire there were now two British-owned lines in Pernambuco, The Recife and São Francisco Railway and The Great Western of Brazil Railway, together with two state-run lines, the Sul de Pernambuco and the Central de Pernambuco. Even before the onset of the republic in 1889, the government was concerned about the drain on the treasury represented by the privately-run railways and complaints about the quality and cost of the service. In 1888, the ministry of agriculture decided to impose tariff controls on the railways, and, as we shall see in a later chapter, the Great Western of Brazil Railway was about to enter a period of uncertainty, but ultimately of unexpected growth.

A Man Of Probity And Integrity
Railways in Alagoas to 1889

Seeking to link the upper and lower reaches of the river São Francisco, there was not, in the survey of this line, any concern to examine the economical-financial aspect of the company, with the result that the studies limited themselves to shortening the distances, taking the line across a sterile region and of sparse population, instead of looking for the fertile regions of the valleys of Pão de Açúcar. The construction of this railway was an economic error.

Estevão Pinto, 1949[136]

Previously a *comarca*, or administrative district, of Pernambuco, the *capitania* of Alagoas was established in 1817, and became a province in Brazil in 1821. In November 1821, Baldwin Sealy was appointed as the British vice consul to serve in Maceió, the site of the best port in the region, that of Jaraguá, and capital of the province (replacing Marechal Deodoro) from 1839. Sealy was the first foreign vice consul in Alagoas, and he was followed by Arthur MacHardy (from 1838), and by James Burnett, who was much involved in the exchange of information on the slave trade with the Foreign Office in London in the 1840s. These appointments reflected the growing presence and importance of the British in Alagoas, especially in commercial houses that initially were branches of companies in Recife and Salvador. The number of British residents rose, so that by 1825 the British government acquired a plot of land for a British cemetery, on the beach of Jaraguá, which today is the Avenida Duque de Caxias. According to Moacir Medeiros de Santana (1970: 56) all but two of the export-import businesses in Maceió in 1828 were British-owned: Mellors & Russel, Humphrey Mitchell, Joseph Wells, Lowes & Johnson, Robert Gray, Diogo (James) Burnett, Guilherme (William) Clark, and Baldwin Sealy.

The economy of Alagoas in the nineteenth century was based mainly on sugar - there were around five hundred *engenhos* in the province in the 1850s. Cotton was also an important product. It had been planted since the late eighteenth century, and enjoyed an immense growth in production during the American Civil War (1861-1865) when cotton became scarce on the world markets. Other agricultural produce included coffee, beans, corn, rice, cassava, wood, and coconuts. Little had been exported during the colonial period and even during the early years of the *primeiro reinado*, the period when Dom Pedro I governed the empire of Brazil, but exports grew following his abdication in 1831, making use of the port of Jaraguá in Maceió. However, before railways were built in the province the existing roads going north and south were in a terrible state, and much of the produce for export from the interior went directly to Pernambuco and onwards by rail to Recife on the Recife and São Francisco Railway, especially from 1862, when the fourth section came into operation.

On 2 July 1864, provincial vice-president Roberto Calheiros de Mello sanctioned Law n° 428, which authorised the government "to arrange for the necessary studies for the costing of a railway that, leaving from Jaraguá, places this capital [of Maceió] in communication with the centre of the province." (translation). Two days later, the imperial government signed Lei n° 439 that gave financial support to this initiative. This was undoubtedly influenced by the existence of the Recife and São Francisco Railway in Pernambuco - the concession given to the de Mornay brothers in 1852, who had close family and commercial links with Alagoas. According to the historian Douglas Apratto Tenório, the de Mornay family had lived in Alagoas since 1844.[137]

The first practical step was taken by a contract signed in 1866 by the provincial government with the Companhia Bahiana de Navegação a Vapor, a company founded in 1839 that in 1862 had become the Bahia Steam Navigation Company with headquarters in London. This involved a six kilometre tramway linking the port of Jaraguá with Trapiche da Barra, from where the company was obliged to establish connecting transport on the nearby lakes. The contract stipulated that "as the means of traction the company will use animal power or steam mechanical power," and that the concession would end in 1882. The provincial government undertook to invest sixty-five *contos de réis* (65:000$000)[138] in the project, to be paid in five instalments. Douglas Apratto Tenório's judgement is that "There is no doubt that this was a measure of great social and economic reach, within the most advanced standards of the time, and brought indisputable practical advantages for the transport of cargo and passengers in the region."[139] This urban train or tramway consisted of two locomotives with two passenger carriages and six wagons for cargo, and was duly opened to traffic as far as Trapiche da Barra on 25 March 1868.

Key to understanding the involvement of the Bahia Steam Navigation Company in this venture, and to accounting for the development of railways in Alagoas, is the name of Hugh Wilson, who was a major shareholder in the company, first with the post of secretary and later as general manager. The company had been founded by British residents in Bahia in 1839, but went bankrupt in 1847 due to poor management, the absence of any government subsidy, and a generally unfavourable economic climate. Brazilian businessmen bought the company, which was renamed as the Companhia Bonfim. The Companhia Bahiana de Navegação a Vapor resurfaced in 1858, as a result of the fusion between two companies, Bonfim and Santa Cruz, who together carried out steamship transport between 1852 and 1858, until the Companhia Bahiana was re-established in 1858 as a single entity. Four years later, in 1862, British investors acquired the greater part of the company shares and, with headquarters in London, the firm became known by the English name of The Bahia Steam Navigation Company. Hugh Wilson soon appears as a leading figure in the company, with the second largest number of shares, after an Englishman named John Watson. The author of his obituary, published in *The Rio News* in October 1888, explains that Hugh Wilson had worked on railways in Venezuela before coming to Brazil in 1863 to work on the Bahia and São Francisco Railway, which was at that time being completed as far as Alagoinhas. "The late Hugh Wilson was a man of probity and integrity, most active and enterprising, and generous to a degree, and his kind nature and liberality won for him the sympathy of a wide circle of friends in Brazil."[140]

He obtained a loan of 160:000$000 réis from the Banco da Bahia on behalf of the Bahia Steam Navigation Company to establish steam navigation on the river São Francisco and the lakes named Norte and Manguaba in the province of Alagoas, and it seems that he began to focus his attentions on this more northerly province. In late 1869, Hugh Wilson left the post of superintendent of the company. He was hired in that year by the Alagoas provincial government to survey a line from Maceió going northwest of Maceió to Vila Nova da Imperatriz (today União dos Palmares). This was a response to the provisions of the 1864 law and an undertaking signed by the provincial president,

"Engineering extraordinary, Alagoas Railway", number 3 of 'Sketches in the northern provinces of Brazil', The Illustrated London News, 14 December 1889, page 768.
Author's Collection

José Bento Figueiredo Junior, on 8 June 1869 for Hugh Wilson to build this railway, with the promise of privilege for thirty years.

Flushed, it appears, with thoughts about the prospects offered by the revolutionary use of steam power, the provincial government also signed a contract for a survey of another railway a month later, on 7 July 1869, offering the same conditions as for Hugh Wilson. This contract was with a competing steamship company, the Companhia Pernambucana de Navegação Costeira a Vapor (the coastal steam navigation company based on Recife in Pernambuco) to survey a line from Maceió to Palmeiras dos Índios via Anadia (to the west of Maceió), and to the north towards Pernambuco via Porto Calvo. The historian Douglas Apratto Tenório sees this as compensation to the Companhia Pernambucana, which vied with the Bahia Steam Navigation for concessions for transport along the coast, across the lakes, and on the rivers. However, this contract was not carried out, perhaps because the clauses of the agreement were rather vague, or perhaps because the Hugh Wilson group turned their guns on this rival concession and had better political influence at imperial and provincial levels.[141]

After the line had been surveyed, provincial Law n° 568 of 24 May 1870 authorised Hugh Wilson "or whomever might offer more advantages" to build a railway from Maceió along the Vale do Mundaú to Vila Nova da Imperatriz, to be built within four years from the approval of the company's statutes by the imperial government. Significantly, this concession also promised a privilege of use lasting ninety years. The provincial decree n° 596 of June 1871 recognised the short Jaraguá to Trapiche da Barra line as the start of a railway going into the interior to Vila Nova da Imperatriz as the Estrada de Ferro da Província das Alagoas (the Alagoas province railway); a move that was polemical and angered those opposed to Hugh Wilson, who was by now becoming a powerful businessman with interests from Paraíba to Bahia.

But Hugh Wilson did not always see off his rivals; on the following day (25 May 1870) provincial Law n° 572 authorised Jacques Bonnefond to build a railway leaving Maceió with the aim of connecting with the Recife and São Francisco Railway in Pernambuco, and the obligation to pass through the towns of Camaragibe and Porto Calvo. This concession was given imperial government approval in 1874 (by decree n° 5,792, of 11 November 1874) and conceded "to Jacques Bonnefond authorisation to extend the Maceió railway to the valley of Jacuipe as far as the Province of Pernambuco and come to a junction with the Recife to São Francisco railway." Despite this backing, nothing was achieved with this initiative. Apratto Tenório believes that Hugh Wilson's group manoeuvred to scupper the project.[142]

On 8 April 1872 a provincial resolution authorised the construction of Hugh Wilson's railway, the Estrada de Ferro Central (central railway). "This was the coup de grâce, delivered by Wilson, a master stroke, silencing the voices of those in opposition to his group, and pushing aside the attacks of other businessmen, since this assured him of the dominion of the economically more profitable regions of the province."[143] The first stretch of ten kilometres from Maceió to Bebedouro (on Lagoa Mundaú) was inaugurated on 19 October 1872 by the concessionaire, with the name of The Alagoas Brazilian Central Railway Company Limited, but also known as the Companhia Anônima da Imperial Estrada de Ferro das Alagoas. The line operated on a gauge of 1 metre 44 cms. with steam locomotive power and also with animals pulling trams. Decree n° 5,672 of 17 June 1874 awarded Hugh Wilson's company a guarantee of 7% interest, but the line to Bebedouro was all that this company achieved, and by 1879 the concession was considered to be lapsed.

It may be that this was, at least in part, because Hugh Wilson turned the focus of his attention back to Bahia in this period. In 1871, the provincial governor of Bahia sent him to London to negotiate the purchase of the bankrupt Paraguassú Steam Tram-Road Company Limited, a company organised by an English engineer named John Charles Morgan with the aim of reaching the diamond prospecting zone of the Chapada Diamantina in the interior of Bahia, but which went bankrupt in 1869 after only twenty-five kilometres of track had been laid.[144] It seems that it was Hugh Wilson who had proposed this course of action and, as a reward, on 26 September 1872 Hugh Wilson was awarded a contract that committed him to assume the bankrupt estate of this narrow gauge undertaking and organise a new company. This contract was ratified by the government of Dom Pedro II, according to imperial decree n° 5,777 of 28 October 1874. Hugh Wilson organised a company in Britain in the following year with the name of The Brazilian Imperial Central Bahia Railway Company Limited, known in Brazil as the Companhia Anonyma da Imperial Estrada de Ferro Central da Bahia, which was then given permission to function in the empire by decree n.° 6,094 of 12 January 1876. Construction did start, with the first stretch to modern-day Feira de Santana opened to traffic in 1876, and the final section inaugurated in 1887, but by this time the diamond rush had lost momentum.

Hugh Wilson was involved in another railway in the province of Bahia; the railway from Santo Amaro to Jacú. The original concession was held by Antônio Salustino Antunes, who transferred the rights to the Visconde de Sergimirin, who in turn commissioned

Wilson to lay the tracks. When the viscount faced certain financial difficulties, the company shares were transferred to the English engineer, and Hugh Wilson started construction in February 1875. However, in April 1878 the provincial government took over operation of this short line. In recognition of his services to that province, in 1882, the president of Bahia made Hugh Wilson a *commendador* of the Imperial Order of the Rose of Brazil. In October of the following year, Hugh Wilson and his son, William (Guilherme), were praised in the press on the occasion of the opening of the third of the six stretches of the Brazilian Imperial Central Bahia Railway: "Hugh Wilson, head of Wilson & Son, of London, and the engineer Guilherme Wilson, his son and representative in Brazil, received significant manifestations of recognition for the great deal they have done for the material development of Brazil."[145]

Returning to the development of railways in Alagoas, in which Hugh Wilson continued to be involved, when the provincial Alagoas Brazilian Central Railway project folded, the central government stepped in and by imperial decree n° 7,517 of 18 October 1879 authorised two businessmen, Manoel Joaquim da Silva Leão and Domingos Moitinho, to undertake new surveys for the railway of one metre gauge from Maceió to Vila da Imperatriz. The decree was signed on behalf of the emperor by João Lins Vieira Cansansão de Sinimbu, later named the Visconde de Siminbu in 1888. He was a former president of Alagoas, and at that time the influential Minister of Transport and Minister of Agriculture (from January 1878 to March 1880). He was also the powerful president of the Council of Ministers of the empire, and greatly enthused by the possibility of promoting railway construction in his native province. The surveys were approved and the imperial government awarded a concession (decree n° 7,895 of 12 November 1880) of ninety years, with a privilege zone of twenty kilometres on either side of the track, and a 7% interest guarantee on a maximum capital investment of 4,553:000$ over thirty years.

Following the usual pattern, decree n° 8,223 of 30 August 1881 authorised a company headquartered in London to take over the concession. This was The Alagoas Railway Company Limited, organised in May that year and set up purposefully to acquire the rights, which absorbed the Alagoas Brazilian Central Railway. The directors in London provided instructions to a general manager in Alagoas appointed by the company. William Rankin was the company representative from 1881, and the first resident engineer, but he returned to England shortly after the line began operating, and was replaced by John Edward Wolfe, his assistant engineer. Hugh Wilson remained influential, and headed the construction company commissioned by the Alagoas Railway Company to undertake the work. According to the historian Apratto Tenório, "The two companies never had any problems between themselves and always walked hand in hand, throwing petals from one to the other."[146] Work started in March 1882 on the eighty-eight kilometre one-metre gauge track, and the first train from Maceió reached Imperatriz on 25 October 1884. The line was officially inaugurated and opened provisionally to traffic on 3 December 1884, and its full operation was authorised by the imperial government in May 1885. This railway mainly transported sugar and cotton from the interior. Later on, a branch was built to Assembléia (opened in 1891) and an extension to São José da Lage (reached in 1894).

While the English concessionaire and Hugh Wilson's construction company worked together harmoniously, there was legal wrangling in 1882 between this consortium and the provincial tax office supported by the president of Alagoas. The issue concerned the owners of land over which the railway would pass who were discontented with the compensation offered, and they took their grievances to the imperial court. The pace of construction work was badly affected, especially when there were disturbances involving armed men engaged by the landowners to attack company property. The owner of the Cariry *engenho*, for example, was accused by the railway company of destroying a bridge and throwing more than one hundred sleepers into the river Mundaú that were swept away by the current. The railway station of Bebedouro was also attacked by a band of more than forty armed men, and the company asked for energetic measures to be taken to stifle this violence. On top of this, the two companies were accused several times of breaking their commitments, whether by disrespecting them or arbitrarily altering their contracts with the empire and with the province. For instance, the municipal government in Maceió in 1882 complained to the president of the province about the excavations being made in different roads in the city that were disrupting public transport.

Held back by these difficulties, the company applied for an extension to the deadline in the contract from March 1884 to the new date of 2 December that year. This request was sanctioned, but they had to pay a fine of 1% per month on the amount of guarantee received - a decision that they argued against, citing force majeure, but lost. The company was so reluctant to pay up that the government was still asking for the fine to be paid in 1886.

Meeting together in 1885, the directors in London were generally satisfied with the first year of operation, and voted dividends to be paid to the shareholders. Having reached the terminus at Imperatriz, this town was now becoming a centre for purchasing, ginning, and pressing cotton, with two factories and warehouses quickly established after the railway arrived. The company experimented with the running of cheap excursion trains in the holiday season, and this initiative was very successful. The general manager's report for 1885 noted encouragingly that:

> We have carried a larger proportion of the sugar and cotton crops, and an absolutely greater quantity of general goods, [which] speaks hopefully for the future prosperity of the railway. The towns on the line, especially Muricy [*sic*], Branquinha and Imperatriz, are rapidly growing, and planting is extending, giving every sign that our business will steadily improve.[147]

However, the board noted that the railway was only carrying 7½% of the total sugar exported through the port of Maceió and only 13% of the cotton, and they concluded that branch lines would have to be built. A provincial law passed in July 1885 responded by authorising the construction of two branch lines. The Alagoas State governor's annual report on 1889 noted that: "For a State like this one, where the main source of public wealth consists of the agricultural industry, the present-day fast and secure communications that it possesses are all insufficient, whether on account of the short extension of the railways, or whether because of the special position in which they are found placed."[148]

The first branch was a sixty-two kilometre line linking Lourenço de Albuquerque with Assembléia (named Viçosa from 1890). This was backed by decree 10,256 of 22 June 1889, which offered a guarantee of interest of 6% per annum on a maximum capital invested of 30.000$ réis per kilometre, taking in the Vale do Paraíba, an area which provided about half the sugar and one third of the cotton exported through Maceió, and this was opened to traffic in December 1891. The second branch line was similar to the failed Jacques Bonnefond project of the early 1870s. A contract was celebrated in September 1885 between the Alagoas Railway and the provincial government for a line that crossed the fertile region of Jetituba, and fulfilled a demand of the municipality of Camaragibe, in the north-east of Alagoas near the border with Pernambuco. Later on, this branch was extended as far as Quebrangulo, where it arrived in 1911, and from there to Palmeira dos Índios, before finally reaching Porto Real do Colégio on the river São Francisco.

In the first two years of operation, 1885 and 1886, as noted in the *Revista de Engenharia* of 1889, "income did not cover costs, and in 1887 and 1888 the balance was insignificant, which must have been absorbed by the expenses of the board of directors in London, so that the state must have shouldered the full burden of the guarantee. With regard to these results, traffic on the line has shown an encouraging movement."[149] This was true, in 1885 there had been 27,039 passengers and 8,915 tons of merchandise carried, while in 1888 these numbers had grown to 52,132 passengers and 18,889 tons. The 1886 annual report showed that 30% more sugar was carried during the year, and that the amount of cotton had increased by 87%. There were now five factories for processing cotton in Imperatriz and eighteen warehouses to stock the cotton. However, passenger numbers dropped by 34% in the second year of operation, now that the novelty of riding on a train had worn off. In 1886, there were eight locomotives, three first class carriages, four second class, and two mixed passenger carriages, together with ninety-two wagons of various types. The directors' report for the year of 1887[150] noted that receipts in Brazil had amounted to £19,557 and expenditure, including loss on exchange, to £91,810, but the interest guaranteed by the imperial government for the year had been received, with which the year ended showing a balance of £21,355, enough for the directors to recommend a dividend of 5½%.

At the beginning of the twentieth century, the Alagoas Railway Company was absorbed by the Great Western of Brazil Railway Company, as was another railway built mostly within Alagoas, and the most intriguing of all the lines taken over by the Great Western, in part because this was the only line never to be physically connected with the network. This was the one metre gauge Paulo Afonso Railway (usually spelt Paulo *Affonso* in older documents) that was named after the main eighty-metre high waterfall of Paulo Afonso in the cataract system of the river São Francisco. Remarkably, when the young emperor Dom Pedro II visited the Paulo Afonso falls in 1859, he decided, after a bone-shaking ride on a donkey, to authorise the construction of a railway to circumvent the rapids and improve transport on the river.

But nothing happened for many years, until 1868, when an engineer named Carlos Krauss was directed by the Ministry of Agriculture to carry out a survey for a railway line that would link the upper and lower reaches of the river. The two river navigations were completely separated by 128 kilometres of waterfalls that made connections between traffic on the two river systems impossible. The plans were delivered, but the project was not taken further until ten years later, triggered in the main by the emergency of the great drought of 1877 to 1878 that inflicted misery on many thousands in the semi-arid regions of the north-east of Brazil. The imperial government sought "to save the lives of the countrymen driven out of their homes in [the provinces of] Piauí, Ceará, Rio Grande do Norte, Paraíba, Pernambuco, and Alagoas, who crowded together, dirty, starving, depressed, on the banks of the São Francisco."[151] Masses of poverty-stricken people also assembled in the cities along the coast, and the provincial governments were goaded into pleading for help from the central government.

In the name of the emperor, Alagoas-born minister Sinimbu issued decree n°. 6,918 of 1 June 1878 that authorised "the extraordinary credit of 9.000:000$000 to pay for the expropriation of the Baturité railway [in Ceará] and to cover the expenses of its extension as far as Canôa, as well as the construction of the Sobral railway [also in Ceará] and the Paulo Affonso railway." In the same month, on 19 June, Sinimbu signed a further decree that was specific to the Paulo Afonso railway: "It is my intention to authorise that on behalf of the state the definitive studies and construction of the Paulo Affonso railway should proceed, for a gauge of one metre between the rails, from the Port of Piranhas as far as Jatobá [today Petrolândia]."[152] Piranhas lies just below the cataracts, at a distance of 228 kilometres from the sea.

A second initial survey was carried out by the American engineer Wilson Milnor Roberts, who died of typhoid fever in Brazil in 1881. A more detailed land survey was undertaken from August 1878, led by a German engineer named Reinaldo von Krüger, and governed by two overriding principles: joining the upper and lower reaches of the river, and taking the shortest possible route. The foundation stone for the future railway has survived, and can be seen in the textile factory museum in present-day Delmiro Gouveia; a town previously named Pedra, and a station on the Paulo Afonso Railway. The legend reads: "EFPA, 1878, P. II," presumably referring to the 'Estrada de Ferro Paulo Afonso' and Dom Pedro II. Construction started very soon afterwards, on 23 October 1878, at Piranhas in Alagoas, and may even have commenced before the final survey and budget were approved. The earthmoving was done by gangs of navies; the drought-exhausted migrants from the *sertão* (semi-arid region) of the north-east of Brazil. Perhaps this early start, only four months after the decree was issued, was due to pressure to get the men working, but the result was that no detailed geological survey was undertaken prior to construction, and the engineers encountered granite in several sections. Several cuttings were dug along the 116 kilometre track; the deepest was near the Olhos d'Agua station, which was 214 metres in length and twelve metres deep at the maximum.

The railway had a dual purpose, as described by one of the directors, Dr. Mello Netto (or Melo Neto):

> 1°. That of linking commercially and socially the upper and lower reaches of the São Francisco, whose extensive length, according to the conscientious studies of the notable and lamented North American engineer W. M. Roberts, was divided into five sections.
> 2°. That of utilising, to hasten this construction, the arms of thousands of Brazilians who, beset by the periodical droughts of the North [of Brazil] and in pitiful and painful promiscuity, emigrated from the high *sertões* of Ceará, Bahia & Pernambuco to the capitals on the coastline, where, for lack of remunerated work, and with great embarrassment, perhaps, they begged for public charity.[153]

The president of the province of Aalgoas noted in his annual report for 1879 (page 5) that of the more than 7,000 *retirantes* (migrants) who had passed through the town of Piranhas, 1,571 had found employment in the construction of the railway, and food was provided for their families as well as for 961 widows, orphans, and blind and crippled people. This must have been back-breaking work. *The Rio News* reported on 24 September 1879 that work was continuing on the first and most difficult stretch, but was hampered by a lack of any means of transportation: "Until recently, all work of that character has been done by men, no mules being available. Besides that, they have suffered from a lack of water which has been transported to the works for a distance of eight or ten miles."

A tragedy occurred during the construction period. The *Jornal do Recife* reported on 24 July 1880 on a disaster on the Paulo Afonso railway one week earlier that involved a train loaded with construction materials for the line, as well as with engineers, workers, and distinguished visitors seated on top of the wagons. The train reached a place known as Cipós, where the driver thought he could uncouple his locomotive and go for water to replenish his tanks. The wagons began to slip backwards, pulled by the force of gravity, and one jumped the tracks in a cutting, stopping the downhill descent. The driver rushed at full speed after the retreating wagons and crashed over the first wagons, killing eleven people, including a provincial deputy, and badly injuring three. Another accident occurred on 20 January 1891, when seven people, including the manager of the line, died during the inaugural run of the PAULO AFFONSO locomotive. In all probability, the driver had got drunk during the inaugural festivities, and he left the station at Piranhas at full speed, derailing at kilometre 1.

On the same day that this account was published, 24 July 1880, the English language *Rio News* reported that the first locomotive, named the MACEIÓ, had run over three kilometres of new track at Piranhas. The railway opened to traffic provisionally on 25 February 1881 after twenty-eight kilometres had been built, and then, still provisionally, along fifty-four kilometres on 10 June 1882. Despite the rushed start to building the line, the entire length of 116 kilometres only reached Jatobá[154] after five years of construction, on 2 August 1883, running over ground in two provinces, Alagoas and Pernambuco. Apart from the accidents, there were several stoppages due to changes of contractor: Reinaldo Von Krüger (in charge of the earth moving), and Jean Guilhaume Monthier (responsible for the bridges and docks). Von Krüger was summarily dismissed in 1880, and so was Monthier. *The Rio News* reported on 24 September 1880 that Von Krüger, "the ex-chief engineer of the Paulo Affonso railway, is charged by the minister of agriculture, on the authority of a report made by the present chief engineer, with dereliction of duty in the matter of avoiding contracts," and not conforming to legal requirements in the awarding of tenders.

There were also financial problems; despite the promises in the decree, credit was sometimes not available - this was a difficult financial period for the government, faced at that time with a huge deficit - and there were allegations that funds intended to help the victims of the prolonged drought had been pocketed. On top of that, there were disagreements over the prices for construction materials and just how exempt imported goods were from being taxed. For example, The English Bank of Rio de Janeiro in 1882 asked to be repaid the 10% duty paid on four locomotives imported in 1880 for the railway, a petition that was turned down by the government, and this led to a quarrel that carried over into 1883, when the request was once again refused. In addition, there were the usual disputes over land ownership and expropriation that required the laborious checking of land titles. These problems were compounded later after the drought ended, when the railway was battered by torrential rains in 1886 and 1888.

The rolling stock in 1886 consisted of six "American locomotives," two first class carriages, four second class, and two mixed, together with two carriages for baggage and mail, two wagons for animals, twenty-nine closed wagons, twenty-five open wagons, five wagons for carrying merchandise, twenty-eight flat bed wagons, and three tankers.[155] In later times, during the Great Western of Brazil period, three types of locomotive were employed on the railway, the Baldwin Consolidation 2-8-0 (an example of which is preserved at Pedra), the Baldwin Double Ender, and the Rogers Tank locomotive.

The railway was a financial disaster, from start to finish. In the financial year 1882 to 1883, when admittedly the line was still not operating across its full length, an income of 59:166$041 was recorded, with total expenses of 226:271$213, leading to a colossal deficit of 167:105$172. But the deficit actually rose in 1884 to a shortfall of 213:007$267, the biggest deficit of all the state owned railways in Brazil. In response, the imperial government altered the contract in March 1885, reducing the number of staff employed and re-classifying the stations in an effort to make economies. This downsizing may have started earlier; *The Rio News* noted on 5 February that six employees had been dismissed by the minister of agriculture "in view of the very small traffic movement on this line."

This was not enough to stem the drain on the imperial government's finances and on 16 October 1886, Antonio da Silva Prado, the Minister of Agriculture, sent a memorandum to the directors of the state-run Paulo Afonso, Sobral, and Baturité railways, as well as the also state-owned extension of the Recife and São Francisco line:

> In response to the imperative need to reduce the expenses of the funding of this Railway you are required to put into practice without delay the salary tables that were approved by yesterday's decree, for which reason make sure that you:
> 1. Reduce as much as possible the number and salary of the drivers, firemen, heads and train staff, workers, attendants, apprentices, etc.
> 2. Classify the several stations that in their majority are no more than simple stops, in accordance with the respective traffic of merchandise and passengers.
> 3. Reduce the number and the speed of the ordinary trains, which only exceptionally will be passenger specials, in conformity with the real needs of the commerce in the region served by this railway.
> 4. Organise with the maximum of economy all the services, so that there will be no more than one man per kilometre of line for the total number of the foremen, overseers, workers, watchmen, guards, workers etc. employed on maintenance, except in the case of force majeure. (translation).

To make sure that the managers paid attention, the new salaries now reduced by the central government were published in decree n° 9,667. Perhaps the Minister of Agriculture was suspicious of whether the Paulo Afonso director, in particular, would heed his instructions, since he had heard allegations of poor management on this line in 1886 - "diverse claims made against the administration of the Paulo Affonso Railway." This was reported in *The Rio News* early in March that year: "The government has appointed a commission for an examination into the administration of the Paulo Affonso railway, against which serious charges have been made. The instructions authorize an inquiry into every branch of the service."[156] The minister proposed the setting up of a commission of inquiry headed by an engineer, Francisco José Gomes Calaça, "with the aim of verifying the grounds that such claims may have, and to whom to attribute the responsibility for whatever irregularity that comes to light."[157] The minister instructed the inquiry to focus on the accounting of income and expenses, as well as all the services provided by the railway, and come up with relevant recommendations.

It is not clear what was reported by this inquiry, but it is certain that the manager of the Paulo Afonso railway was still in the minister's cross-hairs two years later. In 1888, he wrote to the manager drawing attention to the fact that in the previous year the line had spent 60% more than the Sobral railway in the province of Ceará, when both lines were of approximately the same length and subject to the same regime, and therefore "such extraordinary excess of expenses on the Paulo Affonso Railway can have no justification." The minister concluded that, among other causes, the greater number of staff working on that line was a significant issue, for which he recommended that the director reduce this number and reminded him of the need to make savings.[158] In some exasperation, during what turned out to be the last year of the Brazilian empire, the minister sent a directive to the railway superintendent requesting urgently that he be "informed about the state of the bookkeeping since it is not plausible that, with the zeal and competence of the staff, the bookkeeping of the railway is always overdue for a railway with so little traffic."[159] The director was removed soon afterwards, and a commission was appointed to examine the railway's bookkeeping.

The Paulo Afonso railway proved to be a disaster, throughout its history, up to and beyond the Great Western of Brazil assuming management of this line at the beginning of the twentieth century. The Alagoas state president's report on 1889 noted that: "Until this date it has been of little utility for this State, given that its traffic, insignificant at the moment, depends on the river transport of the upper São Francisco".[160] Nevertheless, the president believed that "In the future this railway will be of great advantage for Alagoas since, with the upper São Fransisco in regular river transport, the city of Penedo [on the lower reach, near the mouth of the river] will become the emporium for the transactions made along all the length of the river below the city of Joazeiro." The early signs of this occurring had been slightly encouraging; between March 1881 and February 1882, the steamships SINIMBU and MACEIÓ belonging to the Royal Mail Steam Packet Company had taken to the port of Piranhas for onward transit on the railway, fifty-two European passengers, as well as eighteen from Pernambuco and eleven coming from ports in the south of Brazil.[161] But this was not enough. In his annual report for the year 1924, the Alagoas President, Pedro da Costa Rego, concluded that "This railway failed in its aims, because the only concern for whoever surveyed it seems to have been the joining of the upper and lower reaches of the São Francisco river, across a completely dry, arid and desert zone, completely forgetting the economic objective" (translation). Historians have tended to agree: Douglas Apratto Tenório criticises the fact that the line crosses "an arid and unpopulated zone, simply to shorten the distance."[162] Medeiros de Santana calls the enterprise "a striking example of short-sightedness and the lack of carrying out what we would today call market research."[163]

At the close of the second empire in Brazil, there were the two railways in Alagoas, the state-run Paulo Afonso Railway and the British-owned Alagoas Railway Company, and both were headaches for the Brazilian authorities charged with overseeing operations, but for different reasons. In the latter case, the company was accused of not making sufficient economies to ensure that income increased from the line. As we have seen, there was little stimulus to do so; the interest payments were guaranteed by contract, and were being paid in full since income was not covering expenses. The company was also accused of using inferior materials in the constructions, and of hindering the monitoring of the company by the relevant authorities. Apratto Tenório quotes an exchange between the Fiscal Engineer and the Superintendent of the Alagoas Railway that took place on 9 October 1889, a little over a month before Dom Pedro II was deposed and the new republic inaugurated. The fiscal wrote, pointedly:

> I rejoice to see Your Excellency animated to make economy for the income from the line whose whole interest payments have been paid until today by the Imperial Government. On sharing with you these good desires, I am disposed to carry out a serious study into the various branches of the railway's traffic, and to demand the economies which until today have not been perceived by Your Excellency over unauthorised expenses, in spite of many warnings.[164]

The company's superintendent responded quickly, on 12 October, accusing the head of the Fiscal Department of meddling in the company's administrative matters and complaining at this official's attempt to widen the scope of his monitoring of the company:

Steam locomotive on display at the Pedra textile factory in Delmiro Gouveia, Alagoas near the Paulo Afonso waterfall on the River São Francisco. This engine worked on the Paulo Afonso Railway, and probably was manufactured in 1926 for the São Paulo Railway. More information at: http://www.internationalsteam.co.uk/trains/brazil36.htm, accessed 16 December 2015.

Author

> I cannot, however, admit what Your Excellency wants, [which is] to arrogate to yourself a certain predominance in the administration of the Railway; and I respectfully request Your Excellency permission to remind you that the administration and supervision of a railway is a very serious thing.[165]

The fiscal took his grievances against the company to the president of the province of Alagoas, and the company did likewise, claiming that it could not submit itself to unreasonable demands that were prejudicial to the good working of the railway. In the current circumstances, this seems to have been a risky tactic, since the railway company wanted to build new branches, and new ventures would depend on the income derived from the existing line. However, it is probable that the company realised that change was in the air, and that a new regime would be less cordial in its relationship with the company than the generally compliant Brazilian imperial government had been, and that plans for expansion had better be postponed for the time being. What they did not expect, however, is that their railway would soon be surrendered to the government and then rented out to the Great Western of Brazil Railway Company.

A New Emotion Was Born
Railways in Paraíba and Rio Grande do Norte to 1889

> These English gentlemen are not satisfied with just a little; they want everything straight away; they have an insatiable greed.
>
> *Cartas sobre uma Estrada de Ferro na Provincia da Parahyba do Norte,* 1872[166]

The earliest proposal to build a railway in the then province of Parayba[167] dates from 1867 and was the initiative of two engineers, an Englishman named William Martineau and Manoel Barros de Barreto, a Brazilian, who signed a contract with the president of the province of Paraíba to build a railway from Mamanguape to the "port of Salema," northwest of the provincial capital in Paraíba, but nothing came of this project. According to the author of a short and idiosyncratic book entitled *Cartas sobre uma Estrada de Ferro na Provincia da Parahyba do Norte*, (letters about a railway in the province of Parayba do Norte), who signed himself as "C. M" and wrote the letters ostensibly to "my dear friend," it was another Englishman who undertook the first tentative steps to construct a railway in that province.

This was William Rawlinson, who, it seems, was at that time a director of the Brazilian Street Railway in Recife. "C. M." refers to this Englishman in a letter dated 16 September 1871, and explains that Rawlinson had recently made public three proposals to improve transport communications and public utilities in Paraíba; for a railway, and for gas illumination and drinking water in the provincial capital. While he complains that the direction the railway will take is still unknown, "C. M" is generally in favour of the project:

> The produce of all the centre [of the province] will be sent to the capital and the latter will regain new life; the inhabitants of the city are going to have all the items necessary to life cheap and in abundance, flour, maize, beans, rice etc., and those of the countryside are going to enjoy better their own products; the businessmen are going to buy cotton and sugar more cheaply, and the matutos [country folk] are going to sell them more expensively; in short, there is going to be everything, and lots of it, and everything cheap and everything expensive, thanks to the railway.[168]

But there was still the burning question of which direction the line would take. The 'letter' of the following day commented to his "dear friend" on the rumours that were circulating, chiefly that William Rawlinson wished to take the railway from Paraíba (the provincial capital) through Pilar and Ingá to Campina Grande in the interior, and that he was not up to the task. "C. M." was dismissive of those who entertained doubts about the project:

> There are those who say that Rawlinson is not and never was an engineer and that he simply presents himself as a front man on behalf of the Barão do Livramento in the business that is proposed. [...] I don't care if Rawlinson presents himself on his own or if behind him the Barão do Livramento or someone else can be found. What we have to enquire into is whether his proposal is convenient for the province.[169]

William Rawlinson would almost certainly have known the Barão do Livramento, a baron since 1867 whose real name was José Antônio de Araújo, given that the latter had held the first concession for the *maxambomba* line from the port of Recife to Apipucos. According to "C. M", this was not the only project being discussed; there were two others being considered for railway construction in Paraíba in late 1871. The second came from the company of Saunders Brothers in Recife, who proposed building a railway from Mamanguape to Independência (present-day Guarabira). However, it was the third proposal that had more traction, and enjoyed the impressive seal of approval of no less a personage than the Imperial Princess Isabel, Countess d'Eu. As regent of Brazil during her father's absence in Europe from May 1871, Princess Isabel signed decree n° 4,838 on 15 December that year that awarded a concession to Diogo Velho Cavalcanti de Albuquerque (an imperial counsellor, and from 1888 known as the Visconde de Cavalcanti), Anísio Salatiel Carneiro da Cunha (a general deputy representing Paraíba, as well as an engineer and businessman), and the celebrated Brazilian engineer André Rebouças. The decree offered the privilege to set up a company "inside or outside the Empire" that would construct and operate a railway from the provincial capital to Alagôa Grande, with branch lines to Ingá (south west) and Independência (to the north). There was a deadline of two years for such a company to be established, with the inducement of an exclusive concession that would last for fifty years, and a guarantee that no other line going in the same direction would be permitted within twenty kilometres on either side of the line, unless agreed to by this company. In due course, a company was organised in Britain, with the name of The Conde d'Eu Railway; a deferential homage to Princess Isabel's husband, French-born Luís Filipe Maria Fernando Gastão de Orléans, Count d'Eu, and the imperial princess's consort since 1864.

The imperial decree was backed by a provincial law passed on 22 June 1872, *lei provincial* n° 435, that guaranteed 7% annual interest payments on a maximum capital invested of 5.000:000$000. There were delays in setting up a company to undertake the construction, and the imperial government decreed in 1873 the postponement by one year for the deadline for the railway to be built, and agreed to a further postponement in 1874. But there were still no takers, and so the central government increased its offer to help. Decree n° 5608 of 25 April 1874 confirmed the terms of the provincial offer of 1872, and added a sweetener: article 1 raised the exclusive period for operating the railway from fifty to ninety years. This was still not enough; Anisio Salatiel Carneiro da Cunha and André Rebouças appealed to the imperial government for an increase in the agreed maximum expenditure, and decree n° 5,974 of 4 August 1875 conceded a further sum of 1.000:000$000, "the capital is now raised to 6,000:000$000 or 675,000 pounds [sterling]."

This now proved attractive to investors in Britain, and on 15 September 1875 The Conde d'Eu Railway Company Limited was organised in London expressly to obtain this concession. A new eighteen month deadline for the work to start was granted, but was later extended to the end of December 1880. The survey work for the railway was undertaken by the engineers Teive Argolo and Saldanha da Gama, under the general direction of the company of Wilson, Sons in Recife, and imperial decree n° 6,243 of 12 July 1876 approved these plans. At the request of the British company, decree n° 6,681 of 12 September 1877 was passed, when Princess Isabel was once again regent, in an attempt to consolidate and improve upon all the relevant decrees passed to that date. The imperial government authorised the company to acquire the first tranche of capital for the construction of the initial stretch of the line, totalling £225,000; a figure arrived at by the company in November 1876. This construction was to be completed within two years, and the entire line finished within seven years. The rolling stock was to consist of nine locomotives, six first-class carriages, fifteen second-class, and 150 wagons for cargo.[170] The tariffs to be charged should be computed by the company, but would be subject to government approval. A 50% discount on fares was to be offered to various authorities, such as senior police officials, as well as to settlers and immigrants, including their baggage.

The government reserved the right to expropriate the railway after thirty years, from the date of the completion of the construction, at a price not less than the capital agreed for building the line. Of significance, this decree determined that if dividends were paid at 8%, the excess income would be shared between the company and the government, with the latter reducing its guarantee interest payments by the same amount. And if the dividends paid exceeded 12% in two consecutive years, the government had the right to demand that the tariffs be reduced.

Newspapers in Britain published the company's 'abridged prospectus', such as *The Manchester Guardian* on 18 September 1879:

> This company has been constituted to carry out a concession granted by the Imperial Government of Brazil for constructing and working a railway from the city of Parahyba, the capital and seaport of the province of that name, to the town of Independencia, including a branch through the town of Pilar to Guarita, a total of 87 miles. The Company has also the exclusive right, on terms to be hereafter agreed, to construct one branch from Guarita to Inga, a distance of about 20 miles, and another some 15 miles in length from Mulungú to Alagôa Grande.[171]

In support of this announcement, R. Ringler-Thomson, the company secretary, reproduced in the advertisement a letter from the Brazilian Minister in London to the company, dated 19 August 1979 and signed "Penedo". This acknowledged a letter that Francisco Inácio de Carvalho Moreira, Barão de Penedo, had received from the company informing him of the firm's intention to raise £225,000 by issuing 11,250 shares of £20 each, "being the first issue of the maximum agreed capital of £675,000 (6,000 contos de reis)," and "I hereby certify that such issue is in accordance with the terms of the said decree [n° 6,681], and that the interest of 7 per cent guaranteed thereby is payable half yearly in London."

Construction on the one metre gauge line started in the following year, in August 1880. The Recife company of Saunders Brothers had shown interest in building the railway, but in fact it was Wilson, Sons & Cia. in the same city who contracted to build the railway.[172] This heralded the start of a new era for transport and communications in Paraíba. In his *História da Paraíba*, the Paraíba historian Horácio de Almeida writes that "progress came into Paraíba through the railway. Wherever the train whistled a new emotion was born: that of economic progress, but it was something of little consequence, because the area that was benefitted was too meager."[173] This zone produced sugar, but not cotton, which was harvested much further way in the interior of the province.

The first stretch of thirty kilometres linking Paraíba (capital) to Entroncamento, close to Sapé, was inaugurated in the following year. Appropriately, the word 'entroncamento' in Portuguese means 'junction', and it was from this fork that the railway turned north-west to Mulungú (reached in September 1883), then on northwards to Independência (1884) in the direction of Nova Cruz in the adjoining province of Rio Grande do Norte. The twenty-four kilometre branch line to the south-west of the Entroncamento junction reached Pilar in November 1883, and stopped. In addition to the seventy-five kilometres of railway from the provincial capital to Mulungú, an additional twenty-two kilometres of track were then laid from Mulungú to Independência and opened to traffic in June 1884.

Four months after work started on the railway, in December 1880, the imperial government proposed that the company build an extension from the provincial capital to Cabedelo, just over eighteen kilometres away. It was recognised that the city of Paraíba (nowadays called João Pessoa) was not a seaport - that was the role played by Cabedelo (and still is) - and this would avoid the need to take the treacherous river channel from and to the capital, along which it was common for ships to run aground. In 1882, the central government followed this up by offering a guarantee of interest of 6%. The provincial legislative assembly gave its backing to the proposal, but this was opposed by several businessmen in the capital who, it appears, were fearful of the competition to their business interests that would result from the arrival of a port situated on the ocean front. They argued that the money would be better spent on branch lines to Alagôa Grande and to Campina Grande, and that dredging would suffice to improve communications by river. Writing shortly afterwards, in 1886, Cyro Pessôa Junior concluded that: "There is absolutely no foundation for the panicked terrors of the businesspeople and inhabitants of the capital of Parahyba as regards the disappearance and death of the present city."[174] Nevertheless, emotions ran high, and traffic by rail to Cabedelo was opened only in 1889.

The resident engineer on the Conde d'Eu Railway from 1882 (or 1883) was an Englishman named Ranson Colecome Batterbee. He had experience of working in Brazil, having helped with the management of the Brazilian Street Railway Company until around 1876, before returning to England. Batterbee sent reports to the company board that were the source of information for a shareholders' meeting held on 5 November 1883. The chairman reported that Batterbee "had stated that the traffic had been better than he had anticipated at the beginning, taking into account many disadvantages under which they had opened. [...] The service had been regular, and no complaint had been received from the public."[175] But not all was sweetness and light; Batterbee was actually working under extreme stress, as the author of his 1889 obituary in the Proceedings of the Institution of Civil Engineers explained:

> A difficult task was imposed upon him, owing to disputes between the Company and the Contractors for the line. The worry and responsibility predisposed him to sickness, and an attack of heat apoplexy intervening, he was obliged to come home eighteen months later completely prostrated. Recovering his health, he returned to Brazil in October 1884, and remained in charge of the line till April 1885, when, his health again giving way, he was compelled to resign his appointment. From that time till his death, on the 15th of July, 1888, Mr. Batterbee, though unable to engage in active work, took part in the settlement of the contract accounts, and performed other duties for the Company in London up to the end of 1887. Mr. Batterbee was intelligent, courteous, and amiable, zealous in the discharge of his duties, and honourable in all his proceedings, and was much and deservedly esteemed by those with whom he came in contact. He was elected an Associate Member on the 6th of December, 1882.[176]

The contractor was Wilson, Sons & Company, and disputes between the two companies continued even as late as November 1887 when an agreement was at last reached for the building of the extension to Cabedelo. The contract involved the issue of debentures, but this had proved problematic, and the Conde d'Eu railway was sued by Wilson, Sons. The dispute was settled by each side dropping their claims and agreeing on a new contract, which included the construction of a pier in Cabedelo.

At the general meeting of shareholders held on 17 October 1888, in what turned out to be the penultimate year of the Brazilian empire, the chairman, A. P. Youle, observed that the report for 1887 to 1888 "was satisfactory in so far as it related to the Cabedelo extension being now in course of construction, and to the settlement of the lawsuit with the contractors. It was, however, the reverse of satisfactory in regard to the result of the year's working, which only allowed a distribution to the shareholders of 4¾ per cent for the year."[177] Nevertheless, the railway had carried nearly twice as much produce as in the previous year, and four times what was carried in the year before that, and earnings had risen to £23,570 from £15,690 in 1886-87. On the same day as this meeting was held, a prospectus published in newspapers in Britain boasted that "The Province of Parahyba is one of the most fertile in the empire, and the Railway will serve a country producing sugar, cotton, Indian corn, and other staple productions."[178]

Following the start of the republic in Brazil in November 1889 little further railway construction was undertaken in Paraíba, income from the Conde d'Eu did not improve, and the republican government decided in 1901 to expropriate the company for £615,000, and rent out the existing line and branch lines to the Great Western of Brazil Railway Company.

The fever to build railways in the adjoining and more northerly province of Rio Grande do Norte started around the same time as in Paraíba, and can be traced back to 1870 when sugar estate owners in the Vale Açucareiro (the 'sugar valley' responsible for 65% of all the sugar production in the production) approached the provincial government for their support. Provincial law n° 630 of 26 November 1870 authorised the construction of a railway along the valley of the Ceará-Mirim river north-west of the provincial capital, Natal. The contract was signed two years later by the then president of the province, Delfino de Albuquerque, but no construction work followed. Another concession for a railway intended to link Natal with the Ceará-Mirim valley was drawn up in June 1872. The concessionaires were Major Affonso de Paula de Albuquerque Maranhão and a surveying engineer named João Carlos Greenhalgh, who were offered an exclusive privilege of eighty years and 6% annual interest on a maximum capital investment of 800,000$000. This too was not built at this time; the concessionaires complained that the promised interest payment was not forthcoming, and in fact work on a railway to the north-west of Natal was only started more than thirty years later.

Much more successful was the initiative to build a railway going south of Natal to Nova Cruz in the direction of Paraíba, and it may be that the provision of an interprovincial transport link may have been the main objective of this project. This was kick-started by provincial law n° 682 of 8 August 1873 that voted a concession that was acquired by businessmen in Rio Grande do Norte and Rio de Janeiro. The concession came with a privilege of use over eighty years, and a guarantee of interest at 7% annually over a period of thirty years for a maximum capital expenditure on construction of 6,000:000$000. The historian Wagner do Nascimento Rodrigues comments that "Only after the line was constructed was it shown that the Natal to Nova Cruz [railway] was outside the richest sugar growing region. Not to mention the fact that, on finishing the construction, the region crossed by the tracks was ravaged by a drought and partially depopulated due to epidemics [...] apart from bordering the coastline in its entire length, where there already existed a cheaper and efficient transport system."[179]

The 1873 law stipulated that the line should be finished within six years. The company of Cícero de Pontes & Outros acquired the concession, and signed a contract for its construction in 1874, but they were unable to take this forward. Meanwhile, in the following year of 1875, another railway initiative surfaced in Rio Grande do Norte. Provincial law n° 742 of 26 August 1875 awarded a concession to a Swiss businessman living in Mossoró (a town north-west of Natal) named Johan Ulrich Graf, for an ambitious line that would join Mossoró with the River São Francisco, passing through Apodi and Pau dos Ferros. Nothing came of this project; the finance Graf expected did not materialise and he found it impossible to attract partners to his project and the concession was declared lapsed in June 1882.

In early 1877, work on the Natal to Nova Cruz railway had still not commenced, but a sequence of laws later that year led to a British company taking over the concession. First, imperial decree n° 6.614 of 4 July 1877 authorised the 'Companhia Estrada de Ferro de Natal a Nova Cruz' to function in the empire. Then, in October 1877, the provincial government approved the transfer of this concession to the Imperial Brazilian Natal and Nova Cruz Railway Company Limited, specially incorporated in London to acquire this concession. It is interesting that the provincial contract demanded that the work be completed within eighteen months, and that the company provide the following rolling stock: ten locomotives, ten first class carriages, fifteen second class carriages, and 150 freight wagons.[180] The privilege zone promised was of thirty kilometres on either side of the line, and the track would be of one metre gauge, built with Vignolle rails, for a total extension of nearly 121 kilometres. Finally, imperial decree n° 7.084 of 16 November 1878 conceded the central government's permission for the transfer of contract to the

"Frank Parish, President of the Great Western of Brazil 1880 to 1899". From Estevão Pinto, *História de uma estrada de ferro do nordeste*, Editora José Olympio, Rio de Janeiro, 1949, page 96. However, it seems that Frank Parish was still president of the company in 1901, according to *The Brazilian Review*, 12 March1901, page 196.
Author's Collection

British company. According to Estevão Pinto, this British company had already obtained from the Princess Isabel, imperial regent during the absence of her father Dom Pedro II, permission to function in Brazil.[181]

The construction work was handed to Reed, Bowen & Company, and started in October 1878[182] at a place known then as Nau de Refoles in the city of Natal. However, for reasons that are not apparent, further construction was delayed, and started once again on 27 February 1880, now in the hands of the British company of Sir Charles Fox and Sons. At the same time, the issue of how to serve the rich sugar-growing region north-west of Natal in the Ceará-Mirim valley, where most of the sugar *engenhos* were located, would not go away. *The Rio News* on 15 December 1880 carried news of a request to the imperial government by the Natal and Nova Cruz Railway for an interest guarantee on an additional capital of 800,000$ to construct a branch railway from Natal north to Ceará-Mirim. The central government turned down this request; there was insufficient money left in the fund set aside for such guarantees, and the company did not have the financial resources to undertake this project on its own.

An agreement was eventually signed between the company and the provincial government on 9 October 1882, but no action resulted. The problem seems to have been the estimated budget arrived at by the British company and, as reported in the *Revista de Engenharia* in February 1883, the Minister of Agriculture ordered a new budget to be prepared by the government's tax office "since the budget prepared by the Natal and Nova Cruz Railway Company had not been approved."[183] Nevertheless, the government remained committed to the project, and by imperial decree nº 9.220 published on 31 May 1884, authorised a concession with 6% interest payments over thirty years guaranteed by the provincial assembly of Rio Grande do Norte over a maximum capital invested amounting to 1,417:500$ for the company to build a branch line to Ceará-Mirim.[184] This was in conformity with the clauses of the contract signed by the provincial president, and with imperial law nº 3141 of 30 October 1882 that had set the budget for the biennial 1882-1884, and provided for: "Up to 2,000:000$ for the extension of the Natal to Nova Cruz railway along the Ceará-Mirim valley on the Province of Rio Grande do Norte, not to exceed the interest of 6% per year."

But nothing happened. In 1884, and again in 1885, the company asked for a postponement of the deadline for work to start on the construction of this extension. In some exasperation, the imperial government gave a deadline of sixty days for the company to sign the contract and begin the construction work, at the end of which the concession would be considered lapsed. Writing in 1886, Cyro Pessôa lauded the importance of this railway extension: "Constructing the Ceará-Mirim branch will improve the traffic conditions of the Railway by reaching a region that is considered the most fertile and productive of the province, and where there exists a great number of sugar factories [*usinas*]."[185] The government lost its patience, and in January 1887 declared the May 1884 concession to have lapsed.[186] The project remained untouched until the beginning of the following century.

During this time the Natal and Nova Cruz Railway forged ahead. The first stretch linking the provincial capital with the town of São José do Mipibu was inaugurated on 28 September 1881, and a second stretch from São José do Mipibu to Lagoa de Montanhas was finished on 31 October 1882. Nova Cruz, close to the border with the province of Paraíba, was reached on 1 March 1883. The authorities now realized that a serious mistake had been made. In his annual address to the provincial legislative assembly in March 1886, the president of Rio Grande do Norte lamented that "its income is so very small." An annex to this report covering the year 1885 showed that the total number of trains running, both passenger and freight, had reduced from 853 in 1884 to 747 in 1885, and that there had been frequent delays to the traffic due to accidents, and even a deliberate derailing of a locomotive.[187] The president explained that the drop in second class passenger numbers was due to "the terrible economic conditions of this Province." The trains running on Sundays had been stopped with the permission of the president since 1 May 1885 since they were almost always empty. Overall income had dropped, except that resulting from first class passengers and sugar freight, and the report concluded that the only way to increase income would be for the company to lower freight charges for sugar and cotton.

The Rio News of 24 May 1885 in Rio de Janeiro was unsympathetic.

> This [i.e. the Natal & Nova Cruz] and other railways [...] should not have been built before the probability of a return of 4 per cent on the capital had been demonstrated. [...] The State expected an annual loss of 3,000,000$, at the worst, on the sum of 100,000,000$ to be employed in railways. The indirect profit to be gained would fully compensate for this expense, but the expectation has been disagreeably belied by facts. It has been proved on one side that guaranteed capitals have been exaggerated, and on the other that the supposition of a 4 per cent revenue was not based upon truthful data. The disappointment has been complete.[188]

In December that same year, *The Rio News* reported that the Minister of Agriculture had turned down this railway company's request to increase its guaranteed capital by 582,163$416. The same column (*Railway Notes*) carried the news that the September 1885 receipts for this railway had been 7,406$530, while expenses had totalled 18,597$990.[189] This newspaper reported a similar loss for the month of July 1886; a colossal deficit of 12,103$400.[190] The provincial president's gloomy report on the railway in the year of 1888 sums up the difficulties: "The financial state of this railway is still very little flattering. One of the reasons [...] is the short length over which it runs, adding to this the high tariff and the competition of navigation at some points."[191] Writing in 1949, Estevão Pinto's verdict was:

> What is certain [...] is that from the first year of its operation the above mentioned railway has experienced, continually, a deficit regime, due to its being found almost entirely wedged along the coastal strip, which has no fertility and neither has the means to develop agriculture enough.[192]

As with the Conde d'Eu railway in Paraíba, and other railways in Pernambuco and Alagoas, the Natal and Nova Cruz was absorbed into the Great Western of Brazil Company network at the start of the twentieth century - in this case from 1901 - as we shall see in the following chapter.

And the Ceará-Mirim branch? In 1889, the last year of the empire, one of the original concessionaires of the 1872 concession, Major Affonso de Paula de Albuquerque Maranhão, reappeared and, joined this time by an engineer named Charles Hargreaves, he was awarded the concession for a line to the Ceará-Mirim valley. The Natal and Nova Cruz railway company protested vigorously against this decision. However, this was not the occasion for this extension to be built. The concession was transferred in 1890 to the Companhia Brasileira de Estradas de Ferro e Navegação, and in 1893 the Empreza de Obras Publicas (public works entity) started construction, but work proceeded very slowly, and in fact only in 1904 was any real progress made.

Setting A Good Example
Railways in North East Brazil
1889 to 1913

A glance at the history of Brazilian railways will show that many of them were built long before they should have been — practically they were built for the benefit of contractors and concessionaires — and that the gross traffic being so small it was impossible to make them profitable, for there is, of course, a bed rock below which working expenses per mile cannot go.

Pall Mall Gazette, 29 October 1900[193]

Dom Pedro II was deposed on 15 November 1889, and two days later left Brazil for exile in Portugal. The empire had proved impossible to sustain, especially after the *Lei Áurea* (golden law) was passed in the previous year, finally abolishing slavery within Brazil, and the great landowners - with the grievances that they had been abandoned by the monarchy and had not been recompensed for their losses - clubbed together as the *republicanos de última hora* (last minute republicans) to throw out the emperor of Brazil, as an act of vengeance.

Under the new regime, known as the República Federativa dos Estados Unidos do Brazil,[194] Provinces became States in a federation that inaugurated a period now known as 'the old republic', which lasted from 1889 until 1930. Douglas Apratto Tenório has remarked, insightfully, that: "The proclamation of the Republic meant, from certain aspects, the liberation of Brazil from the old links that fastened her to England."[195] The monarchy was gone, and the constitution adopted in February 1891, clearly inspired by the American federalist constitution, signified a shift towards the United States and away from Europe, especially Britain. This constitution proved to be durable; it lasted throughout the 'old republic'.

At the close of the Brazilian empire, railway companies with guaranteed interest payments financed by the state accounted for 43% of the country's railway network, and operated alongside companies belonging to the government (34%), and railways owned by Brazilian nationals and foreigners that operated without state financial support (22%).[196] Among the railways supported by the imperial government, only the São Paulo Railway had profits exceeding 7%, and when this happened, this railway left the guarantee regime. Josemir Camilo de Melo comments that: "The English railways [...] never managed an income from traffic that reached the 7% of the guarantee rate, distributing dividends practically according to that rate and not to the productivity of the railways."[197]

During the period of transition, before the adoption of a new constitution, the provisional republican government in January 1890 convened a commission to present a General Plan of Federal Transport (*Plano Geral de Viação Federal*) in the shortest possible time. The chief aim was to integrate the country better, covering rail, river, and road communications. Douglas Apratto Tenório believes that road transport was now given the attention that had been denied for some time while railways were in prominence, and that Brazil began to lose its fascination with railway construction.[198] A flurry of decrees followed, many of them in haste and ill-judged, and several related to the pressing issue of what to do with the hemorrhage on the national treasury represented by contributions made to railways owned by foreign companies, and the embarrassing fact that, despite all the investments made over the previous decades, the country was still largely disconnected and not governed by a rational transport system. Decree n° 862 of 16 October 1890 conceded "privilege, a guarantee of interest and other benefits, for the establishment of a general transport system linking the various States of the Union between themselves and with the Federal Capital," Rio de Janeiro, which remained the capital of Brazil (until 1960). This was in consideration of "the high expedience of narrowing the ties of political and commercial relations of the different States of Brazil between each other and the Federal Capital."

While this decree did not specifically refer to the north-east of Brazil, other decrees followed that had a direct bearing on the railway companies there. Noticing that the Paulo Afonso line was making a huge loss, and was not connected to any other railway, decree n° 993 of 8 November 1890 confirmed "a guarantee of 6% per year for 30 years, guaranteed by the Governador of the State of Alagôas, over a maximum capital of 30:000$ per kilometre, destined to the construction of a railway that, leaving the city of Alagôas [Maceió], will make junction with the Paulo Affonso Railway." Decree n° 1,060 of 22 November 1890 awarded "privilege and guarantee of interest for the construction of a railway between Caruarú, in the State of Pernambuco, and Crato, in that of Ceará. [This came with] A guarantee of interest of 6% per year for 30 years over the capital, up to a maximum corresponding to 30:000$ per kilometre, [which] should be fixed by the Government as necessary for the construction and compete establishment of the railway." The Caruaru to Crato railway would have measured 600 kilometres, and the Maceió to Paulo Afonso track 384 kilometres. Josemir Camilo de Melo concludes that: "The federal government started a virtual festival of railway concessions, many of them following a completely inoperable route."[199] Neither branch was ever built, although Crato was joined to the northern Baturité railway of Ceará in 1926.

All of this took place against the background of a deepening crisis for the new republican government, which had inherited a huge annual deficit in the country's external and internal debts. As a result, the republic ushered in a period of instability in Brazil that lasted until 1898. The international exchange rate of the *milreis* suffered a rapid depreciation, and with this came the imminent threat of national bankruptcy. Julian Smith Duncan notes that in 1889 one *milreis* was worth fifty-three cents of an American dollar, but only fifteen cents ten years later.[200] The crisis was particularly acute in the early years of 1889 to 1892, in a period now known as the *Crise do Encilhamento* - literally 'saddling crisis', or harnessing a horse prior to a race when betting rises to a peak - in a period of volatility during a bubble in the economy when investors were looking for quick gains. This crisis broke out during the period of the provisional government led by Deodoro da Fonseca between 1889 and 1891, when, in the face of a reduction in foreign investment into Brazil, the Treasury Minister Ruy Barbosa decided to free up credit by printing large amounts of money, in the hope that new limited companies backed by Brazilian shareholder deposits would stimulate investment in industry. This stimulated a boom, but it didn't last. Many of the companies that were founded were just a façade, or based on unrealistic business plans, and when investors realised that the shares on offer did not have secure financial backing, they panicked and the bubble burst.

The issue of the continuing drain on the federal budget represented by the guaranteed interest payments to foreign-owned railways was focussed on in 1891. As we have seen, this was a stimulus to inefficiency since, however badly managed, the railway company was guaranteed an injection of funds from the Brazilian government to pay dividends abroad, mainly in Britain. But what to do about this? The companies could be expropriated and run as state enterprises, as provided for in the contracts, but this was seen as unattractive, in part because pension and other social benefits would have to be paid. Law n° 3,397 of 24 November 1888, a year before the republic started, had established a *Caixa de Socorros* (social security) for workers on the state-owned railways when they were ill or incapacitated. Soon after the republic began, decree n° 221 of 26 February 1890 introduced pensions for employees of the state-run Estrada de Ferro Central do Brasil, a benefit that in July 1890 (decree n° 565) was expanded on as a right to be enjoyed by workers on all the railways in the republic.

The sugar industry was another issue of pressing importance to the provisional government, and of great relevance to the north-east and the railway network established there. In 1890, 38.2% of the sugar produced in Pernambuco was still transported to the port of Recife by water, while various forms of animal transport carried 3.9%. The railways carried 57.3%, with the Recife and São Francisco Railway - the line in Pernambuco that carried the most sugar - accounting for 36.4%, followed by the Great Western of Brazil (16.8 %), and the Estrada de Ferro Central (4.1 %).[201] But these were not the only railways carrying sugar cane; the usinas also had their own networks, and they were considerable in size.

> The railways, essential to the functioning of the *usinas*, spread out like virtual tentacles, over kilometres of distance, linking the lands of the old *engenhos* to the new factories. It was through them that the *usinas* extended their area with the acquisition of *engenhos*, and their influence, taking into their domain the sugar plantations of private *engenhos*. (Manuel Correia Andrade).[202]

One of the ways that this happened resulted when owners of *usinas* paid for the right of way when crossing private *engenhos* that, over time, led to their incorporation into the lands of the *usinas*.

An interesting case is that of Alagoas, where several of the State's important *usinas* built narrow gauge lines to convey their product for onward shipment on the Alagoas Railway. The Usina Central Leão is an example. This was the second *usina* to be established in Alagoas and was apparently the first to be financed by capitalists in that State. Founded by Luiz de Amorim Leão, established on the lands of the old *engenhos* of Utinga, Oficina, and Boa Paz that were inherited by his father, and belonging to the Sociedade Agrícola e Industrial Usina Leão, this factory began to mill sugar in 1894.[203] Much of the rudimentary machinery in use at this *usina* came from the firms of George Fletcher & Company, of Derby, and Watson, Laidlaw & Company, an associate company of the Mirrlees Watson Company in Glasgow. In 1897, more modern equipment that provided for double milling was installed by the Mirrlees Watson Company. Another *usina* with its own railway network was the Usina Serra Grande in São José da Laje, which also started milling in 1894, and linked to the Alagoas Railway Company line, later part of the Great Western of Brazil railway. Both of these *usinas* are still milling sugar today.

In 1890, the writing was on the wall for the British-owned railways in Brazil, and with hindsight we now realise that the arrival of the republic signalled the end of the golden era of British railways in Brazil. In a period of social convulsion, there were strikes by workers in Pernambuco, partly fuelled by the crisis of the *Encilhamento*, and also by the greater number of workers available and competing for jobs - at least 45,000 former slaves came into salaried work in Pernambuco in this period. And there were strikes, for

"William Boxwell, negociante. Grupo de ingleses, Rede ferroviária 1900-1920" (William Boxwell, businessman. Group of Englishmen, Railway network 1900-1920). (This is the work of the French photographer Louis Piereck taken in the district of Jaqueira in Recife, probably between 1905 and 1909, when John Lorimer was the local manager of the Great Western in Recife. Standing: Mssrs. Daniel, Riley, Fletcher, C. Conolly, Cláudio Dubeux, John Lorimer, William Boxwell, Harding, Swift. Seated: Mssrs. Robson, R. Conolly, Webster, John H. Boxwell, Ernest Brotherhood, Foy. Reclining: Mssrs. Felton, Dick Conolly. John H. Boxwell in the photograph was the uncle of William Boxwell, whose full name was William Ewart Gladstone Boxwell, and married to Lucy Needham. Author's interview with a grandson of William Boxwell, also called William Boxwell, in 1994).

Courtesy Biblioteca Central Blanche Knopf, photograph library, Fundação Joaquim Nabuco, Recife. Ref. F.R. 6.331.

better salaries by workers on the state-run Sul de Pernambuco in 1891, and for a salary increase of 35% by workers on the Recife and São Francisco Railway in 1894. In spite of these problems, between 1890 and 1895, 3,383 kilometres of railways were actually inaugurated, comparing favourably to the previous five years (3,281 kilometres), but the second half of the 1890s decade saw a fall of 31% in railway building.[204]

An early step taken by the government of significance to the north-east of Brazil was enshrined in federal decree n° 624 of 2 August 1890, which set out, among other measures, to "separate the administrations of the state railways in Pernambuco." The lines connecting Recife to Caruaru (the Central de Pernambuco railway) and Palmares to Garanhuns (the Sul de Pernambuco railway) would now be independent of each other and directly subordinate to the Ministry of Agriculture, Commerce, and Public Works. Three years later, by decree n° 1,551 of 27 September 1893, the federal government removed from Sul de Pernambuco management the branch lines of Timbaúba to Pilar, Guarabira to Nova Cruz, and Mulungú to Campina Grande, and incorporated them into the Central de Pernambuco's administration. Still not satisfied, the government divided the management of both administrations in 1894 (decree n° 1,705-A of 30 April 1894) in an effort to improve the service offered. The Sul de Pernambuco was split into two entities: Palmares to Garanhuns (headquartered in Palmares) with the name 'Sul de Pernambuco Railway', and Paquevira (Glicério) to União (União dos Palmares today) with Barra do Canhoto (later named Rocha Cavalcanti) to Aguas Bellas called the Norte das Alagoas (north of Alagoas) railway, headquartered in União. Similarly, the Central de Pernambuco was divided into two parts: the original Central de Pernambuco, headquartered in Recife, and the Timbaúba to Nova Cruz railway that consisted of the proposed lines from Timbaúba to Pilar, Guarabira to Nova Cruz, and the extension of the Conde d'Eu railway from Mulungú to Campina Grande, headquartered in Pilar. Josemir Camilo de Melo describes the latter as "a virtual assault on the public purse."[205]

The strategy did not work, and in 1896 the government decided to change tack; instead of extending the state-owned railway network in the north east, they would rent out the lines. As a result, work on joining the various lines in the four States into one network was suspended. Brazilian finances had deteriorated to the point that leasing some of the state railways to private operators for cash payment was now very attractive, and accordingly, Law n° 427 of 9 December 1896 authorised the government to rent out the state railways by means of public tender. The Brazilian Vice President, using the authority of this law, emitted a decree (n° 2,413 of 28 December 1896) that set out the details of how the railways were to be rented. Rentals were to be for a period of sixty years; a down payment was required on signing the rental contract; an annual payment would be charged based on net operating income; and the government reserved the right to expropriate the main line and any branches after thirty years, the value of the expropriation to be paid in gold in a calculation based on the average net income over the previous five years plus the reimbursement of the costs of any works carried out in the previous three years. It was hoped that the money saved in this way could be used by the government for new construction.

But by 1898, national bankruptcy was a very real possibility, and it was this fact that spurred the government into considering the renting out of the privately-owned railways. The country was in financial turmoil, and the president-elect of Brazil, Campos Sales, and his Minister of the Treasury, Joaquim Murtinho, decided to approach European bankers for a substantial, and controversial, funding loan to avoid default. The government needed a breathing space, and the hope was that by consolidating Brazil's debts while simultaneously securing a moratorium on their repayment, in exchange for a programme of austerity and strengthening of the national currency, that this would give time for reorganisation of the financial workings of the country. A financial agreement between the national treasury in Brazil and the banking firm of N. M. Rothschild & Sons[206] was duly signed on 15 June 1898 "recognising that [the government] cannot pay in money the interest on the loans of its foreign debt [including] the sums paid to the several companies of the guaranteed railways." In return for the loan of £10,000,000 to pay off the national external debt, the government would emit securities through Rothschild denominated as 'United States of Brazil 5% Funding Bonds', to be redeemed within the period of sixty-three years from 1 July 1898. This loan would be paid back after a period of thirteen years, and was secured against the customs receipts at Rio de Janeiro, and other customs houses if necessary. It was cheaper for the government to pay interest on this loan that made it possible to expropriate the railway lines with these securities than to continue paying the guaranteed interest payments. The list accompanying the contract with Rothschild specified which railways would be affected, and these included: "The Alagôas Railway Company (main line). The Alagôas Railway Company (Assembléa branch). The Great Western of Brazil Railway Company. The Conde d'Eu Railway Company. [...] The Natal and Nova Cruz Railway Company. [...] The Recife and São Francisco Railway Company."[207]

Public portfolio British investment, which had been more important than other investments before 1885, maintained a share of about 50% of total investment between the mid-1880s and mid-1890s. But it rose steeply again after 1898 as a result of the funding loan operations, the large 1901 loan to finance the rescission of railway guarantees, and new loans floated immediately after the turn of the century for the federal government, several states and major municipalities. By 1905 public portfolio loans corresponded to 2/3 of sterling investment in Brazil. The nine years before the World War I marked the heyday of British private investment in Brazil: no less than £10 million entered the country on average every year. (Marcelo de Paiva Abreu, *British Business in Brazil: Maturity and demise, 1850-1950*).[208]

This spelt disaster for the twelve British-Brazilian railway companies in Brazil; from June 1898 they received funding bonds in lieu of interest payments. The problem was that these securities were quoted at between 15 to 20% discount, representing an immediate loss when converted, and all cash payments to the companies were suspended. *The Investors' Review* commented succinctly in June 1898 that:

The fact that the Brazilian government proposes to pay its railway guarantees for the next three years in funding bonds is a serious matter for the Brazilian guaranteed railways. These lines are in a railway sense most miserable concerns, the only important companies being those that work without a guarantee. Not one of the guaranteed lines earns anything like the interest upon its debenture capital, and the majority of the companies operate at an absolute loss. [...] Scattered up and down the country, without much connection one with the other, and often without any objective point, their only advantage is that they usually connect a part of the interior with a port on the sea-board. [...] The default of the Brazilian Government aggravates an already unsound position, and may lead to awkward disputes.[209]

Just prior to the funding loan measure, The Great Western of Brazil Railway in 1897 carried 333,063 passengers.[210] The company's annual report for that year showed a net revenue of £400, and it had received a guaranteed payment from the government of £39,374. The Recife and São Francisco Railway had a better net revenue, of £6,849, but had received a much larger guarantee payment, of £80,282. Of the other guaranteed lines in the north east, only the Alagoas Railway had demonstrated a positive net revenue, of just £90, with a guarantee payment of £39,254 - all the others recorded a loss and received substantial guarantee payments. The Great Western paid a dividend of 3 ½% in 1897, but no dividend was awarded in 1898; passenger numbers had dropped to 296,299 although net revenue was slightly higher. The directors' report for 1898 was upbeat:

The directors have pleasure in stating that their relations with the Government have, under the new regime, been of a satisfactory nature, and during the past year several of the pending questions have been arranged.[211]

One remaining problem for the government, and for the Great Western, was that there was still a substantial gap of about forty kilometres between Timbaúba in Pernambuco (the northern limit of the Great Western) and Pilar in Paraíba (the southern terminus of the Conde d'Eu). The *Pacific Line Guide to South America* of 1895 described how "From Timbauba the diligence can be taken to Pilar, a station on the Conde D'Eu Railway, which runs to Parahyba. This is the only overland route from Pernambuco to Parahyba, and takes about thirty hours."[212] In addition, there was a gap of around fifty kilometres between Independencia (Guarabira today) in Paraíba and Nova Cruz in Rio Grande do Norte, begging for a connection to be built between the Conde d'Eu and the Natal to Nova Cruz lines to make possible continuous communication from Natal to Recife in Pernambuco. All work funded by the federal government on these links had been suspended in 1896, but the Great Western offered in 1898:

> [...] to complete the section between Timbaúba and Pilar, asking only to be permitted to utilize the work already done and the materials already accumulated for the completion of the line. [...] Government, we believe, desires that the company should pay for the work already done as well as the accumulated materials. [...] By leaving the line to go to rack and ruin, as it will every year if it remains unfinished and unworked, not only will there be no profit but a certainty of dead loss to Government itself and to the district it is intended to serve. [...] Local opinion at Pernambuco and Parahyba seems unquestionably in favour of the concession, to which great importance is attached as a factor of industrial development.[213]

1899 was a difficult year for the Great Western. In July, *The Brazilian Review* reported: "The shrinkage of traffic which has been so prominent on this line for so long in consequence of the terrible drought that desolated the northern Atlantic States [but] now seems to be declining."[214] However, in August, the same journal congratulated the Great Western management on its energy in solving problems: "If other companies would only follow their example and give up the endless whining and regret for diminished dividends there might be some chance of their increasing. [...] The Great Western is setting a good example."[215] The *Review* carried an advertisement for the Great Western in October that year that gave the names of all the stations in operation from Recife to Timbaúba: Recife, Encruzilhada, Arraial, Macacos, Camaragibe, São Lourenço, Tiuma, Santa Rita, Pão d'Alho, Carpina, Lagôa do Carro, Campo Grande, Limoeira, Tracunhãem, Nazareth, Lagôa Secca, Barauna, Alliança, Pureza, Timbaúba.[216] One daily train left Recife at 07:00 and arrived in Timbaúba at 12:00, returning at 13:10 to arrive in Recife at 18:12. There were also trains on working days between Recife and Arraial, Recife and Limoeira, Recife and Tiuma, plus trains on Sundays only between Recife and São Lourenço, and between Carpina and Limoeira.

At the turn of the century, in round numbers, the four north-eastern States possessed the following railway lengths: Alagoas (269 kilometres), Pernambuco (646), Paraíba (141), and Rio Grande do Norte (122),[217] all of which were soon destined to be amalgamated within a network operated by the Great Western of Brazil railway. Estevão Pinto provides the following account of the railways operating in Pernambuco in 1900:[218]

> • Recife and São Francisco Railway, Recife to Una (Palmares): 124 kilometres 739 metres.
> • Sul de Pernambuco railway, Una to Garanhuns: 157,801 metres. When the extension from Glicério to Imperatriz (União) was included, this grew to 193 kilometres. This line belonged to the central government and was in constant deficit.
> • Great Western of Brazil Railway, Recife to Limoeiro: 152,631 metres.
> • Central de Pernambuco railway: 179,900 metres.
> • Paulo Afonso railway (the part in Pernambuco): 30,783 metres.

The prospects for these railways in 1900 were mixed, but the Great Western was in reasonable shape. On 30 July, two years after offering to build the key link from Timbaúba to Pilar - the ´linha norte' (northern line) that the Central de Pernambuco had failed to complete - the budget presented by the Great Western to conclude this stretch of track was approved by federal decree n°3,723. This was at the time that A. H. A. Knox-Little was general manager of the company, resident in Recife.[219] At the half-yearly meeting of the Recife and São Francisco Railway held on 24 April 1900, the chairman, W. B. Greenfield, was deliberately upbeat about the future for the company; he reported that traffic receipts in the second half of 1899 had amounted to £106,858, the best recorded in a corresponding period. "Generally, the affairs of Brazil seemed to be improving, and this company might expect to benefit from any additional prosperity that the country enjoyed." But this was not to be; in August 1901, the Recife and São Francisco Railway passed a resolution to voluntarily wind up the company and appoint liquidators at an Extraordinary General Meeting held in London.[220]

The situation in Alagoas in 1900 was as follows:

• The Alagoas Railway Company: consisting of the earlier Central de Alagoas railway and União branch, plus the branch line to Assembléia (Viçosa): 150 kilometres in all.
• The part of the Glicério branch line extension of the Sul de Pernambuco railway that lay in Alagoas: 35,847 metres.
• The part of the Paulo Afonso railway that lay in Alagoas: 83,269 metres.

The relationship between the Alagoas Railway Company and the provincial government had been fraught, as we have seen, and with the change of regime on the arrival of the republic several suitors appeared intent on breaking the monopoly of this British railway, sensing that this time they would be successful.

This sudden festival of requests for the construction of railways in Alagoas demonstrates a good dose of opportunism or adventurism by the interested parties, most of which had neither technical nor economic foundation, all of them infected by the national fever of obtaining new companies, backed by the resources of the stock market and also by political patronage. (Douglas Apratto Tenório).[221]

The federal government was equally keen to take on the Alagoas Railway. At the beginning of the twentieth century, income was more or less equivalent to expenses, and so the government was paying the company the whole of the guarantee. In May 1890, the company was advised in an official communication that if it did not provide a full statement of accounts - specifically, bills that related to construction work carried out in 1884 - then the government would suspend the payment of the amount based on the capital guaranteed. The company argued that surely the issue in question had lapsed in time, and that, had they been asked for this at that time, the company would have requested the contractors to provide these bills. Furthermore, these accounts in many cases no longer existed; an admission by the company that only served to irritate the government.

The company was targeted too by the government of the State, and by public opinion. There was a growing revolt against the Alagoas Railway among the population of that State, egged on by vociferous attacks in the local newspapers, and even a certain dose of xenophobia against the foreign company.[222] The company attempted to brush off the growing criticisms in the popular press, even those that were openly hostile. The company's general manager wrote on 16 January 1890 to the State governor to say that they gave little importance to articles published in newspapers, but that if anyone had a complaint to make personally or in writing the company would be glad to attend to this promptly. However, public opinion was galvanised when Brazilian workers at the company were dismissed in favour of workers from Britain in February 1890. The newspapers admonished the company for dismissing Brazilian workers in the name of economy, and then hiring British workers at higher salaries. The company's superintendent, J. E. Wolfe, responded by saying that he was responsible to the directors of the Alagoas Railway, whose shares had lost a third of their value, and that he had to justify his decisions to them. He pointed out that:

> In the company there is no distinction between Brazilians and foreigners. On my part, I am at peace with my conscience and I give no importance to these anonymous accusations from those who have no understanding of the matter. The affairs of administration are of my competence. If the governor of this State wishes to know something I will be pleased to inform him verbally, but officially it seems to me that we can consider the incident terminated.[223]

Perhaps he realised soon afterwards that this arrogant tone was not helpful, and that the climate for relationship building had in fact changed since the arrival of the republic, so the general manager looked for a diplomatic way out of his problem. Writing again to the governor, in March 1890, the superintendent set out to politely explain that there were many Brazilians working for the company, and that the Alagoas Railway could not do without them; there had been a reorganisation of the company and some posts had been lost while others were created. "I ask the government to believe in this explanation as being frank and satisfactory, putting an end to an incident which I regret."[224]

But the State government kept up the pressure. One event that showed which way the wind was blowing took place in June 1890. The Juiz de Direito (court judge) of the *camarca* of Imperatriz complained to the Repartição Fiscal (tax office) that the company had refused to embark a police escort on its way to Maceió, arguing that the necessary paperwork had not been received in time. A memorandum from the head of the Repartição Fiscal dated 31 October 1890 dismissed the company's rebuttal over the matter in Imperatriz, and added that as a Brazilian and a public servant it sorrowed him every time that "I see the foreign companies [that] only remember about their contracted commitments when they need the Government to pay the guarantees of the concession, and their managements with the greatest lack of embarrassment are guided only by their interests and at times their whims."[225] Accordingly, the company was fined for being in contravention with its contract. The Alagoas Railway took their grievance to the federal government, with a request that the *engenheiro fiscal* responsible for these actions be removed, but this was turned down by the Ministry of Agriculture in Rio de Janeiro, underlining the fact that the generally cosy relations with the central government in imperial times had come to an end.

At the same time, local media and public opinion would not let the matter drop, until there was a new focus for their attentions - the choice of where the railways of the States of Pernambuco and Alagoas were to meet. The company had an opinion on this matter, and a clear interest in the decision, but had by now learned to be more discreet in their efforts to influence developments. The question was delicate; public opinion in Alagoas was roused against the 'imperialists' in Pernambuco set on dominating the economy in Alagoas. In September 1890, a memorandum from concerned citizens to the government of Alagoas drew attention to Pernambuco's plan that, in their view, aimed to siphon off produce from the interior of their state beyond Imperatriz (União), as well as to build a branch to "the insignificant traffic on the English railway of the São Francisco;" that is, the Paulo Afonso Railway.[226]

The federal government let it be known that they were inclined to expropriate the

Alagoas Railway Company; a move that was vigorously opposed by the chairman, John Beaton. It was reported at the annual general meeting held on 29 April 1902 that the government had offered in December 1901 to pay £700,000 in "four per cent rescission bonds." This had not only been rejected by the board, they had not even brought the offer to the attention of the shareholders; "It was not sufficiently good enough to submit to you for your adoption, and we therefore declined it."[227] Nevertheless, the government's determination proved irresistible, and at an extraordinary general meeting held in London on 29 August 1902 a resolution was passed to voluntarily wind up the company and appoint liquidators.[228]

In Paraíba, the Conde d'Eu Railway in 1900 possessed nearly 141 kilometres of track. With few exceptions, the line was in deficit every year, and generally speaking, the government was paying the total of the guarantee. The chairman reported at the annual general meeting held on 22 January 1900 that: "The company had a very bad year [with] considerable decreases in their passenger and goods traffic."[229] This railway was bought out by the federal government in 1901 for £615,000, and rented to the Great Western in July 1901.

The Imperial Brazilian Natal and Nova Cruz Railway in Rio Grande do Norte possessed 122 kilometres of track and also ran at a loss, with the total of the guarantee effectively being paid every year by the government. As a sign of the poor receipts, an announcement placed in the newspaper *Rio Grande do Norte* in September 1891 informed the public that with immediate effect a mixed cargo and passenger train would run during the sugar harvest period from Natal to Nova Cruz on Tuesdays, Thursday and Saturdays, and in the opposite direction on Mondays, Wednesdays and Fridays.[230] And yet the chairman, Louis Hirsch, put on a brave face at the general meeting of the railway company held on 25 April 1893, and was able to say that: "they had met under much more favourable circumstances than they had done at any time in the history of the company," and an annual dividend of 4½% was being recommended by the board.[231] But the tide could not be turned; at the extraordinary general meeting of the company held in London on 16 December 1901 a resolution was passed voluntarily winding up the business and appointing a liquidator.[232] The line was expropriated at the price of £427,800, and by decree n° 4,111 of 31 July 1901 rented to the Great Western of Brazil Railway. The rental contract came with an obligation, that the Great Western construct the often yearned-for link between Nova Cruz in Rio Grande do Norte south to Independência (today Guarabira) to join up with the Conde d'Eu railway in Paraíba, and on 1 January 1904 this stretch was opened to traffic. Since the extension from Timbaúba to Pilar had been opened, on 3 July 1901, for the first time it was now possible for a train to pass over a network linking the three States of Rio Grande do Norte, Paraíba, and Pernambuco.

The republican government also turned in 1904 to the question of the link north from Natal to Ceará-Mirim, so long delayed, but this authorisation to start work coincided with a severe drought in the interior of Rio Grande do Norte, a time when whole families abandoned their farms and fled for the State capital, and further afield to the more prosperous south-east of Brazil. A commission headed by the engineer Sampaio Correia duly arrived, and they were charged too with carrying out studies for another new railway - the Central do Rio Grande railway - which would cross the regions in the interior that had been hit by the prolonged drought, but whose starting point had still not been determined. As with other railways in the north-east during the severe drought of the late 1870s, the plan was to use unemployed and hungry migrants as work-gangs on the construction.[233] The thirty-four kilometre line from Natal to Ceará-Mirim was opened to traffic in 1906, the same year that the Central railway was also inaugurated, leaving from the estuary of the river Potengi near Natal. Neither of these lines ever belonged to the Great Western.

The sequence of events leading to the Great Western of Brazil operating most of the railway lines in the north-east is worth exploring in more detail. At the beginning of 1899, the general manager, Follett Holt (later president of the company) suggested that the federal government set up just one railway network in the four States. This plan was at first rejected by the government, which saw piecemeal renting of some of the lines as a viable alternative. In April 1899, the Ministry of Industry, Railways and Public Works invited proposals (adverts were placed abroad in English) for the lease of "the Paulo Affonso Railway in the State of Alagoas" which had traffic running on a line that measured just short of seventeen kilometres in traffic! An initial down payment was required, of "not less than 25:000$ (twenty five contos de réis)." This was hardly an attractive investment; in 1990 the railway carried just 3,967 passengers, compared to nearly 7,000 in 1883. In the same month, a separate tender offered a lease of sixty years for the Sul de Pernambuco railway (194 kilometres in traffic) and the São Francisco railway in the State of Bahia, with the government reserving the right to expropriate after thirty years. There were no takers.

The government was now getting desperate. On the penultimate day of the century, 30 December 1899, *The Economist*, taking stock of the situation in an article headed 'Brazilian Railway Prospects', reported that the government had attempted to construct the extension from Timbaúba to Pilar, but had stopped after only six miles.[234] The first thought had been to abandon the project and pull up the tracks, but then the government decided in a decree published on 30 October to lease the line as a concession to the Great Western of Brazil Railway.[235] A contract was signed on 23 November for a lease lasting fifty-three years, with construction to be completed within twenty months. The government ceded all the existing materials in store or along the line that had been acquired for the construction of the line. "Any excess over 8% earned on the capital employed in completing the line will revert to the Treasury in payment of the materials and works handed over to the company." The *Brazilian Review* was unimpressed and argued in favour of amalgamating the three railways of the Conde d'Eu, the Natal to Nova Cruz, and the Great Western. The total length of these lines running from Recife to Natal would be 474 kilometres, including branches. "As a joint concern these railways have some chance of perhaps not only paying expenses, but of giving a small dividend in the days when guarantees shall be no more. As three separate and independent, and to some extent, competing railways they are predestined to hopeless insolvency."

The Economist was of the opinion that the Great Western was "in a very poor position, although it is shortly to build an extension [Timbaúba to Pilar] which the directors hope will bring considerable traffic to the line." *The Economist* concluded that:

> It may very much be doubted if the building of this branch is financially advisable by the Great Western Railway, although no doubt the directors, in view of the fact that in a very few years their guarantee will expire, feel called upon to try something to ameliorate the company's present poor condition. The Natal and Nova Cruz is also in a very poor condition with decreasing traffics and dividends, as is also the Conde d'Eu. All three are very closely situated to each other, and amalgamation, which has been suggested, would probably benefit the shareholders of all three, at least to some extent.

Federal decree 3,723 of 30 July 1900 approved the GWBR budget for completing the railway from Timbaúba to Pilar; the first stretch from Timbaúba to Rosa e Silva was inaugurated in 1900, and traffic to Pilar was authorised to start provisionally on 1 January 1901.

This hardly affected the larger picture, and the federal government was in a bind. The main conundrum was that the government could exercise its leverage over tariffs to keep them low, which pleased the landowners, but this meant paying out more in guarantee payments, as required by the contracts when revenue did not meet expenses nor cover the dividends to shareholders. According to Rory Miller (1993: 167), in 1898, at the end of the empire, one third of the government budget was being spent on railway guarantee payments, usually in gold. Another headache was that the guarantee terms expired in different years: 1909 for the Great Western, 1910 for the Natal and Nova Cruz, 1911 for the Alagoas Railway, 1914 for the Conde d'Eu (although most of the guarantee would expire in 1911), and 1944 for the Recife and São Francisco Railway. The republican government decided that it had no alternative other than to purchase the railways where they were obliged to pay guarantees of interest. In 1900, there were 3,110 kilometres of railway in this category, with a total net burden for the country of £964,248.

The government sent José Carlos Rodrigues to London in 1900 as its representative to negotiate an agreement for the purchase of railways on which a guarantee of interest was payable, all of which were owned by British companies. By 1902, 2,148 kilometres had been recaptured. According to Smith Duncan (1932: 50) the price to be paid for this was £14,605,000 in government bonds, payable in gold and bearing interest at 4%; a lower rate of interest than the rate paid under the guarantee regime. Essentially, the government sought to consolidate the existing small lines into five larger systems, one of which was in the north east. Recognising that state operation was less efficient and more onerous than private operation of these railways, the government decided that the best option was to rent out the lines.

The government's decisions sparked a great deal of comment in the British press and Brazilian English language publications in the years 1900 and 1901. This was at a time when the Great Western was in good shape; the chairman described the annual report on 1900 as "one of the best ever presented." 120,000 tons of goods had been transported, compared to 105,000 tons in 1899, and there had been "a steady development" in passenger traffic. In April 1900, *The Times* quoted the chairman of the Great Western, W. B. Greenfield, who reported that: "Generally, the affairs of Brazil seemed to be improving, and this company might expect to benefit from any additional prosperity that the country enjoyed." However, funding bonds received from the government had been sold at an average price of 85 per cent, and he calculated that the loss on receiving these bonds instead of the full guarantee so far had amounted to £25,282.[236] In October, the *Pall Mall Gazette* reported that the Great Western was "in a much more favourable position than most of its neighbours, for its net earnings in the half year were £15,338, but as £10,103 of this was earned by its main line [i.e. Recife to Limoeiro], the latter sum had to be returned to the Government, the balance being retained in respect of the extension, which receives no guarantee."[237] In the following month, November 1900, the *Gazette* concluded that:

> what the present Brazilian Administration undoubtedly wants is to liquidate the financial obligations left by predecessors of many years ago in the easiest manner possible. [...] There are only a few companies over which the Government have at present the right of expropriation, and to successfully carry that out would require the issuing of between £20,000,000 and £30,000,000 of bonds, and the Government would then have to work or

lease the lines, and are not likely to be successful with either.[238]

Surprisingly, the same publication also carried an advertisement urging the public to purchase "12,500 preferred shares of £20 each" in The Imperial Brazilian Natal and Nova Cruz Railway Company Limited, earning a guaranteed dividend of 7%.

By the end of 1900, rumours were circulating regarding the possible merger of the railways in the north-east. *The Brazilian Review* on 25 December carried a denial from the secretary of the Great Western that there was any discussion with the Brazilian government about commutation of the guarantee.[239] In February of the following year, the *Review* commented on the company's recent Extraordinary General Meeting, at which the chairman, Frank Parrish, had announced that he would be stepping down "in view of his advancing age".

> It would seem that many shareholders [...] did not appear to look with very great favour upon the resolution regarding the proposed amalgamation with the Conde d'Eu Railway; [...] as the Great Western of Brazil is a profit-making line, which the Conde d'Eu is not, they were naturally afraid of the latter getting the best of the bargain.[240]

Frank Parrish had reassured his shareholders that: "The amalgamation is not proposed to take effect until after the guarantees expire, by which time the Conde d'Eu will have redeemed all its debentures, and the line will then be dependent upon its earnings for ordinary dividends."[241] Parrish was still presiding at the Extraordinary General Meeting held in March 1901 at River Plate House, Finsbury Circus, in London when two resolutions were passed.[242] The first provided for the creation and issue of debentures for the Tambaúba to Pilar line secured against the company's property, and the second gave approval "of an agreement with the Conde d'Eu Company for unification of management, working, and eventual amalgamation." Parish argued strenuously that since the government guarantee for the Great Western would expire in ten years' time, "it was manifest the lines should be worked together for their joint benefit." The two resolutions were carried.

This union of the two companies had already been sanctioned by the Conde d'Eu Railway Company at their Annual General Meeting held on 3 February 1901. *The Brazilian Review* noted that: "The amalgamation with the Western of Brazil Ry. Co. was carried with one dissentient." The Conde d'Eu board announced an extraordinary general meeting of shareholders to be held on 29 October 1901 "to consider a resolution empowering the directors to sell the company's railways and all its properties to the Brazilian Government." Shareholders had approved a direct sale to the Great Western - many Great Western shareholders were also shareholders in the Conde d'Eu - but this had been vetoed by the Brazilian government. The resolution was carried by twenty-seven votes to eight. The expropriation of this line cost the government £700,000.

Although negotiations with the government were protracted, the Recife and São Francisco Railway was also fused with the Great Western. The board's report on 1900 explained that: "In accordance with the resolution approving the agreement embodying the terms of the sale of the company's undertaking to the Brazilian government, the directors have signed the agreement on behalf of the company, and the document has now been formally executed by his Excellency, the Brazilian Minister."[243] The cost to the Brazilian government of the expropriation in 1901 came to £1,500,000, mostly paid for in 4% government bonds. All that remained was for the Great Western to take over the operation, and in June 1901 the board sent a circular to shareholders explaining a provisional agreement reached with the Brazilian government:

> The Government will grant to the Company a seventy years' lease of the Recife and S. Francisco and the Sul de Pernambuco lines, rent free until 1911, when those two systems will be worked by the Company for 85 and 95 per cent of the gross receipts respectively. [...] Should the Government purchase the Conde d'Eu and Natal and Nova Cruz systems they will be leased to the Great Western. The Company for its part surrenders all claim on the Government on account of the guarantee as from the date it takes over the leased lines, retaining, however, all the profits arising from its own property.[244]

Government decree n° 4,111 of 31 July 1901 approved "the contract with the Great Western of Brazil Company for rescission of the guarantee of interest on the capital expended on the construction and maintenance of the Recife to Limoeiro railway [...] and the lease of the following railways: Recife and S. Francisco, Sul de Pernambuco with the Glycerio-União branch, Conde d'Eu, Natal & Nova Cruz, Central Alagoas and Paulo Affonso, in case the government should acquire the said Conde d'Eu, Natal & Nova Cruz, and Central Alagoas lines."[245] This was followed in August 1901 by a contract signed with the Great Western that confirmed the surrender of the guarantee payments in exchange for the company operating most of the railways in the north-east under a rental agreement. This represented a sudden and enormous increase; Estevão Pinto (1949: 128) estimates that the network now extended for 872 kilometres, in addition to the Great Western's own line.

The rental period was for sixty years. In return for the more complicated lease of the Recife to São Francisco and the Sul de Pernambuco lines, the Great Western agreed not to accept the interest payments (amounting to £39,375 per year) that under the original concession were payable to 31 December 1910. For all the lines taken over, the Great Western could keep all the revenue, and from 1 January 1911 pay the government a set percentage of the gross earnings which varied from line to line (15% for the Recife and São Francisco, 5% for the Sul de Pernambuco, 8% for the Conde d'Eu, and 12% for the Central Alagoas). However, if the gross revenue on any of the leased lines exceeded 5,000,000$ (five thousand *contos*) the Great Western would have to pay the government 15% of gross revenues, or if the gross revenue of all the leased lines together exceeded six thousand *contos*, then also 15% was to be sent to the government.

As previously, the government reserved the right to expropriate before the rental agreement expired. Article VIII spelt this out:

> Duly authorised by the Legislature, [the] Government may, 30 years from this date, acquire the lessee's interest in the leased lines and their extensions and branches constructed by said lessee, by rescission of the contract and payment of indenisation to the amount of ten (10) times the average net Revenue of the previous five years for the leased lines, and an indemnity equal to the Capital actually expended plus twenty per cent (20%) of same for the extensions and branches.

Reflecting in 1902 on what had happened, *The Economist* was not surprised that Brazil had "got tired of this very one-sided condition of affairs," which entailed paying year after year a guaranteed income to small and wasteful railways. Having obtained control of the railways by "spending a little more than guarantee liability," the government could then amalgamate the small lines into larger concerns to be leased to "responsible people", in exchange for a fixed percentage of gross revenue.

The Recife and São Francisco Railway was managed by the Great Western from July

1901. One issue unique to this line was the 5 feet 3 inches broad gauge that was later changed to the standard metre gauge of the rest of the network, with work starting on new track in December 1904 and completed by September 1905. The Sul de Pernambuco Railway was rented from 23 August 1901.

The Conde d'Eu in Paraíba joined from 1 January 1902, and this proved to be more contentious. An Extraordinary General Meeting was held on 29 October 1901 expressly "to consider a resolution empowering the directors to sell the company's railways and all it property to the Brazilian Government" following an agreement reached between the two parties on 23 October. The chairman, G. P. Torrens, proposed that the resolution be carried.[246] At a later meeting, held on 4 November, the chairman reported that agreement had been reached with the Brazilian government for the purchase of the line on 31 December 1901, with the company receiving £600,000 in Federal Government 4% bonds, starting in1905, and repayable after sixty years, on 1 July 1962. The guarantee would continue to be paid up to 31 December 1901. Torrens admitted that: "In spite of all efforts […] the company never succeeded in paying its way, and the interest received by the shareholders was from the guarantee. They had received an average of 4½% up to 1898 and from that time 3%. […] He thought [the agreement] was the best that could be done, and he advised its acceptance."[247] *The Brazilian Review* carried a report on this second extraordinary general meeting:

> A shareholder asked why, on the advice of very large shareholders, the board had decided to recommend the sale of the Conde d'Eu when the Great Western of Brazil Railway had agreed to take it over and pay a rent to the Brazilian Government for its use. The answer was that the latter company had, the directors understood, entered into an agreement with the Government whereby they had the working as a whole of a large system of railroads, which include the Conde d'Eu line. This was a very different matter from working the Conde d'Eu line alone in competition with a powerful neighbour. The Great Western of Brazil Railway paid a percentage of gross receipts on the Conde d'Eu line to the Government in consideration of the privileges which they obtained from the Government elsewhere. Their own agreement with the Great Western Company, which the shareholders approved, although it was not nearly so favourable to them as was the present sale, was vetoed by the Brazilian Government and was therefore abandoned.

The Conde d'Eu was not in good shape; it was recording an average loss of £5,000 per annum, with a staggering £11,800 loss on the year ending June 1901. The chairman explained that the decision for shareholders was either to accept the government offer of rescission bonds expected to pay 3% per annum interest to be redeemed within sixty years, or to continue earning 4% interest each year for the next ten years under the guarantee, with the risk that the line could not continue to pay its way and unredeemed debentures at the close of this period would lead to foreclosure. The latter course of action was accepted by a show of hands at the meeting, but a call for proxy votes to be counted meant that the resolution was not accepted by the shareholders; the required three-quarters of the votes was not reached.[248]

In Rio Grande do Norte, the Natal to Nova Cruz was purchased by the government for £427,000 on 31 December 1901 and rented to the Great Western from January 1902. The agreement reached with the government allowed the Great Western to work the line rent-free for ten years and afterwards pay 5% on gross receipts. A year later, in January 1903, the Alagoas Central and Paulo Afonso lines were handed over by the government to the Great Western, which in that year awarded a 6% dividend to its shareholders.[249]

According to Reginald Lloyd (*Impressões do Brasil no Século Vinte*, 1913), at the start of the century the railways that subsequently came under the control of the Great Western comprised a total of 871,230 metres, and consisted of the Recife and São Francisco (124,739 metres), the Sul de Pernambuco with a branch from Glicério to União (193,908 metres), the Conde d'Eu (166,000 metres), the Central de Alagoas and branch (150,000 metres), the Paulo Afonso (115,583 metres), and the Natal and Nova Cruz (121,000 metres). The Central de Pernambuco line was added to the Great Western's portfolio in October 1904.

The Great Western could not have been happier with the deal. The chairman enthused at the ordinary general meeting held on 26 April 1904 that:

> The report which we have the pleasure of presenting to you on this occasion is the most satisfactory which has fallen to the lot of the directors to compile for a good many years past. [...] The [government] has been relieved from a very serious responsibility in connection with the payment of the guarantee and for meeting the losses on working of the Sul de Pernambuco and Paulo Affonso sections, whilst [our customers] are now provided with a service of a better and more efficient character than they have ever before enjoyed.[250]

In July 1904, the government revised the contract with the Great Western, and set out very detailed regulations and norms for the transport of goods, baggage and passengers.[251] The contract also stipulated that the Central de Pernambuco would become part of the Great Western's network, and that this line should be extended from Antônio Olinto to Pesqueira. In addition, the Great Western was to build a branch from Itabaiana to Campina Grande in Paraíba. The decree also gave authority for the company to acquire a concession for a branch line in Pernambuco from Ribeirão to Bonito, but only if the existing line to Cortez (half way to Bonito) was rebuilt. In return, the lines operated by the Great Western would revert to the government on 31 December 1960, with the government redeeming the cost of the line from Recife to Limoeiro including the branch line from Carpina to Nazaré (the original Great Western line), the line from Nazaré to Timbaúba, and the extensions Antônio Olinto to Pesqueira and Itabaiana to Campina Grande. The rest of the lines, all *leased* to the Great Western, would revert to the government on that date without indemnity.

An extraordinary general meeting of the Great Western was held on 3 September 1904 "to consider resolutions approving a revised contract between the company and the Federal Government of Brazil, providing for the construction, leasing, and working by the company of certain additional railways." The chairman, Jason Rigby, set a positive tone:

> The proposals now submitted would undoubtedly prove of great future benefit to the company as well as to the country served by their system. [...] By incorporating the Central Railway with their own they obtained control of the whole of the railway system of the northern district of Brazil, and by linking up the two present disconnected systems, the northern and the southern, with the Central railway they would get one united whole, over which they would be able to transfer and make the best use of their rolling stock.

Rigby concluded that he "did not think that there could be any question as to the benefit to be derived from the proposed scheme."

A further revision of the contract followed in October 1909.[252] Essentially, the Great Western could keep the net receipts from its own original line and pay the government a percentage on the receipts for the other leased lines on a sliding scale of between 4% and 15%. This new agreement also obliged the company to construct three extensions:

Independência to Picuí in Paraíba (which was never built); Pesqueira to Flores in Pernambuco (which was built as far as Albuquerque); and Viçosa to Palmeira dos Índios in Alagoas (which was built) - all of which would revert to the government with no payment of indemnity. A short private railway from Ribeirão to Barreiros in Pernambuco was also acquired by the Great Western at this time.

This was a period, up to the outbreak of the First World War, of intense activity for the Great Western of Brazil Company, overseen by a succession of general managers: A. H. A. Knox-Little (1900-March 1905); J. A. Lorimer (1905-1909); A.T. Connor (May 1909-October 1913); and H.O. Jungstedt (1913 to 1919). David Simson was the company president from 1909 to 1913. Knox-Little was especially busy; during his term as superintendent in Recife the following lines were absorbed by the Great Western:

• 1 July 1901: The Recife and São Francisco. (Recife to Una [Palmares]).
• 23 August 1901: Sul de Pernambuco (Una [Palmares] to União [Imperatriz]), and the branch line from Glicério to União.
• 1 January 1902: The Conde d'Eu, including the branch line Pilar to Independência, and the extension from Paraíba [João Pessoa today] to Cabedelo, plus the branch line Mulungú to Alagoa Grande. The Natal and Nova Cruz railway.
• 1 January 1903: The Paulo Afonso Railway from Piranhas to Jatobá [Petrolândia today], and the Central de Alagoas, including the Assembléia branch.
• 1 October 1904: The Central de Pernambuco railway (Recife to Antônio Olinto).

The Great Western was now one of the biggest railway companies in Brazil; the third in terms of kilometres of track in traffic. The railway lines in Pernambuco accounted for around 75% of the company's total income,[253] and the Recife and São Francisco line was especially profitable, accounting for around one quarter of the company's total income. Perhaps because the railway from Recife to Una was doing well, there was a strike by workers on this line soon after the lease started in support of a salary increase. Management resisted, arguing that to raise wages would lead to an unacceptable increase in the tariffs charged to their clients in the sugar producing region that the railway passed through. There were other grievances too: Knox-Little had suspended the free passes issued to workers on the line when they were off duty (a discount of 50% had been introduced), and, allegedly, he had declared the summary dismissal of any worker absent for more than thirty days, even if due to illness. A commission of three strikers came from Cabo to Recife on the timetabled train to talk with Knox-Little, but failed to reach agreement, and on impulse they commandeered the train and returned to Cabo.[254] Orders were given for the three strikers to be arrested, and the strike lasted for only three days, with traffic restored on 7 October 1901.[255]

Knox-Little faced another strike during his time in Recife. In January 1902, strikers led by locomotive drivers and office staff on the network demanded a 50% salary raise. They also insisted on a daily working shift of eight hours, free passes on the railway when not working, and a guarantee that workers would not be dismissed without the consent of the 'Centro Protetor dos Operários'. This 'Protecting Centre of the Workers' had been founded in 1900 in Recife and had its own journal, the 'Aurora Social' (social dawn). This strike too was quickly resolved. The report presented to the Great Western General Meeting held on 22 April 1902 noted:

The labour and difficulty in taking over the leased lines has been very great and has been increased by the disturbances amongst the men: unfortunately a number of socialist agitators have established themselves in Pernambuco [...] misleading the men and

RAILWAYS OF BRAZIL
Viçosa on the Alagoas Section of the Great Western of Brazil Railway
Bringing in Cotton for transport

The township of Viçosa (formerly named Assembleia) on the Great Western of Brazil Railway in Alagoas, with cotton waiting for transport by rail.
Dodd, Mead, and Company, 1906. Author's Collection

inducing them to strike. We have had several strikes amongst the engine drivers and firemen. I need scarcely say in our case they were absolutely unwarranted, both as regards pay and working hours the employees of our Company have nothing to complain of. Owing to the firmness and tact displayed by Mr. Knox-Little and his assistants these strikes have ended without any ill effect except a slight stoppage of the traffic. In every case the men have given way and come back to work on our terms.[256]

In early 1903, upset by a decision to suspend trains from Recife to Paraíba (João Pessoa today), in order to improve traffic directly from Recife to Natal, businessmen in Paraíba helped by the local community pulled up around twenty kilometres of track at Coitezeiras on the Conde d'Eu line.[257] Despite such difficulties, the Great Western was soon recording good results: the annual report on 1905 showed an increase of 64.17% in receipts (£458,451), and an increase in gross profits of 82.14% (£143,418) over the previous year, and the board recommended a 6% dividend be paid for the year.[258]

While the strikes could easily be suppressed in this period, two 'Kings of the Cangaço' appeared to trouble the Great Western in the twentieth century, the first one in 1906. This was the *cangaceiro* Antônio Silvino, whose real name was Manoel Batista de Morais, who terrorised the north-east for sixteen years. He was called the 'bandido cavalheiro' (gentleman bandit) and 'the terror of the Great Western', and he also enjoyed the nickname of 'rifle de ouro' (golden rifle). The term *cangaço* derives from the word 'canga' - the wooden yoke used on oxen - and was inspired by the fact that these outlaws had to carry everything with them, often festooned round their necks, like a yoke. In a general sense, the *cangaço* was the semi-arid region (the *sertão*) that covers much of the north-east of Brazil, where *cangaceiros* (bandits) found it easy to hide from the authorities in a period that lasted from around the mid nineteenth century to 1938. Antônio Silvino and his gang of *cangaceiros* pursued British engineers working in the *sertão* of Paraíba, threatened the workers, cut telegraph lines, damaged tracks, and extorted money from passengers.

On one famous occasion he sent a letter to the directors of the Great Western saying that he would allow the construction to take place in exchange for thirty *contos de réis*. The newspaper *A Província* on 10 November 1906 told the story. On the previous day, at 8 o'clock in the morning, a train taking material and a large number of workers helping with the construction of the branch from Itabaiana to Campina Grande was stopped near Mogeiro by Antônio Silvino and twelve *cangaceiros*, all armed with rifles and garlanded with bullet belts. Prior to the arrival of the train, Silvino had captured a worker on the line and had asked him if the locomotive would stop at his signal. The worker said yes, but Silvino piled up some sleepers on the track, just in case. Having stopped the train, and living up to his 'gentleman' fame, Silvino requested a word in private with Coronel Francisco de Sá, one of the constructors responsible for the new line, and asked him for thirty *contos de réis*, for having crossed lands that belonged to him (!) without his consent. The coronel replied that, unfortunately, this would have to be taken up with the directors of the Great Western. Silvino noticed a young Englishman, an engineer, among the workers, and asked if perhaps he was one of the directors. The coronel explained that no, the directors were to be found in Recife. Silvino then threatened to pull up the rails every day, and that if he was not paid the line would never reach Campina Grande. Despite this setback, the extension to Campina Grande was opened in October 1907, climbing a rise of 462 metres, as was the Antônio Olinto to Pesqueira link.

Silvino's luck ran out on 27 November 1914, when he was wounded in a shoot-out with the police in Taquaritinga, from where he was taken to the railway station in Caruaru, where, fittingly, a Great Western special train waited to take him to Recife. Silvino was condemned to 239 years and eight months in prison, but was pardoned in 1937 by President Getúlio Vargas, after spending more than twenty-three years in jail.

The Great Western's business continued to flourish; the annual report on 1906 recorded a 4.82% increase in gross receipts, a 5.89% increase in passengers carried, and a 13.8% increase in tons of goods hauled, mainly sugar, cotton, maize, and manioc. Another dividend of 6% was paid in 1906, and in the same year, the Great Western introduced a pensions scheme for employees. The report also mentioned the new President of Brazil, Afonso Pena, elected in March 1906, who was a great advocate of improving communications, especially railways. He famously asserted that: "To govern is to populate; but you don't populate without opening roads, of all kinds. To govern, then, is to make roads." Afonso Pena travelled on the Great Western in 1906:

> He joined our railway at Maceió, and went practically all over the system before arriving at Natal. [...] His Excellency not only expressed his satisfaction with the arrangements made for the comfort of himself and suite, but also his pleasure at seeing the many improvements and extensions which were carried out, and he expressed his intention of making the railway development of the country one of the most important points of his programme during his term of Presidency of this great country. (GWBR annual report for 1906).

This augured well for the company, but the weather did not help. Drought had returned during 1906, and the Great Western lowered transport rates to help the sugar producers:

> This had the desired effect, and the area planted for the last crop was large, but unfortunately, though the beginning of the season promised well, the promise was not fulfilled, and the partial drought which followed seriously affected the growing cane. [...] We have [...] been approached by the Federal Government, who are very anxious to provide work for the people in the Northern States who have been seriously impoverished by the drought of last year, inquiring as to the terms under which we would build for their account some small extensions.[259]

But the directors were not willing to contribute to construction programmes "which are more or less in the nature of relief works."

With the following year, 1907, came a deepening of the crisis in the sugar industry - a crisis that continued to 1914. In general, the sugar cane plantations had not modernised sufficiently, and the industry was holding back on investment, since this contributed to the already high costs of production. Brazil was also producing more sugar than could be absorbed by the internal market. Not all the surplus was being exported, and what remained was not being sold on the national market since this would bring down the domestic price paid. One outcome was that the owners of the *usinas* demanded a better regulation of the policy for awarding tariff increases on the railways that crossed the States of the north-east. Another complaint was that since the gauge used on the *usina* railways was narrow - usually between sixty and seventy-five centimetres - this led to difficulties in the integration of the two systems. Above all, what the sugar industry needed was a network of railways that could take sugar (the main source of revenue for the railways) efficiently and economically to the ports. In the case of the north-east of Brazil there was also the problem of increasing competition from sugar produced elsewhere in Brazil, in Bahia, São Paulo, and Rio de Janeiro.

Nevertheless, the company paid a dividend of 6% in 1907, and again in 1908 when gross receipts rose by 5.13% compared to the previous year.[260] The produce carried by the Great Western at this time was varied, and tended to differ in some respects from one line to another. The 'Sul de Pernambuco' transported sugar, cotton, maize, beans, manioc, coffee, tobacco, and cottonseed oil. The 'Recife and São Francisco' relied mainly on sugar, serving twenty-eight *usinas* in 1908. The 'Central de Pernambuco' carried sugar, manioc, cotton, maize, beans, coffee, and hides. The 'Recife to Limoeiro' line dealt in sugar (with *usinas* established near Tiuma, Mussurepe, and Pau d'Alho), as well as cloth (Apipucos), and bricks (Camaragibe). The 'Conde d'Eu' carried sugar, and served a soap factory. The 'Natal and Nova Cruz' carried sugar and some cotton.

A major strike - the first on a regional scale in the north-east of Brazil - took place on 13 January 1909, towards the close of J. A. Lorimer's period as general manager, and this affected the entire network spread over four States. The strikers alleged that after the amalgamation of the lines into one network, workers had been dismissed and wages held down with the promise that they would be raised later. Their demands included a salary increase and two days' rest every thirty days worked for drivers, stokers and conductors, as well as a guarantee that no worker could be dismissed on grounds of ill health. The strike enjoyed strong support in the local newspapers and among workers' groups, such as the União Operária Alagoana in Maceió, and the Liga Artística e Operária in Natal.

The *Diario do Natal* in Rio Grande do Norte editorialised on 13 January that:

> As a general rule, we are not apologists for strikes, but in the case of the Great Western we find that the attitude of the national workers and operators is just, whose rights have not been attended to by the powerful company. After the leasing of the railways to the Great Western, the latter reduced the number of workers and lowered the salaries, promising to raise them later, which to date they have not fulfilled, despite the constant argument of their revenues. We advise all calm to our countrymen and that they stay firm in their resolution until they are properly attended to.[261]

A strike on this scale sent out shockwaves, both nationally and even internationally. The British Consul in Alagoas sent the governor an official communication saying that there was no truth to the rumour that Britain was sending a cruiser! The federal government caught fright and advised the Great Western to reach an agreement quickly with the striking workers. *The Brazilian Review*, however, was not sympathetic:

> A commission sent to represent the men interviewed the Manager and asked for increases in salary varying from 25 to 50 per cent; full day during sickness; the non removal of an employee from one place to another without his consent, and a few other minor conditions of the same impossible character. As the Company naturally could not accede to such terms, the men went out on strike. [...] It seems absurd that a few politicians and discontented men can stir up the personnel of a big Railway to making the most extravagant demands under threat of striking and it is clear that if the Company gives way in the very slightest degree, it will be subject to continual recurrence of strikes, which are so prejudicial to commerce and to the inhabitants of the districts served by the Railway.[262]

Management at the Great Western decided to stick in their heels, and announced that they would only discuss the claims if the workers returned to work. The newspaper *A Província* in Pernambuco was surprised by this tactic, and on 20 January gave its opinion: "We cannot allow to pass without [expressing] how strange is the calm with which the Great Western sits and waits so that, of itself, a situation is resolved that only it is responsible for resolving, [especially considering] the very abnormal state of affairs that for eight days has afflicted the populations of this capital, of the interior, and of the neighbouring States."

> A peaceful strike is not a crime in the face of our legislation; and for having been born of the blatant contempt for the most just of the complaints of a great number of our countrymen, it has attracted the sympathy and even the enthusiasm of all the classes of Brazilian society of the four States interested in it.[263]

The strike ended on 24 January after mediation by the state president of Pernambuco.

In July 1910, during the period when A. T. Connor was general manger, a federal decree gave approval to the plans and budget presented by the Great Western to build the first forty-one kilometres of an extension from Pesqueira on the old Central de Pernambuco line towards Flores at a cost of £35,066 (2,162:672$880), but Flores was never reached during the time the company operated railways in Pernambuco. In May of the following year, a federal decree approved the studies and budget for the Great Western to reconstruct the tracks going north-west from Riberão to Cortez and continue on to Bonito, as allowed for in the decree of 1904, but the line beyond Cortez was never built by the company. The annual report for 1911 noted, rather lamely, that:

> Unfortunately, for reasons entirely outside the control of the management, they were finding themselves unable to carry out these extensions with the rapidity which was hoped for, owing to a great shortage of labour in this part of Brazil, which was partly due to the increased cultivation going on, and partly to the large public works being carried on by the State of Pernambuco, which included an extensive drainage scheme in the capital itself.

The chairman Jason Rigby had died in the interim, and the report introduced his successor, David Simson, who commented:

> He was sure they would all be pleased to note, from a study of the figures given in the report, that the year under review had been a prosperous one, indeed the results formed a record, since the receipts, amounting to £604,188, were £76,739 in excess of the highest

limit hitherto reached. Altogether the year had been an important one, since it marked the conclusion of one epoch and the beginning of a new one in the history of the company.

Passenger traffic had indeed improved, but sugar receipts were down by about 19,000 tons (equivalent to £8,804 in receipts) due to crop failure caused by drought affecting the northern part of the network. However, both cotton and general goods "showed considerable increases".

In 1911, the Great Western earned £467,000 from carrying 146,000 passengers; compared to 43,000 passengers in 1902. Income from cargo amounted to a similar figure, £433,830, which, in round numbers, broke down into: sugar, £110,000; cotton, £60,000; foodstuffs, £22,000; cotton seed, £20,000; wheat flour, £16,000; sugar cane, £15,000; cloth, £15,000; manioc, £14,000; alcohol, £14,000; dried fish, £11,000; kerosene, £11,000; and coffee, £10,000. The company had 1,329 employees, including fourteen British, and during harvest time the railway employed 122 drivers and 129 stokers.

In 1912, on average, 1,517 kilometres of track were in operation, including 360 kilometres that belonged outright to the Great Western. The branch line from Ribeirão south-east to Barreiros (just over fifty-five kilometres) was acquired in this year; a railway that belonged to the Companhia Geral de Melhoramentos de Pernambuco. This line followed part of the intended track of the old Estrada de Ferro de Tamandaré, which aimed to link the port of Tamandaré with the banks of the river Una,[267] but was never built. In 1893, the concession was handed to the Companhia Estradas de Ferro Norte do Brazil, but, once again, nothing had happened, and the terms of the concession were declared lapsed five years later.

Another development in 1912 for the Great Western was the setting up of a subsidiary company called The Alagoas and Northern Railway, formed expressly in England to exploit an Alagoas State government concession for a line known in Brazil as the Estrada de Ferro do Norte de Alagoas. This railway was to be built northwards from near Maceió (either from Bom Jardim or Lourenço de Albuquerque) northwards to Jacuhype (Jacuípe today) on the river Jacuípe, a tributary of the river Una, where Pernambuco and Alagoas meet. A contract was signed on 3 April 1912, with the general manager, Alberto Theodoro Connor, representing the company.[268] Echoing practice in imperial times, the State offered a guarantee of 5% on a maximum capital invested of £3,000 per kilometre, and privilege of use for ninety years.[269] While surveys were undertaken and some construction work was started, this line was never completed. Follett Holt, the company chairman, explained in 1929 that the Great War had intervened; it coincided with a difficult time when tariffs could not be raised; and heavy rainfall had washed away several of the cuttings. As a result, "It was impossible in the circumstance to obtain materials, or to carry on the work, and in the passing of time there has been little encouragement to us to proceed."

At the Ordinary General Meeting held in London on 29 April 1913, the chairman, David Simson,[270] cautiously noted "a gradual development in the whole business." Receipts for 1912 had exceeded the highest previous record by £40,097, and passenger numbers had increased. However, while the transport of cotton and wood had increased, and "the import traffic" into the interior had "showed considerable increases," sugar cargo had decreased.[271] This was at the time when British investment in Latin America probably reached its zenith, when nearly 224 million pounds were invested in Brazil, second only to investments in Argentina.[272] But then the Great War intervened, and this proved to be a watershed from which British involvement in Brazil never recovered.

We Fall Between
These Rival Parties
The Great Western of Brazil
Railway 1914-1950

I see through the window of my train
the Sundays of the little citizens,
with little girls and lasses,
and starched clerks who come to look at
the dust-covered passengers of the wagons.
This Great Western railway
made to order for the north-east
is the most picturesque of the universe,
with its sleepy Baldwins
and its wagons of Ôlho matchbox trademark.

Jorge de Lima, *G.W.B.R.*, 1929, translation[273]

The year of 1914 marks the end of British predominance in Brazil. This hegemony was already under attack from other countries from the start of the new century, especially the United States and Germany, and it withered as the realisation set in - that Brazil's continuing modernisation no longer depended on input from Britain. The industrialisation of Brazil can conveniently be said to start in 1914, given impulse by the sudden shortage of products internally once war broke out and the shortage of foreign capital for investment. The outbreak of the Great War in August 1914 is a key watershed for understanding British involvement in Brazil; in the post-war period war debts created a huge burden, and Britain lost its supremacy in key industrial sectors due to a loss of competiveness internationally, and this meant too that countries looked less and less to Britain as a source of capital for development.

In 1914, the Great Western of Brazil Railway had 1,476 kilometres of track in operation, centred on Recife. Writing in 1916 while the war still raged in Europe, Frederic Halsey wrote encouragingly in his book *Railway Expansion in Latin America* that: "The Great Western of Brazil Ry. operates about 1,010 miles of main track extending from Pernambuco [i.e. Recife] into the interior and northward along the coast. The railway handles a considerable traffic in sugar, cotton, timber etc., and is a successful enterprise."[274] The company's network was made up of 224 miles owned directly by the Great Western, in which they had invested £1,500,000, and 786 miles of track under lease from the government, on which the company had spent around £2,500,000 on improvements and extensions.

The period immediately before hostilities broke out actually augured well for the Great Western. Speaking at the annual general meeting held in London on 28 April 1914, chairman Follett Holt called attention to the record volume of traffic carried in 1913, despite difficulties resulting from restrictions on credit. The profit margin had increased to £31,000. But this was the zenith of the company's fortunes;

> From 1914, with the exception of just one year, the Great Western did not distribute dividends to the shareholders, prevented by the progressive lowering of exchange, by the correlative increase in the price of fuel, by the increase in the salaries, and by the growing necessity to repair the company's material, increasingly worn out by use, or deteriorated by the sun, by the dust, and by the salty waters of the north-east. (Estevão Pinto).[275]

Receipts fell in the years 1914 and 1915, and the crisis caused by the war very nearly brought the Great Western to its knees. Ironically, the company was unable to cope with the increase in demand for transport after war broke out; there simply were not enough locomotives and wagons available. Estevão Pinto estimates that the amount of rolling stock available had been reduced by 10% just prior to the war.[276] Firewood was being used as fuel, and the danger of sparks starting fires meant that cotton had to be transported in closed wagons.

In 1914, goods traffic dropped by 15%, and passenger numbers by 14%. At the ordinary general meeting held in London on 4 June 1915, Follett Holt reported on how the outbreak of war had been a burden for the company; Brazil had faced a serious financial crisis and had declared a moratorium, "and for many weeks business was at a standstill and the exchange market was completely demoralized." Thirty of the company's employees had joined up, and one had died in the Dardanelles. The way out was to earn more from the rates they charged, and the company was now negotiating for a revision of the contract on the leased lines; "an equitable adjustment of their tariffs", since "values had so changed since this contract was made that they believed the Government would eventually realize that the conditions under which they were working must also be changed." The chairman "had no doubt that they would be given a favourable hearing," but this was not to be.[277]

At the ordinary general meeting held in June two years later, Follett Holt lamented that 1915 and 1916 had been disastrous years, due to bad weather and the exchange rate, until a good sugar cane crop in October 1916 "brought with it a great revival of business." At the same time, there was the overriding need for an increase in tariffs that, he now admitted, the government was reluctant to award. While business was generally prospering in the region served by the railway, "we were called upon to carry goods at less than real cost for clients who were fully able, and I believe willing, to pay a proper rate. [...] We are, of course, wholly dissatisfied with the results," and the company had been negotiating yet again with the government.

On top of this, "New officials have read new meanings into old contracts, and closed accounts have been reopened in order to establish claims for additional payments by the company for past years." Nevertheless, he was hopeful of a good outcome: "The work done by this company in the North of Brazil during the last 35 years has been of such great value to that country, and our case is so straightforward and honest, that I firmly believe, judging from my own happy experiences in Brazil in the past, that the Government [...] will arrive shortly at a satisfactory agreement."[278]

1918 was dominated by discussion of the tariffs and the need for a new contract with the government. At the ordinary general meeting held on 4 July, the chairman, H. C. Allen (in the absence of Follett Holt) reviewed the history of negotiations with the Brazilian government in recent years and the status of the contract. The 1901 agreement had allowed the Great Western to lease railway lines in four north-eastern States, but this contract was different from agreements with other similar companies in Brazil;

> In return for giving up the guarantee, the Government transferred on a 60 years' lease, under conditions then favourable to the company, some 540 miles of railway which they had either acquired or intended acquiring. [But then] altered conditions in 1904 rendered a revision of the 1901 agreement necessary for the purpose of providing for the inclusion in the lease of the Central Railway of Pernambuco, [...] the construction of extensions to Pesqueira and Campina Grande, the reduction of the gauge of the Recife and São Francisco line from 5'6" to metre, and the linking up of all the lines entering Pernambuco.

The 1909 contract, he emphasised, had obliged the Great Western to construct certain extensions with no recourse to future indemnity. In other cases in Brazil, the lines were taken over and then rented to companies that merely came in with the capital for their exploitation, and any extensions were paid for by the government. "There is still much to be done before our tariffs bear any relation to the increased cost of working and the enhanced market value of the goods we transport." The chairman tried to keep positive:

> There is every hope of this business being satisfactorily settled upon terms which, while providing the government with a fair rental for the leased lines, will leave the company with an equitable proportion of the profits realized.[279]

But for this to happen the government needed to submit a bill to Congress, and was loath to take this step. At the next annual general meeting, held on 11 July 1919, Follett Holt (back in the chair) presented "a very unsatisfactory report" to shareholders, and excoriated the government for its "apathetic policy":

> As the exports of Brazil and the future development of that huge country depend upon the efficient development of the railway system, there is nothing good that can be said by even the best friends of that country in defence of the apathetic policy that has ruled during the past few years and which has brought the greater part of the railway system of the country into disrepute and almost to disaster. [...] The policy, or lack of policy, that has brought the present state of affairs about can only be condemned. It has not been malicious. [...] It has been simply apathetic. [...] For the past four years it must have been perfectly obvious to everyone able to add two and two together and make it four that as working costs increased on the railways, charges would have to be increased if the railway services were to be maintained and improved.[280]

But there was some light at the end of tunnel - the newly elected president of Brazil, Epitácio Pessoa, had visited the Great Western office in London and "he has promised us that one of his first acts when he takes up the reins of government will be to see that justice is done to the transport companies [of Brazil]."

This pressure led to agreement over a new contract in August 1920, in which both sides made concessions.[281] The Great Western handed over to the government all the lines which were its property: the Recife to Limoeiro plus Carpina to Nazaré branch, as well as the extensions Nazaré to Timbaúba, Antônio Olinto to Pesqueira, Itabaiana to Campina Grande, Riberão to Barreiros, and Riberão to Bonito (Cortez). This all came to nearly 354 kilometres. In exchange, the company had to forgo the indemnities that the previous contract had promised for end 1960. These lines, along with the leased lines, were then rented to the Great Western until 31 December 1960, at a rate of 4% of gross receipts, but if this exceeded 15:800$000 per kilometre of line with traffic, then 10% was to be paid over the amount exceeding this sum.

In return, the government would guarantee to raise the tariffs in such a way that there would be sufficient income to pay the company's commitments to shareholders and holders of debentures. Clause 19 of the contract allowed for the Great Western to use the yearly balance to service interest payments and redeem debentures plus pay a dividend of 6% on shares, both ordinary and preferential. Any balance left over was to be shared in equal parts between the company and the government. Clause 40 allowed for consultation on raising tariffs every three years, by initiative by either of the parties, taking into account the balance between income and expenses, including the servicing of the company's capital.

Initially, this looked satisfactory to the Great Western, and in the same year of 1920, preliminary studies were conducted into building a branch from Atalaia, on the line from Maceió to Assembléa in Alagoas, to link up with the railway in the State of Sergipe at the São Francisco river. This was authorised by the government in 1921, as was an extension of the 'Central de Pernambuco' from Rio Branco to Petrolina on the bank of the river São Francisco. Neither of these lines was ever built by the Great Western; the tariff issue remained as a major stumbling block.

Follett Holt called an ordinary general meeting in March 1921 for shareholders to review the 1919 accounts and to discuss the new contract. This report had been delayed, presumably so that a final agreement could be reached on how much money was owed to the government. The chairman summed up the current situation:

> During the last six years the company has suffered almost every possible ill a railway a railway can suffer - labour troubles, enormously high costs for fuel and materials, inadequate tariffs, adverse exchange, and the payment of an altogether disproportionate part of our revenue to the Brazilian Government. [...] We endeavoured fruitlessly to bring the fact home to the public and to the Government officials that it was impossible to maintain a first-class service for a third-class tariff.

The problem was, as Follett Holt recognised, that raising the tariff was "a delicate matter. [...] The temper of the public and the rates that traffic can bear without prejudice to trade or its development are factors that have to be considered." The new contract had helped mitigate rental payments, but had not adequately addressed the tariffs issue: "We have obtained no benefit from the tariff clauses of the new contract, but we have obtained for these years under the new contract a very substantial reduction in the amounts paid to the government in the form of rental." Nevertheless, prospects for the coming year of 1922 looked good; the general manager had just cabled to say that they expected to carry about 1,000,000 sacks of sugar and 100,000 sacks of cotton. The report was approved, which meant that shareholders accepted the provisions of the new contract.[282]

Three months later, at the ordinary general meeting held on 14 July 1921, Follett Holt reported sadly that: "We just scrape through, but, unfortunately, show no balance available for shareholders' dividends." On top of that, the prospects for that year looked very poor. "The only advantage which the new [1920] contract with the Government brought to us came from the reduction of the amount payable in the form of rental; no advantage accrued from the increased tariffs to which we are entitled in due course." Given the current exchange rate, Follett Holt estimated that a 75% increase in tariffs was needed.[283]

A company advertisement published in *Wileman´s Brazilian Review* in August 1921[284] provides an interesting snapshot of operations that year in Brazil. The total network in traffic had reached 1,621 kilometres, up from 1,276 kilometres in 1905, serving a combined population in the four States of 3,720,075 (in 1918). "Owing to its advantageous situation, Recife is the port for most of the produce of the rich tropical zone of north-eastern Brazil, a fact which cannot fail to contribute considerably to the progress of the neighbouring zones likewise. The favourable conditions and steady progress of this zone should attract the attention of European and American investors to the zone served by the Great Western Railway."

This painted an alluring picture, but the reality was somewhat different; the company had requested an increase in tariffs in May 1921, but the government had not approved this measure. They were more successful in October 1921; authority was given to raise tariffs by 16%, but, as Follett Holt reported at the annual meeting in May 1922, "as soon as the increase was announced, the Government, under the pressure of public clamour, ordered its withdrawal."

> The position, therefore, is that although we have, in accordance with the contract [of 1920], agreed to hand over the whole of our assets to the Brazilian Government at the end of the leased period without indemnity, we have not been permitted to increase our tariffs to enable us to meet the obligations [...] to our debenture and shareholders.

Despite everything, Holt was still cautiously optimistic about the outcome, and hoped that the recent period of "apathy of officialdom" was now behind them. Looking back,

> we were forced quite unnecessarily to work at starvation tariffs when the Northern States were enjoying the abounding prosperity of war prices for produce, and the result is a creeping paralysis of poverty reflect to-day by our inability to carry out many schemes we had in view for the betterment of our railway, and a body of very indignant shareholders.[285]

But matters did not improve. At the ordinary general meeting held in February 1923, Follett Holt announced that the accounts for the two previous years, 1921 and 1922, had been withheld due to disagreements arising over the tariff question - the company had resorted to the only leverage available to them; they had simply not paid the rent in this period. In his opinion, the blame fell squarely on Epitácio Pessoa, president of Brazil until November 1922, who had failed to comply with the terms of the contract and was "responsible for the great shortage of revenue shown by our accounts." As a result,

> An examination of the present worth of [the] capital [invested by British railways in Brazil] is really less than shocking. We, at any rate under present conditions, are unable to raise further funds for the railway development of the four Northern States which we serve, and it is even impossible to maintain our track and rolling stock [to a proper standard].

Follett Holt stressed that "our position is becoming very serious." There is no doubt as to his exasperation and frustration with the authorities:

> We were told by the late government that it is impossible to raise rates further in the North of Brazil. I do not for one moment agree with this view, but if we accept it then our railway is a luxury which the inhabitants of the North of Brazil cannot afford, and certainly should not enjoy at the expense of English shareholders. (Hear. hear). [...] We are met with endless delays, caused hitherto by the inability of the Government to adopt any decisive policy or action.

The chairman's speech ended with these words: "In conclusion, gentlemen, I cannot tell you how indignant and distressed we all are at having to present to you such a very bad report, but we know that with fair treatment by the authorities this old established and at one time prosperous Anglo-Brazilian company should recover the position which it has, we hope only temporarily, lost."[286]

Local authorities were just as displeased. Pernambuco continued to be badly served by the railway network, according to the president of the State in his annual report on 1923. The Great Western had been in crisis since the Great War, leading the company to paralyse all new construction and limit traffic on the older lines due to the poor state of the rolling stock. The president blamed the original contract and the later revisions as the main causes of present state of affairs - "our great poverty of railways" and "the absolute deficiency that we note in the present transport services maintained by the company."[287] The president outlined three options as he saw them: (1) that the federal government expropriate the company, at a cost of four million pounds sterling, which represented the amount of capital that the Great Western had invested in Brazil, and then pass the network on to another company to exploit the lines; (2) that the federal government expropriate the company and then rent out the lines again, and in return the company renting the lines would invest a million pounds sterling in the much needed improvements; (3) that a revision of the contract be signed with the Great Western so that it would run its services from 85% of its gross income, with the federal government covering the remaining 15% and the further amount really needed to pay off the company's financial commitments.

The crisis only worsened. At the ordinary general meeting held in June 1923, Follett Holt reminded the representatives of around 6,000 investors in the company that it had been impossible to negotiate with Epitácio Pessoa - "it is useless flogging a dead horse." He deplored "the treatment we received during that never-to-be-forgotten period." Although negotiations had started again with the new government, led by Artur Bernardes, the central issue of the tariffs remained unresolved:

> The users of the railway [in the north-east] form to a certain extent one political and economic body, and the Federal Government another, and the latter has to endeavour to find a means of satisfying the exigencies of the former without unduly prejudicing their resources. For some years past we have suffered between these two forces.

The results had been "calamitous" for the company, caused by the government not meeting its contractual obligations and by the collapse of the exchange rate. Follett Holt concluded that: "We must struggle on, and as long as possible maintain as a going concern the railway system," although "carrying on the affairs of the railway in the present circumstances is anything but an agreeable task." Nevertheless, he ended on a cautiously optimistic note: "Believing that a settlement is near, we are very unwilling to break up the organization which has taken years to create."[288] In September 1923, the Minister of Transport and Public Works decided to grant an extension to the deadline for the remittance of the rent quotas for 1921 and 1922 until the situation resulting from the 1920 contract was normalised.[289]

In an effort to break the impasse, and with the backing of the other three States, the President of Pernambuco took the initiative in 1923 to call a meeting of regional representatives, the Great Western management, and the federal inspector of railways. As "an emergency measure" they called on the federal government to provide rolling stock and other necessary material to the company, and agree to a tariff revision "that

NORTH BRITISH LOCOMOTIVE COMPANY, LIMITED.
QUEEN'S PARK WORKS, GLASGOW.
Reference No. L 153.

Steam locomotive manufactured for the Great Western of Brazil by North British Locomotive Company Limited, Glasgow. Original factory specifications. Author's collection. This was one of the engines in the series 17226-8 manufactured in 1906 and acquired by the Great Western in 1910. The photo shows the wheel configuration 4-4-0, but it was converted at the Great Western's Jaboatão workshop in 1949 to burn fuel oil instead of wood, with a new wheel arrangement as 2-6-2, and also to increase its maximum speed from 20 to 30 kilometres per hour. More information at: http://www.internationalsteam.co.uk/trains/brazil36.htm, accessed 16 December 2015.

Author's Collection

would permit a fair increase in income within the economic capacity of the regions served by the railways." An increase was granted, although this provoked "strong complaints" and the Alagoas State government, for one, had to employ "energetic measures" to ensure that the increases were imposed in 1924.[290] This was the year that J. G. Castles was succeeded by Joaquim de Assis Ribeiro as resident general manager, and from this time on all local superintendents were Brazilian.[291]

This was still not enough. At the ordinary general meeting held in July 1924, Follett Holt supposed that since the railway had operated at a loss the previous year, "you were not therefore unprepared for the extremely disappointing accounts which we have called you together to consider today." The chairman had been to Brazil to meet with the president and the ministers of Railways and Finance. Their meetings had been courteous, but had not resolved their differences. "We do not ask a favour; we only ask that the price for which we sold our birthright in 1920 should be delivered to us. The price was a tariff sufficient to enable us to amortize our capital and provide modest dividends to our shareholders, and this has not been paid to us." Follett then added a warning: "If eventually it is found that the capital invested in our undertaking is unprotected by the Brazilian Government and unsafe, then, in my opinion, no British capital invested in that country will be safe." He begged shareholders for a bit more patience so that the board could continue with "our unpleasant task in the endeavour to avoid a crash which would seriously affect not only Brazilian credit, but would land us regretfully in litigation with a country which was our ally and old-time friend."

Shareholders at this meeting were equally indignant: "a complete disregard on the part of the Brazilian government towards its contractual obligations"; "the effect of such actions […] reacts prejudicially on the credit of Brazil in the world's financial markets"; "The position is indefensible - nay, it is in some respects immoral - that the Brazilian public should expect to receive such services as we render in the development of their country without reasonable compensation being offered. (Cheers)." E. P. Mousir, a shareholder, suggested a resolution be passed "to call public attention (1) to the persistent ill-treatment of their property by the Brazilian Government ; (2) to the fact that the Brazilian Government has completely defaulted on its 1920 contract with the company; and (3) that the many promises that the Brazilian Government has made to remedy the railway's position have in no instance whatever been carried out." The resolution was unanimously adopted.[292]

Hemmed in on both sides, the federal government finally gave in to the pressure, and in September 1924 the Minister of Transport authorised an increase in tariffs. *Wileman's Brazilian Review* reported that: "The pending settlement of the Great Western Railway's tariff question has been received with much satisfaction both here and in London."[293] The expectation was that a tariff would be awarded from 1 November that would increase income by 50%. The Great Western had scraped through. Follett Holt was much relieved when he addressed shareholders in June 1925 and reminded everyone that "When we met you last year the company was very near to the rocks. […] Last year we were in a serious condition, being on the point of retiring from Brazil with a lawsuit against the Government for the recovery of their capital." New tariffs had been introduced in November 1924 "without, as far as we are aware, real prejudice to any individual or industry." Recognising the plight of the company, the government had advanced funds to be spent on improvements, and had waived rental payments for the period 1921 to 1924. This all "marks the turn in the tide that commenced to run against us some ten years ago." The loss of £9,400 made in 1923 had turned into a profit of £39,000 in 1924. The chairman concluded by saying that "Our prospects are better now than they have been for many years."[294]

The President of Pernambuco was a great deal more gloomy. In his report on 1924 he referred to "the protests, the complaints, the outcries [that] arose from all the points of the State," and he again recommended that the Great Western be expropriated and rented out again for a period of twenty years, presumably to another operator.[295] In his narrative on the same year, the President of Alagoas recalled that after disturbances had broken out in Pernambuco he had ordered that the company's railways in his State be defended by the "public force." But he had also written to the federal government to protest the 'prohibitive' tariff increase and to declare his support for "the legitimate complaints of the producers of my land."[296]

On a more positive note, it was in this period that landmark legislation was passed that is considered today as the starting point of social security in Brazil, and this was embraced first by the Great Western of Brazil company. Decree n° 4,682 of 24 January 1923 (known as the Elói Chaves law) determined that all railway companies in Brazil set up a pensions scheme for all their workers, and the pioneer in establishing this scheme was the Great Western, from 20 March 1923. The law provided for a monthly contribution of 3% of the workers' salaries, and an annual contribution from the company of 1% of its gross income.

At long last, the Great Western's fortunes seemed to be improving. *The Railway Gazette* published a lengthy article in December 1926 on the company with the heading: "This Line, which is over 1,000 miles long, is on the metre gauge, and handles a big Traffic in Sugar Cane, Sugar and Cotton. Record receipts were earned in 1925." The text refers to "The more favourable terms of the 1920 contract [that] chiefly refer to revisions of tariffs periodically." 2,829,065 passengers had been carried in 1925, compared to 2,442,688 in the previous year, and passenger traffic revenue had increased by almost 41 per cent. Similarly, the total of goods, parcels and livestock for 1925 was 1,781,137 tons, representing an increase of nearly 24 per cent over 1924. However, "More than 50 per cent of the traffic is sugar cane, which is very low rated, and thus accounts for about 8 per cent of the gross receipts."[297]

But, despite the 1924 tariff agreement, the company was still in trouble. In May 1927, Follett Holt dropped a bombshell; tariffs had not been raised sufficiently - he calculated that £1,500,000 had been lost in revenue in recent years - and "it is obvious, therefore, that, whilst we are deprived of this large amount, we are not in a position to pay rental." The chairman put a brave face on the situation, and reported that discussions were in hand with the federal government over "the serious position that has been created." The new president of Brazil, Washington Luís (who had assumed office in November the previous year), had sent a telegram through the Minister of Public Works: "President of Republic declared prepared to raise rates to comply with contract within limits economic possibilities zone," and the chairman welcomed this declaration.[298]

In June 1928, Follett Holt's report to shareholders began: "Again the results of another year's working of this railway [...] have demonstrated that so long as it is compelled to work with an inadequate tariff, burdened with liabilities to the Government, and with an exchange which has been stabilized at the low rate of a trifle under 6d., the company cannot expect to provide remuneration for its long-suffering shareholders." The currency had depreciated by 16% during 1927 and this had affected the pound sterling value of remittances to Britain. A tentative agreement had been reached with the federal government, and this was "communicated to the Governors of the States of the States which we serve, who at once raised objections and used their influence to secure a delay in which to devise an alternative scheme."

The company now altered tack, and by talking directly with the State presidents, they came up with a mutually agreed plan, but the Brazilian president refused to accept it and insisted on the wording of the original scheme for tariff increases. Then, in May 1928, "to our intense disappointment, we were informed that the President preferred to postpone the matter for some other opportunity." The essential difficulty, as Follett Holt correctly summarised, was that the people who benefitted from the railway network "wish to pay as little as possible for its use and direct all their political efforts towards forcing the financial burden on to an unwilling Federal Government. We fall between these rival parties. [...] Railways we know how to deal with, but politics, State and Federal, are beyond our scope and comprehension." He concluded his address to the shareholders: "The starvation we have suffered during the last 14 years has been almost unendurable."[299]

Once again the incessant pressure paid off, and decree n° 5,630 of 31 December 1928 authorised the government to make changes to the 1920 contract: the rent quotas could be reduced and the company's debts with the federal government could be paid in instalments, after confirming that the gross income of the network was greater than what was necessary to cover expenses and contracted capital obligations. One provision did not change; the government reserved the right to expropriate the company, as provided for under the 1920 contract. At the annual general meeting in June the following year, Follett Holt expressed his immense relief: "We can put the last 15 distressing years into the limbo of the past." The government of President Washington Luís had awarded an improved tariff, on a sliding scale, and the future now looked more promising.[300]

Estácio de Albuquerque Coimbra, President of Pernambuco since December 1926, saw no reason to celebrate. His report on the year 1929 grumbled that: "There is no other solution for our railway problem than the removal of the Great Western," which had become a "serious obstacle" to railway development of the State. He complained that construction works on the network had been interrupted for fourteen years, and had only begun again in 1926 when he, with the help of the presidents of the other States served by this company, obtained a line of credit from the federal government. But the extensions and branches contemplated by this credit had not been open to traffic, although some work was going on. He appealed to the federal government to indemnify the Great Western, terminate the rental contract, and hand over responsibility to the States for the railways crossing their territories, as had been tried with success in the States of Rio Grande do Sul and Minas Gerais. A key issue, in his opinion, was that the progressive tariff increases had forced agricultural producers and industrialists to seek alternative transport solutions; by sea in the region near the coast, and by road in the interior "even by bad tracks."

Albuquerque Coimbra returned to this theme in his annual report of 1930, shortly before he was dismissed in the October 1930 revolution: "As long as the railway network in Pernambuco is yoked to a joint exploitation with the lines in the adjoining States, in charge of the Great Western, by means of a contract of a purely commercial nature, we can achieve nothing in the sense of confronting efficiently the convenient solutions for the economic development of the State." He argued strenuously for an "expropriation on the part of the Federal Government of the capital invested by the Great Western in the railway network."

The government's intention of guaranteeing a return on capital invested by means of progressively raising tariffs was destined to bring problems. This device had worked with the São Paulo Railway and other lines in Brazil, but the difference was that these lines carried coffee. On the Leopoldina Railway, for instance, 14% of the produce carried was coffee, but this accounted for almost half of its receipts. In contrast, almost half of the produce carried by the Great Western was sugar cane, which produced only 8% of its gross income, and there was no compensating high value product to be transported. And there had been little investment in rolling stock; to make matters worse, the rolling stock on the 'Recife and São Francisco' line no longer served since the gauge was changed. The general manager reported that, for example, if the 1923 sugar cane harvest had been better they could not have transported it all. Several of the bridges and viaducts were not in good shape, and the company suffered from periods of drought. On top of this, it was common for passengers in this period not to pay their fares, by giving a tip to the conductors.

We are fortunate to have the memoirs of Terence Hanson, who arrived in Recife in 1927 during this turbulent period to work on the Great Western, and stayed with his family there for thirty-two years, until 1959. He published an account of his experiences in 1989; a book entitled *A railway engineer in Brazil*. His first appointment was as one of the district engineers, starting with responsibility for Alagoas and for the branch line to Garanhuns, working from the office in Maceió, then as Engineer-in-charge of Betterment Works in 1939, and eventually promoted to the Chief Engineer, Ways and Works of the northeastern network of the Brazilian Federal Railways, once the Great Western had been nationalised, but with duties still covering 1,700 kilometres in the same four States of the previously British network.

His train journey from Recife to Maceió with the train swaying from side to side introduced him to the problems of his district: "Fifty per cent of the sleepers were rotten; rails and fishplates were badly worn; and the budget for maintenance was slender. The line got worse in the rainy season. It was now up to me to do all I could to put things right, and keep the trains running on time." The Assistant Chief Engineer, Duniam Jones, accompanied Hanson and was not very encouraging; Hanson's predecessor had only worked in Alagoas for five months. "Six months was the longest period ever served by a District Engineer in Alagoas," which he put down to the lawlessness of the State.

Hanson was soon told of a new band of marauding *cangaceiros* led by a man with the nickname Lampião, who, "with his cut-throats, infest the Sertão, ranging entirely at will over the vast region from Alagoas to Ceará, robbing, terrorizing and murdering. Some of the big landowners in the Interior are hand-in-glove with Lampião, and freely connive at his atrocities; others have no option but to do so, if they want to survive."[301] Virgulino Ferreira da Silva - alias Lampião (lantern) - was the most famous of the *cangaceiros* and assumed the mantle of 'King of the Cangaço' that Antônio Silvino had been stripped of in 1914. His nickname apparently derived from the speed at which he could fire his rifle, that at night seemed like a lantern in the darkness. Formerly in the national guard, and blind in one eye, Lampião roamed practically all the States in the north-east in the 1920s and 1930s. Maria Gomes de Oliveira, known to her family as Maria Déia, joined the outlaws in 1931, and later, as consort to Lampião, became known as *Maria Bonita* (pretty Mary, although she was far from that).

The root causes of the *cangaço* were unemployment, drought, famine, and the pervading sense of injustice and a thirst for vengeance that broke apart family and community ties among people in the countryside. While Lampião and his gang cultivated a Robin Hood legend for themselves, they harboured a hatred for anything connected with authority and government, and were often very brutal. However, the stories of how they outwitted police and soldiers, disappearing and reappearing, seemingly at will, became part of folklore and greatly entertained the general public. Lampião and nine of his followers were finally corralled by soldiers in 1938, at a farm near Moxotó - a station on the Paulo Afonso railway. In the firefight that followed Lampeão, Maria Bonita, and many of the *cangaceiros* were shot and killed. The soldiers severed the heads of the gang and took them to the station at Pedra, where they were pickled in glass jars of alcohol, according to Hanson,[302] and taken by a Great Western train to Piranhas to be exhibited as proof that Lampião was actually dead.

Three years earlier, Hanson had had his own brush with Lampião. One late afternoon in 1935, Hanson was on the track two kilometres from the Mimoso station, situated between Pesqueira and Arcoverde on the line running west from Recife, when his railcar broke down. The problem was that "the seats and floor of my car [were] cluttered with bags of silver currency" to make payments to the construction gang in Rio Branco, further down the line. Suddenly a *delegado* (policeman) and a trooper arrived on foot from Mimoso with news that *cangaceiros* had been spotted in the area, and advised Hanson to reverse and go back to the previous station of Pesqueira. Hanson tried to make contact by telephone and telegraph from Mimoso station, but the lines had been cut by the bandits. With remarkable coolheadedness, he decided to go ahead with the journey, since he felt an obligation to the workers who were waiting for the wages.

Knowing the line well, Hanson worked out where the *cangaceiros* were probably lying in wait to make an ambush, in a cutting, and consulted with his co-workers as to where the bandits would probably be placing sleepers on the track. He then made a plan to trick the bandits. He found an old discarded trolley and tied this to the rear of his railcar. On arriving at the place where he imagined there would be sleepers placed across the track the plan was to unfasten the old trolley and, in pitch darkness, Hanson would shout out loudly in Portuguese to his companions that they would return the way they had come, and push the trolley back down the descent. Hoping that the bandits would race after the retreating trolley, Hanson and his companions would take the railcar forward in silence, removing any obstacle they found on the track. This was the plan, and it worked!

Hanson travelled extensively on the network in an inspection carriage, for which he provides a description:

> In the rear part of the saloon of the observation coach there were a pantry, an oil stove, table and chairs, and a toilet and washbasin. The three sleeping cars [which accompanied] had individual cabins equipped with a toilet and shower for each officer, while at the end of the train there was a dormitory car for the crew. All meals were prepared by the restaurant car cooks. According to regulations, a baggage van was coupled immediately behind the engine tender. This was compulsory on all trains which carried passengers, as an added safeguard for them in case of collision.[303]

Three years after Hanson's arrival, Follett Holt reported in May 1930 that a dividend of 6% on preferred shares and of 3% on ordinary shares had been agreed - the first dividend to be paid in sixteen years, and, as it turned out, the only dividend ever paid in the post First World War period. The stock market had crashed in the previous year, but optimism was in the air: "The total ton-miles handled by the railway was the greatest in our long history;" the sterling balance was slightly better than the record year of 1913; and "our relations with both Federal and State authorities in Brazil, I am happy to say, have been most cordial throughout the year."[304] This did not last; the chairman in April 1931 reported that the results for the previous year were very disappointing, and that tariffs had been lowered in order to meet competition from the roads and the fall in the value of sugar and cotton.[305]

After breaking the record for a district engineer's stay in Alagoas, Hanson subsequently moved to the same post in the Limoeiro district, which included responsibility for lines in both Pernambuco and Paraíba, and he witnessed first-hand the revolution of October 1930 in which the State of Paraíba played a major role. This was a coup. President Washington Luís was ousted on 24 October 1930, and the revolutionaries prevented the inauguration of president-elect Júlio Prestes. Getúlio Vargas assumed the leadership of the provisional government in November 1930 and began to rule by decree. Hanson remarks that the provisional government had made a favourable impression on the company, "making good progress in straightening out the affairs of the country."

A second revolution followed in Brazil: the Constitutionalist Revolution of 1932 against the coup d'état led by Getúlio Vargas. Looking back on 1932 in May the following year, Follett Holt felt that the overall picture for the company was reasonable, despite a number of problems. There were worries over the prevailing sense of insecurity in the world, and the federal government's "bitter struggle with the State of São Paulo" (the revolution). In addition, restrictions on remittances in sterling from Brazil had meant that "the company's cash in London was becoming depleted." Local problems exacerbated these general difficulties: tariffs had been reduced in the face of "the advent of lorry competition," there had been a serious drought, a poor cotton harvest, and disputes with workers - "the company suffered in Pernambuco repercussions with a certain section of labour from which they were only now beginning to recover."[306]

Follett Holt resigned in January 1934, and G.H. Harrisson took over the presidency of the company, a position he held until 1938. Presiding at a meeting of shareholders in May 1934, Harrisson reported that the previous year had been "a truly disastrous one" for the company. There was strong competition from lorries that "had a stranglehold on the company," since they were not subject to the same limitations of tariff and norms of operation. The sugar harvest had been poor due to a serious drought, and the company laboured under "a tariff system unsuited to modern conditions." As a result, "the line was one of low traffic density." The company hoped that the government would recognise that railways were

> a vital necessity for the present needs and future development of their country, [but] if the directors were wrong in assuming that the Government wished them to maintain those railway services, and were unable or unwilling to grant the essential help, the company's only alternative was to ask that the Government should take over the property under the terms clearly and adequately provided for in the contract.

Negotiations with the government were ongoing, and the company had submitted four main proposals in writing: that the government provide a loan for "vital works of renewal and improvement;" that the road transport companies be subject to the same government controls (such as health and safety, and payment of taxes); and that the tariff system be modernised. The fourth request to the government was to urge the abandonment of the Paulo Afonso railway line, "The traffic was not, and never had been, sufficient to warrant the operation of the line, which involved the company yearly in considerable losses."[307]

The Paulo Afonso Railway had become the subject of ridicule. The train was sometimes taking six hours to cover the fifty-four kilometres from Piranhas to Pedra. In his book *Delmiro Gouveia: O Mauá do Sertão Alagoano*, Félix Lima Júnior describes how the rolling stock was poorly maintained: "It was said, jokingly, that behind the train that went up or down the line there came a locomotive with a cargo wagon, picking up the fallen pieces from the locomotive and the carriages in the other composition." There was a weekly train from Jatobá to Piranhas on Tuesdays, carrying few passengers and little cargo. In Piranhas, the train met the steamboat SINIMBÚ from Penedo that had spent the night in Pão de Açúcar. The boat arrived at mid-day on Wednesday and returned to Penedo on Thursday in the afternoon. The train then travelled back to Jatobá on Thursday in the morning. "The railway agent and the telegraph operator died of boredom at Pedra, a post to which they sent, as punishment, lazy workers or those who had committed some mistake."[308]

A journalist named Oleone Coelho Fontes rode on the Paulo Afonso railway in 1937, and recorded his experience of taking the train from the station at Piranhas in his book *Lampião na Bahia*:

> I ran greedily to the railway station in order to acquire my ticket, and I bought it with the warning that the train did not keep to a strict timetable, neither leaving, nor arriving, since it depended on the presence of the *volante* (police escort) to defend it along all the route from possible attacks by Lampião's band, unpredictable in their tricks. "However, there was no risk of missing it," the head of the station assured me, "even if the *volante* was to arrive on that day, they would have to enjoy at least one night's rest before setting off again."[309]

On his journey the train stopped at Pedra, today named after the eponymous Delmiro Gouveia, the legendary businessman who built the first hydroelectric station in north-east Brazil at the Paulo Afonso falls and established in 1914 a sewing and embroidery thread factory in Pedra - the Companhia Agro-Fabril Mercantil - which still makes thread in Pedra. His company competed directly, and often bitterly, with the firm of J. & P. Coats, established in São Paulo in 1907.

This initiative had only been possible because of the access to hydroelectric power and the railway, and at first the factory gave a new lease of life to the Paulo Afonso railway, transporting cotton for the machines and exporting the products. But this did not last long - Gouveia was an enthusiast for road transport from the outset; he built 520 kilometres in all before he was assassinated in Pedra in 1917, in circumstances that are still considered mysterious. A popular refrain ran: "There are two things in the world, that I see and I admire, it's the train there from Piranhas, and Delmiro's car."[310]

In July 1935, chairman Harrisson announced to shareholders that the company had presented a note to the government "emphasizing the critical position of the railway, and outlining our suggestions for rehabilitation as a satisfactory and reliable going concern, including a considerable grant to overtake deferred maintenance and renewals." The recent "almost tragic depreciation in the Brazilian exchange" had led to net results that "indicate the impossibility of our being able to maintain the property at the high standard which is desirable in the important area we serve." This had led to "a vivid anomaly"; the general manager had cabled London in alarm to say that "the crops are likely to be so far in excess of those during previous years that it is doubtful whether the physical condition of the track and the rolling stock available are sufficient to deal properly and adequately to the satisfaction of the shippers."[311]

Harrisson visited Brazil in April 1936 and in an interview with the president, Getúlio Vargas, he made "a personal appeal" for more understanding, stressing that: "if the Government did not feel disposed to find an early solution, as an alternative it was suggested that the Brazilian Government should acquire the line, on terms so clearly defined in the [1920] contract." He reported back to shareholders in June that the president had promised to give the matter his attention and that "there should be little doubt as to the result, as in equity the company's claims were essentially just and reasonable."[312]

Adding to the difficulties faced by the firm, this was a period of agitation by communists who targeted the foreign-owned business. In March 1936, the Minister of Work, Industry, and Commerce ruled, in response to a request from the Great Western, that they could dismiss six named individuals, believed to be communists, in accordance with a law passed in December 1935.[313] In April 1937, the same ministry authorised the firing of more workers identified as members of the Communist Party.[314]

The company's business prospects did not improve, if anything the situation worsened. Exasperated by the lack of progress in negotiations, Harrisson reported to shareholders in May 1937 that: "The time has now arrived for the Brazilian Government to take a more helpful interest in the property we lease from them. [...] As I have said before, we have made the suggestion to the Government that if they prefer to take over the operation of the line, we should be perfectly willing to retire on the terms laid down in our contract of 1920; but they have expressed themselves against any such desire or intention."[315] Given this position, the company had requested a loan from the government to put the railway in order. The mood at the ordinary general meeting held in June 1938 remained sober: the government needed to come to their rescue in order to "enable us partially to re-equip the line with urgently needed rolling stock and permanent way material."[316] The same was true in June 1939, by which date Harrisson had resigned, where the new chairman, W.M. Codrington, lamented the condition of the track and bridges that "has given cause for considerable anxiety during the last five years. [...] We are only lessees of the railway, and the whole of the track and equipment is the property of the Federal Government."[317]

In 1939, the government took a significant step. By decree n° 1,475 of 3 August 1939, the 121 kilometre line originally known as the Imperial Brazilian Natal and Nova Cruz Railway was separated from the Great Western's network, together with the rolling stock in permanent use on this line, and returned to federal administration at no cost to the government. This was at the request of the Great Western: "This section for years past had been operated at a loss, and we could see no prospect of an increase in traffic through greater prosperity coming to that particular zone." The line was taken over by the Central do Rio Grande do Norte Railway, and adopted a new name - the Sampaio Correia Railway, in honour of the engineer who had carried out the original studies for the Central line in Rio Grande do Norte. In the same decree the government promised a significant loan to the Great Western to restore, improve, and re-equip its lines and rolling stock, to be repaid in instalments between 1939 and 1942 from income, but only when this exceeded 6% of the corresponding capital. This was welcome news. Not so sweet was the government's insistence that, in return, the company had to desist from all its claims under the 1920 contract.

The government loan was received in 1940, by which time the Second World War had broken out. Under the direction of the general manager, Manuel de Azevedo Leão, several bridges affected by flooding were rebuilt or reinforced, and the old viaducts of the Serra das Russas on the line going to Caruaru were replaced with reinforced concrete; they had not been conceived to carry the weight of traffic which was now common. New railway stations were completed and inaugurated, such as at Rio Largo and João Pessoa. The company sought also to attend to the welfare and education of the workers: the 'Sousa Brandão' school and a technical training school were opened in Jaboatão, and the 'Assis Ribeiro' school in Palmeiras. Cafeterias were opened for workers in the general workshops in Jaboatão, and another in Edgard Werneck, with meals subsidised by the company.

Coal was scarce because of the war, and the company turned to using firewood - 90% of fuel consumption in 1942 - exhausting forest reserves. A reforestation programme began in 1940, with nurseries for tree seedlings at Jaboatão, Cabo, Escada, Palmares, and Primavera. The war also meant that the Great Western's workshops were compelled to start manufacturing such parts as axles and cylinders, parts that previously were imported from abroad. One benefit to the company of the conflict was that that parts and tyres for vehicles could not be imported, and petrol was rationed, which practically wiped out the competition from road transport. Passenger numbers rose exponentially, from 3,200,000 in 1938 to more than 8,000,000 in 1945, but numbers dropped thereafter.

Brazil entered the war on the side of the allies in August 1942, and suddenly the Great Western had an important role to play in the conflict. Military personnel and goods were taken to the airport in Natal for onward flights with the allied forces. Terence Hanson explains that: "The Americans had a Naval-and-Air base in Recife, and an Air base in Natal. [...] The port at Natal was too shallow for big ships. Consequently, masses of war materials were constantly arriving in Recife by the shipload, to be transported by rail to Natal Airport."[318] He describes accompanying 400 American soldiers on a special troop train from Recife to Natal, straight off a troopship and en route for North Africa. This involved coordination between the Great Western and the state-owned Sampaio Correia railway. The locomotive had to be changed at Nova Cruz station since Great Western locomotives were too heavy for the line inside Rio Grande do Norte. Military teletype wires were carried on railway posts to connect the airfields at Recife and Natal. Parnamirim airport in Natal was the primary airfield for trans-Atlantic crossings to Africa until the end of the conflict, and for a time became the busiest airport in the world; flights were taking off and landing on average every three minutes. It is estimated that during the war between 3,000 and 5,000 Americans were stationed at Parnamirim airport, and tens of thousands of Americans and British passed through Natal in transit.

Not surprisingly, the chairman reported on the "much improved results achieved during 1942" when he met with shareholders in September 1943. There had been a reduction in the tonnage of sugar and cotton carried, but this had been compensated for by the fact that "there is at present an acute shortage of petrol, rubber tyres, and spares for motor transport, with the result that a great deal of the traffic which would in normal times have been carried by road has been forced back on to the railway. At the same time the military activities of both the United States and Brazilian Governments in the areas served by the company have also provided additional traffic."[319] However, this increase in traffic was taking its toll on the track and rolling stock.

At long last, in March 1943, the government acted on the issue of the leased Paulo Afonso railway, and authorised the Great Western to remove this line from its network.[320] Any reusable materials from this railway were to be used to build a line from Palmeira dos Índios to Colégio on the river São Francisco, but this was not carried out, and - remarkably - the Paulo Afonso line managed to stagger on until 1964.

1944 saw record gross receipts, which, in chairman Codrington's opinion, "reflect the increase of tariffs put into force in 1942-43, the virtual absence of road competition, and additional traffics brought by war conditions." The government had authorised an increase in tariffs by 20%, with the exception of certain foodstuffs, and this had come into force in September 1944. Finding firewood had become a problem, and seven locomotives had been converted that year to burn fuel oil. Despite the generally good news, the chairman closed the meeting with shareholders in October 1944 with a warning that "such prosperity as we have enjoyed since 1942 is unlikely to endure under peace conditions […] unless we are protected in some measure from road competition which is bound to revive when petrol and tyres are once more easily available."[321]

When the war ended in 1945, the Great Western had a total of 1,657 kilometres in operation. Codrington reported to shareholders on 15 August 1945 (the same day that the Japanese forces surrendered) that gross receipts in currency had reached a new record, but that this gain was offset by a rise in working expenses.[322] More oil fuel and imported coal had been used, since wood fuel was scarce, in order to keep traffic on the move. He proposed that a local committee be set up in Rio de Janeiro to cope with the financial complexities of running the company in the aftermath of the war, and, accordingly, the first meeting of the 'local council' was held at the Great Western's office in that city in March 1946, "with all the powers demanded by Brazilian laws for the representation of foreign stock companies in Brazil."[323]

When Codrington reported on the year 1946, he stressed that it had been "again one of intense activity in all departments. We were favoured by an exceptionally good crop of both sugar and cotton." He had recently visited Brazil, and his mind was turning increasingly to the option of selling out to the government:

> I inquired whether the Brazilian Government had at that time any intention to exercise the right which it possesses to buy out the company under Article 52 of our lease contract. They replied that they had every confidence in the present Anglo-Brazilian administration and had no desire to make any change.[324]

He had also pressed the government for an understanding of "the plight of the stockholders in this company who had been furnishing an admittedly efficient service without enjoying any reward since 1929;" that is, they had received no dividend payments.

Despite the government's assurance that they had no intention of taking over the running of the Great Western, chairman Codrington reported in August 1948 that "during

Saddle tank locomotive manufactured by R. & W. Hawthorn Engineers, Newcastle Upon Tyne, in 1882. This locomotive was acquired by the Alagoas Railway Company as number 1, later number 156 with the Great Western of Brazil. Today this locomotive carries the number 3, but there is no evidence that this was the number used when it was in service. Photograph taken at the Museu do Trem in Recife before the locomotive was removed in 2015 to Natal in Rio Grande do Norte as part of the railway museum focussed on a railway turntable in the new campus of the Federal Institute of Science and Technology in that city. More information at: http://www. internationalsteam.co.uk/trains/brazil36.htm, accessed 16 December 2015.

Author

the year rumours were at times started to the effect that the Brazilian Government were likely to buy us out;" a right enshrined in the 1920 contract.

> It is perhaps necessary to state [...] that up to the present no intimation of any kind has been received from the Brazilian authorities of any such intention. [...] It remains to be seen whether the Brazilian Government will desire to exercise [this right] at this juncture. Meanwhile we continue to press for conditions which will not only enable us to improve our service, but which, in the absence of any more radical solution, will also provide some remuneration for our long-suffering stockholders.[325]

In the following year of 1949, the Great Western was confident enough to place orders for two new Garratt-type steam engines to be manufactured by Henschel & Sohn in Germany, and thirteen diesel-electric locomotives from the English Electric Company.[326] This was also the same year that Estevão Pinto, who had worked for the company, published his study of the Great Western of Brazil Railway. He too felt confident about the future: the company was planning a renovation and improvement project to be carried out over five years with a budget of "more than 100 million cruzeiros." The sum proposed by the government was actually 200 million cruzeiros, equivalent then to £2,650,000; a grant spread over ten years to help with renovation of the line.

But this was not to be carried forward by The Great Western of Brazil Railway Company. In 1950, the company was nationalised. Two administrations were established in Recife, one British and the other Brazilian, to effect a transition to Brazilian ownership under the name of the Rede Ferroviária do Nordeste.

Adeus!
1950 and Beyond

The bell tolls,
the driver blows the whistle,
the iron train lets out a shriek,
and then starts to move.

…

Rustic huts immerse
in the wet mangroves,
young kids, mulattos,
come watch it pass by.
Adeus!
- Adeus!

Trem de Alagoas, 1951,
Ascenso Ferreira. (translation)[326]

The inevitable took place in mid 1950. Law no. 1,154 of 5 July 1950 authorised "the Executive Power to enact the expropriation of the contracts of The Great Western of Brazil Railway Limited," followed in November that year by a resolution passed at an extraordinary general meeting of the Great Western that the company be wound up voluntarily and that liquidators be appointed.[327]

But just how inevitable was this? The demise of the Great Western was just one example of what was happening on a large scale in a wider scenario - the decline of the British business presence in Latin America at this time. While there is no consensus among historians as to exactly what went wrong, Rory Miller provides three plausible explanations in his book *Britain and Latin America in the nineteenth and twentieth centuries.* First, that the British government and British business leaders were simply incompetent, and British business interests were allowed to rust away while new ventures that might have been tried in order to sustain the relationship with Latin America were either not tried or were officially discouraged. Second, that Britain retreated from a region where the United States possessed a natural hegemony and this was part of a rational decision to concentrate on interests in other parts of the world, especially in what remained of Britain's empire. Thirdly, the adverse effect of events that could not be predicted in the twentieth century; especially the First and Second World Wars and the Great Depression. Rory Miller points out that these possible explanations are not mutually exclusive, and that in fact what happened may have resulted from a combination of all three.

In an earlier study, entitled *The decline of British interests in Latin America,* the same author makes the interesting point that while the Second World War, unsurprisingly, contributed further to the decline that had started earlier in the century and hastened the nationalisation of British companies in this period, this was actually fortunate for many boards of directors, since the assets of these companies were generally run down due to a lack of investment, and there was no longer any real enthusiasm to hang on to their property in the longer term. According to the Brazilian economist Marcelo de Paiva Abreu in his article *British business in Brazil: Maturity and demise (1850-1950)*, the British-owned railways in Brazil "were rather rundown concerns. Prevented from increasing tariffs, the majority had to confront exchange losses and capital scarcity. Unable to maintain profitability in sterling or secure new funds overseas, they cut depreciation provision to the bone. The consequence was a sharp deterioration in the quality of services provided and further aggravation of the difficulties between the companies and the government."[328] The companies were also the target of attacks by nationalists in the region.

At the outbreak of the Second World War, around 40% of British capital investment in the region was in railways alone, which were ripe for expropriation. Britain no longer held sway, was severely weakened by the war, and British companies looked old-fashioned and vulnerable. A contributing factor was the incapacity of some British boards, thousands of kilometres away in London and Liverpool, and certain of their managers in Brazil, to really understand and assimilate the culture where they found themselves working. At the same time, The United States emerged from the war politically and economically dominant - the nineteenth century *de facto* arrangement whereby the United States predominated in Central America, the Caribbean, and the northern nations of South America, and left much of the Southern Cone to Britain (and others) had begun to erode after the First World War, and was now very much in evidence as American businesses successfully challenged the British for supremacy in Brazil and the neighbouring countries.

Brazil had benefitted from the six years of the war, from high prices for its produce, including a second rubber boom in the Amazon, and, significantly, from the building by the American government of the Volta Redonda steelworks in the State of Rio de Janeiro under the terms of the May 1942 'Washington Accords'; an inducement to Brazil to drop its neutrality and enter the conflict on the side of the allies. At the same time, Britain no longer had the wherewithal to provide the expertise, the machinery and other resources needed in Brazil in its commitment to industrialisation. As a result of all these factors, between 1941 and 1950 the value of British investments in Latin America fell by more than 50%.

From the perspective of Brazil, as we have seen, and as is well summarised in the official site of the Instituto do Patrimônio Histórico e Artístico Nacional (IPHAN) in a text entitled 'Histórico das ferrovias no Brasil' (history of the railways in Brazil):

> The changes in the relations of production and consumption, (the decadence of the plantations of coffee, cotton, tobacco, etc.), resulting from the Second World War, meant that many lines lost their income (the transport of these products) and, for this reason, started to lose money. As a consequence, several companies came under state control, which acted in the sense of recovering them, equipping them, and extending their lines between the various regions of the country, as the result of several prepared transport plans. However, by the middle of the twentieth century, the railways offered few axes of national integration, consisting of disconnected archipelagos of dense and disintegrated networks, the result of the initial project that concentrated only the link between the producing regions and the ports for outflow.[329]

Having decided to expropriate the Great Western in July 1950, the Brazilian government had now to make key financial decisions. The first, curiously, was the law approved by the National Congress the following month that authorised "the Executive Power to open a line of special credit to help The Great Western Of Brazil Railway Company Limited with the increase in the salaries of its workers."[330] The Ministry of

One of the six Garratt-type locomotives delivered in 1952 according to Great Western of Brazil specifications by Henschel & Sohn, Germany, on display at the Museu do Trem in Recife. The original contract was signed with the company of Beyer Peacock of Manchester, and this firm subcontracted to Henschel. More information at: http://www.internationalsteam. co.uk/trains/brazil36.htm, accessed 16 December 2015.
Author's Collection

Transport and Public Works opened a credit of Cr$ 94,500,000.00 for this purpose, "not available for any other application," with one-third of the amount destined to increase salary payments in the second semester of the previous year and two-thirds for the current year of 1950. The actual cost to the government of rescinding the lease to the Great Western came to £3,798,750, a sum that pleased (and very probably surprised) shareholders in the company. In January of the following year, the liquidators invited all creditors of the company to send them details of their claims by the deadline of 26 February 1951.[331]

The government created the Rede Ferroviária do Nordeste (north-eastern railway network) in 1951 to take over operation of the Great Western's network and other railways in that region. This was superseded in 1957 when the Rede Ferroviária Federal Sociedade Anônima (RFFSA) was created by Law no. 3,115 of 16 March 1957 as a mixed economy limited company indirectly administered by the federal government and tied managerially to the Ministry of Transport. With its headquarters in Juiz de Fora in the State of Minas Gerais, the RFFSA brought together eighteen regional railways, all of which continued to operate as separate entities. In the case of the northeast of Brazil, the RFFSA was divided into three regional superintendencies: SR 1, SR 11, and SR 12, with SR 1 covering the States of Alagoas, Pernambuco, Paraíba, and Rio Grande do Norte.

A railway timetable published in 1976 provides a snapshot of the reduced extent and regularity of services on the SR 1 network at that time, based largely on the original Great Western lines.[332] The 'Linha Centro' following the old Central Railway route from Recife through Caruaru had reached Salgueiro in 1963, without intersecting with any other line in the region, and there were trains four times a week in both directions. The 'Linha Norte' line from Recife to Souza in Paraíba (538 kilometres), passing through Carpina, ran two trains a day, one of which was an 'express' that continued over the railway system of Ceará State on to Fortaleza. From Souza to Mossoró (243 kilometres) trains ran twice a week. From Recife to Natal (422 kilometres) there were two trains a week. In addition to these longer journeys, there were suburban services from Recife to Carpina, the junction for Bom Jardim, and to Cabo on the line to Maceió in Alagoas, as well as to Jaboatão on the Central line where the principal railways workshops had been established in the days of the Great Western. The Central Line ceased operating officially in 1996.

From Recife to Maceió (348 kilometres), a 'fast' train ran along the 'Linha Sul' three times a week, taking around eight hours, together with a daily train stopping at all stations, operated separately from both ends to Paquevira (ex-Glicério) but apparently not connecting with each other or with the 'fast' train. The service from Paquevira to Garanhuns no longer operated. From Maceió there was a suburban service to Lourenço de Albuquerque (32 kilometres), the junction for the line south to Porto Real do Colégio on the River São Francisco (299 kilometres) reached by a train three times a week that then crossed the river bridge (built in 1972) to continue further south to Aracaju in the State of Sergipe. The Paulo Afonso railway had stopped working several years previously, in 1964. The Recife to Maceió line stopped working before the end of the 1970s decade, as did the railway from Carpina to Nazaré da Mata that followed the original branch line of the Great Western Recife to Limoeiro railway. The latter is currently the focus of an NGO campaign by the Pernambuco branch of *Amigos do Trem* to see this line reactivated so that passengers can travel by rail from Recife to Nazaré.

The RFFSA was included in the National Privatisation Programme of 1992, and this gave rise to studies commissioned by the Banco Nacional de Desenvolvimento Econômico e Social (BNDES) that recommended the transfer to the private sector of the rail cargo transport services. This transfer was carried out between 1996 and 1998. In January 1998, a new company was set up - the Companhia Ferroviária do Nordeste S/A (CFN) - that operated the railway network from the State of Maranhão to Alagoas. The RFFSA was disbanded in a sequence of decrees starting with legislation passed on 7 December 1999[333] and the disposal of its assets was initiated on 17 December that year. The operational resources (infrastructure, locomotives, wagons, and other assets tied to railway operation) were leased to the operating concessionaires of the railways in Brazil, including the CFN. The RFFSA was finally declared extinct in 2007, when Medida Provisória (provisional law) no. 353 was converted into Federal Law no. 11,483 on 31 May 2007. In the following year of 2008 the company name of CFN changed to Transnordestina Logística S/A, a private company within the CFN Group that manages the railway network in the northeast of Brazil that was acquired from the RFFSA.

Following the winding up of the RFFSA, its non-operational assets were transferred to the federal government, and IPHAN (the national heritage institute) assumed specific duties and responsibilities for the preservation of railway memory.[334] Starting in 2007, IPHAN has been preparing an inventory (Inventário de Conhecimento do Patrimônio Cultural Ferroviário) that now catalogues more than six thousand buildings in various states of conservation. IPHAN's 'railway cultural heritage' list, updated in January 2015, gives an account of those assets considered to be of value according to the institute's mission. As an example, this list includes several railway stations in the State of Pernambuco: the Central Station of Recife (where the Museu do Trem functions today); the railway station of Brum in Recife (where the original Great Western line started from); and of Pombos, Vitória de Santo Antão, Gravatá, Bezerros, São Caetano, Caruaru, Pesqueira, Mimoso, Petrolina, Maraial, Pátio de Jaboatão dos Guararapes, Paudalho, and of Arcoverde. Given the huge controversy caused in Recife during 2015 by the proposal to build thirteen high rise apartment towers in the non-operational part of the Cinco Pontas railway yard (where the original Recife and São Francisco line departed from), in an area known as Cais José Estelita, it is interesting to note that IPHAN published in March of that year a ratification notice that declared the operational part of the yard to be of historic, artistic, and cultural value.

Almost nothing remains in operation today of the Great Western railway network. The Companhia Brasileira de Trens Urbanos (CBTU), arising out of the RFFSA, operates the Metrô do Recife that follows the route of the first Great Western line, reaching

Camaragibe and Jaboatão. It is striking that, with the exception of Belo Horizonte in the State of Minas Gerais, all the metropolitan transport systems currently operated by the CBTU in Brazil are focused on State capitals where the Great Western operated in the past - Recife, Maceió, João Pessoa, and Natal.

In the case of Recife, the decision to install a metro was taken at the federal level by the Ministry of Transport when, in September 1982, the METROREC consortium was established, consisting of the RFFSA and the Empresa Metropolitana de Transportes Urbanos (EMTU, which today is extinct). This consortium started construction of the metro in January 1983, in the same year that the Central Station in Recife received the last passenger train, on 26 August. In March 1985, the first stretch of the metro line was officially inaugurated. In January 1988, the CBTU began to manage the suburban line of Recife, now known as the Linha Sul do METROREC, that reaches Cabo following the route of the first of all the railways in the northeast of Brazil, The Recife and São Francisco Railway.

It is possible for tourists to travel on a passenger train pulled by a steam locomotive in several places in Brazil, but, sadly, not in the northeast. However, there remains a great deal to see and to remind us of the golden age of travel in trains pulled by steam locomotives that Brazilians call *Marias Fumaças* (literally, smoky Marys). The first railway museum to open in Brazil, in 1972, and the second of its kind in Latin America, is accommodated within the Capiba Central Station in the district of São José in the centre of Recife. The museum closed for renovation in 1983, but was reopened in December 2014, after a renovation costing 2.5 million Reais, with an exhibition that embraces more than 500 items collected from the old railway stations in Pernambuco. Among the locomotives under cover that line the now-discontinued railway platform in the museum, there is an impressive Garratt articulated locomotive ordered from the company of Beyer Peacock in England in 1949, but subsequently sub-contracted to Henschel & Sohn in Germany and built by them in 1952. At the side of the Garratt there is the wheel arrangement of a locomotive that very probably once ran on The Recife and São Francisco Railway. On display in front of the Garratt there is one of the thirteen diesel-electric locomotives manufactured by the English Electric Company in 1954 that was acquired by the Rede Ferroviária do Nordeste in 1955.

On the other side of the platform, there is a steam locomotive built in 1906 by the North British Locomotive Company in Glasgow, Scotland. However, the oldest steam locomotive associated with this museum, known familiarly as *Catita* and built in 1882 by the company of R & W. Hawthorn Engineers in Newcastle Upon Tyne in England, was removed in October 2014 and taken to Natal in the State of Rio Grande do Norte. This followed a court decision won by the Instituto dos Amigos do Patrimônio Histórico e Artístico-Cultural of Natal and the Instituto Federal de Educação, Ciência e Tecnologia in Rio Grande do Norte. This locomotive was built for the Estrada de Ferro Central of Alagoas and, later, it is alleged, this locomotive inaugurated in April 1916 the Igapó iron bridge in Natal. It is intended that this engine will be the central attraction for the Museu do Trem de Natal, to be established on the site of the *Rotunda*, the old locomotive and wagon workshop belonging to RFFSA. In a decision by the Secretaria do Patrimônio da União of the Ministry of Planning, this structure has been handed to the federal institute of education in the district of Cidade Alta in Natal, which needed to expand the area of its campus.

Other museums have connections with the history of the Great Western. The Museu do Sertão inside the original Paulo Afonso railway station was inaugurated in 1982 as an integral part of the Casa de Cultura in Piranhas, Alagoas, and the museum has artefacts

Steam locomotive manufactured by Swiss Locomotive and Machine Works, Winterthur, Switzerland, in 1922, that operated during sugar harvests until the middle of the 1990s. Author's photograph showing the locomotive taking sugar cane to the *usina* of Serra Grande in Alagoas, 1993.

Author

linked to the history of this railway and the period of the cangaço when Lampião and his bandit companions terrorised the northeast of Brazil. Not far away, the only steam locomotive that has survived that once ran on the Paulo Afonso line is preserved in the Fábrica de Pedra, as is what appears to be the foundation stone of this railway with the legend "EFPA, 1878, P. II" that presumably refers to Dom Pedro II. Another museum that functions on the site of an old Great Western railway station is the Museu de História e Tecnologia do Algodão in Campina Grande, Paraíba, which has several artefacts connected with the railway age and a preserved 1922 Baldwin locomotive that may have been originally purchased by the Inspetoria Federal de Obras Contra as Secas (federal inspectorate for drought-related public works) that sub-contracted work to The Great Western Railway Company.

It is perhaps a fitting conclusion to this book to mention the two mosaic murals on display in the main station of the Recife Metro, beyond the preserved railway platform of the museum, and along the wall just beyond the turnstiles used by around 280,000 passengers daily. These are the work of the British artist Walter Kershaw undertaken in 1986, and they contrast the past - a *maria fumaça* locomotive with a seated mulatto woman in a rural scene that includes the façade of the church of Nossa Senhora dos Prazeres - with more recent times as represented by a diesel-electric locomotive in the second mosaic. As a curiosity, the two murals only really make sense to passengers as they rush to and from the trains, since they have to be viewed from an angle, and are difficult to make out when viewed from directly in front.

Historical Timeline

1373: The Anglo-Portuguese Treaty is signed between King Edward III of England and King Ferdinand and Queen Eleanor of Portugal.

1703: The Methuen treaty between England and Portugal was concluded in December 1703.

1808 (22 January): Prince Regent Dom João Maria de Bragança arrived in Salvador, Brazil, escorted by British naval ships, having fled the forces of Napoleon.

1808 (28 January): Dom João issued a decree that permitted "friendly nations" to conduct commerce in Brazilian ports.

1810 (19 February): Treaties were signed in Brazil between Portugal and Britain: The Treaty of Friendship and Alliance & The Treaty of Commerce and Navigation.

1815 (16 December): The United Kingdom of Portugal, Brazil, and the Algarves was created.

1817: The Portuguese Convention agreement gave the right to the British navy to stop and search merchant ships for the presence of slaves.

1821 (April): Dom João left Brazil for Portugal, leaving his eldest son Dom Pedro behind as regent of Brazil.

1822 (7 September): Brazil's independence from Portugal was announced. Dom Pedro became Dom Pedro I, emperor of Brazil.

1825 (August): The Treaty of Peace and Alliance between Britain and Portugal was signed in Brazil.

1826 (23 November): The Anglo-Brazilian Abolition Treaty was signed, and ratified by Brazil in 1827.

1827 (August): The Treaty of Friendship, Navigation, and Commerce was signed between Britain and Brazil.

1831 (7 April): Dom Pedro I abdicated and returned to Portugal.

1835 (31 October): Law no. 101 (the Lei Feijó) authorised the Regency to award railway concessions in Brazil (during the regency of Padre Diogo Antonio Feijó).

1839: Dr. Thomas Cochrane signed a contract to link Rio de Janeiro and São Paulo by railway.

1841 (July): Dom Pedro I's son was crowned Pedro II, Emperor of Brazil.

1845: Britain passed The Slave Trade Suppression Act (commonly known as the Aberdeen Act).

1850 (4 September): Lei no. 581 (Eusébio de Queirós Law) was passed by which Brazil undertook to no longer import slaves into Brazil.

1852 (26 June): Law no. 641 was designed to kick-start railway building in Brazil. This decree gave priority to lines that would link the Court in Rio de Janeiro with the provinces of São Paulo and Minas Gerais.

1852 (7 August): Imperial Decree no. 1,030 granted a concession to Edward and Alfred de Mornay for the construction of a railway between the city of Recife and Água Preta in Pernambuco.

1853: The Recife and São Francisco Railway Company was organised in London, the first to be backed by the articles of concession in the 1852 law.

1854 (28 January): The first case of cholera was reported in Recife.

1854 (30 April): Brazil's first railway was opened, covering 16 kilometres from Mauá to

Raiz da Serra in the province of Rio de Janeiro.

1855: The bank of N. M. Rothschild & Son in London was appointed the sole agent and banker for the Brazilian government in Britain.

1855 (September): George Furness arrived in Recife, as chief engineer, and construction on the Recife and São Francisco line started soon afterwards.

1858 (8 February): The first stretch of The Recife and São Francisco Railway was opened to traffic, running 31.5 kilometres from Recife to Cabo in Pernambuco. This was the second railway to operate in Brazil, and the first of economic importance.

1858: The first railway workers' strike in Brazil: Belgian workers complained about wages and working conditions on The Recife and São Francisco Railway.

1870 (16 July): The second Barão da Soledade (José Pereira Viana) was awarded the concession for a railway linking Recife to Limoeiro in a contract awarded by the Province of Pernambuco.

1871 (28 September): Law no. 2040, known as the Free Womb Law was signed by Princesa Isabel in the name of the Emperor Dom Pedro II, and legislated that all babies born of slaves from that date onwards were considered to be born free.

1872 (19 October): The Alagoas Brazilian Central Railway Company inaugurated a railway from Maceió to Bebedouro in Alagoas.

1872 (21 December): English capitalists met in London to incorporate a company named The Great Western of Brazil Railway expressly to take advantage of the concession awarded to the Barão de Soledade.

1873 (September): Imperial Decree no. 2,450 was passed to promote railway construction in the provinces that could improve communications between the centres of agricultural production in the interior and the exporting ports.

1874 (28 February): Imperial Decree no. 5,561 sought to regulate the laws of 1852 and 1873.

1874 (April): Imperial Decree no. 5,608 authorised the construction of The Conde d'Eu Railway in the Province of Paraíba.

1875 (20 February): Decree no. 5,877 authorised the construction of The Imperial Brazilian Natal and Nova Cruz Railway in the Province of Rio Grande do Norte.

1875 (15 September): The Conde d'Eu Railway Company Limited was organised in London expressly to obtain the concession for a railway to link Parahyba (João Pessoa today) with Indepêndencia (Guarabira today) in the Province of Paraíba.

1875 (6 November): Decree no. 2,687 was passed; the first legislation to encourage investment in usinas centrais (central sugar mills).

1877 (17 November): Decree no. 6,746 of 17 November 1877 authorised the construction of The Great Western of Brazil Railway, from Recife to Limoeiro in the Province of Pernambuco.

1878 (23 October): Work started at Piranhas in Alagoas on The Paulo Afonso Railway.

1881 (30 August): Decree no. 8,223 authorised The Alagoas Railway Company Limited to acquire the concession for a railway linking Maceió and Vila da Imperatriz.

1881 (28 September): The first stretch of The Imperial Brazilian Natal and Nova Cruz Railway linking Natal with São José do Mipibu in Rio Grande do Norte was opened to traffic.

1881 (24 October): The first stretch of The Great Western of Brazil Railway from Recife to Pau-d'Alho was inaugurated.

1881: The first stretch of the Conde d'Eu railway of thirty kilometres to Entroncamento was opened to traffic in the province of Paraíba.

1882 (28 July): Decree no. 8,627 granted The Central Sugar Factories of Brazil Company permission to function in Brazil.

1882 (December): The first stretch of the Sul de Pernambuco Railway (state-owned) from Una to Catende was opened to traffic.

1883 (17 February): Decree no. 8,882 granted The North Brazilian Sugar Factories Company permission to function in the Brazilian empire.

1885: The first stretch of the Central de Pernambuco Railway (state-owned) was opened to traffic from Recife to Jaboatão.

1889 (15 November): Emperor Dom Pedro II was deposed, which inaugurated the Federal Republic of the United States of Brazil — the 'old republic' that lasted until 1930.

1901 (1 July): The Recife and São Francisco railway was rented to the Great Western.

1901 (31 July): Decree n° 4,111 approved the lease to The Great Western of Brazil Railway Company of the following railways: the Recife and São Francisco, the Sul de Pernambuco, the Conde d'Eu in Paraíba, the Natal and Nova Cruz in Rio Grande do Norte, the Central Alagoas, and the Paulo Afonso Railway.

1901 (23 August): The Sul de Pernambuco Railway was rented to the Great Western.

1902 (1 January): The Conde d'Eu Railway in Paraíba and the Natal and Nova Cruz in Rio Grande do Norte were rented to the Great Western.

1902 (29 August): A resolution was passed to voluntarily wind up the Alagoas Railway Company.

1903 (1 January): The Alagoas Central and Paulo Afonso railways were rented to the Great Western.

1904 (1 October): The Central de Pernambuco railway was rented to the Great Western.

1912: The Great Western set up a subsidiary company called The Alagoas and Northern Railway.

1920 (August): A new contract was signed between the Great Western and the Brazilian government.

1923 (24 January): Decree n° 4,682 (the Elói Chaves law) established a pensions scheme for all railway workers, and the pioneer was the Great Western of Brazil, from 20 March 1923.

1939 (3 August): Decree n° 1,475 separated the line originally known as the Imperial Brazilian Natal and Nova Cruz Railway from the Great Western's network.

1950 (5 July): Law no. 1,154 authorised the government to expropriate the contracts of The Great Western of Brazil Railway, and in November 1950 the company passed a resolution to voluntarily wind up affairs and appoint liquidators.

1951: The government created the Rede Ferroviária do Nordeste to manage lines previously operated by the Great Western.

1957 (16 March): The Rede Ferroviária Federal Sociedade Anônima (RFFSA) was created by Law no. 3,115. Regional Superintendency SR 1 covered the States of Alagoas, Pernambuco, Paraíba, and Rio Grande do Norte.

1964: The Paulo Afonso Railway finally closed to traffic.

1983 (26 August): The last passenger train pulled into the Central Station in Recife.

1998 (January): The Companhia Ferroviária do Nordeste S/A (CFN) was created to operate the railway network from the State of Maranhão to Alagoas.

2014 (December) The railway museum accommodated within the Capiba Central Station in the centre of Recife reopened to visitors following expensive renovation works.

Footnotes

Introduction

1 Richard Graham, *Britain and the Onset of Modernization in Brazil*. 1968: 73.

2 Josemir Camilo de Melo, *Modernização e Mudanças: O trem inglês nos canaviais do Nordeste (1852-1902)*, doctoral thesis. 2000: 89, translation.

3 Colin M. Lewis, *Public Policy and Private Initiative: Railway Building in São Paulo 1860-1889*. 1991: 12.

4 John Casper Branner, *The railways of Brazil*. 1887: 20.

5 Estevão Pinto, *História de uma estrada-de-ferro do nordeste*. 1949: 218, translation.

6 Josemir Camilo de Melo, *Ferrovias Inglesas e Mobilidade Social no Nordeste (1850-1900)*. 2008: 78-79, translation.

7 The Great Western of Brazil was not the only company outside Britain to borrow the name, there were also The Argentine Great Western Railway; The Midland Great Western Railway in Ireland; The Great Western Railways of Ontario and Saskatchewan in Canada; The Great Western Railway (Tasmania); and in the United States: The Atlantic and Great Western Railroad; The Chicago Great Western Railway; The Great Western Railway of Colorado; The Great Western Railroad (Illinois), and The Great Western Railroad (Ohio).

8 D. C. M. Platt, *The British in South America: An Archive Report*. 1965: 172.

Marvellous Ineptitude

9 Richard Burton, *The Highlands of the Brazil*. 1869: 226.

10 *The Rio News*, Brazil, 24 April 1887. Quoted in *Railways of Brazil*, Branner 1887: 11-12.

11 See Alan K. Manchester, *British Preëminence in Brazil: Its rise and decline*, 1933, chapter 1, for a detailed account of relations between England and Portugal in the times of the Crusades.

12 Alan K. Manchester, op. cit., 1933: 16.

13 The Kingdom of England, which after 1284 included Wales, was a sovereign state until 1 May 1707, when the Acts of Union put into effect the terms agreed in the Treaty of Union the previous year, resulting in a political union with the Kingdom of Scotland to create the Kingdom of Great Britain. This book will refer to the nation of England for events to 1707, and to Britain thereafter.

14 Manchester, op. cit., 1933: 18-19 & 54.

15 Dom João was officially named Prince Regent in 1799, after his mother Dona Maria I was declared mentally incapable. Dona Maria I died in 1816.

16 Salvador had been the capital of colonial Brazil until 1763; thereafter Rio de Janeiro became the capital until Brasilia was built. Captaincies became provinces in Brazil from 1815.

17 Manchester, op. cit., 1933: 91.

18 Maria Graham, *Journal of a Voyage to Brazil, and Residence There, During Part of the Years 1821, 1822, 1823*. Journal entry for 28 October 1821.

19 Manchester, op. cit., 1933: 108.

20 Richard Graham, *Britain and the Onset of Modernization in Brazil: 1850-1914*. 1972: 82.

21 A second loan of £800,000 with the bankers N. M. Rothschild & Sons was agreed in 1829.

22 William R. Summerhill. *Market Intervention in a Backward Economy: Railway Subsidy in Brazil, 1854-1913*, 1998: 545.

23 Thomas Cochrane lived with his family at the Chácara da Tijuca, also known by the name of Castelo, and later as Parque Cochrane, which he bought on 21 November 1855. On 30 January 1858, Thomas Cochrane inaugurated in Rio de Janeiro the first tramline in Brazil, with horsedrawn carriages. He died in Brazil in 1873, and there are descendants in Brazil. The Morro do Cochrane (Cochrane Hill) in the Tijuca National Park, Rio de Janeiro, is so named in his honour.

24 Douglas Apratto Tenório, *Capitalismo e Ferrovias no Brasil*. 1979: 37, translation.

25 Colin Lewis, *Public Policy and Private Initiative: Railway Building in São Paulo 1860-1889*, 1991: 8.

26 Apratto Tenório, op. cit., 1979: 38 & 61, translation.

27 See Leslie Bethell 2009, page 58, "this is the most convincing explanation for the origin of this

expression."
28 It is estimated that at least 500,000 slaves were imported into Brazil in the decades of 1830 and 1840, and around one million in all from 1800. Some historians place this figure higher: Douglas AprattoTenório, for instance, calculates that in the first half of the nineteenth century 1,600,000 slaves were brought to Brazil, and in the period 1840 to 1845 alone, 239,800 slaves were brought into Brazil. Given the average price of a slave at 300 mil-réis, this amounted to almost the amount earned from the export of coffee in the same period. The slave population in Brazil dropped from around 2,500,000 in 1850 to around 1,500,000 in 1875 (Tenório 1979: 20).
29 The Fundação Joaquim Nabuco exists today in Recife, and was founded in 1949.
30 Apratto Tenório, op. cit., 1979: 21, translation.
31 Lucia Lamounier. *The 'Labour Question' in Nineteenth Century Brazil: Railways, export agriculture and labour scarcity*, 2000: 3.
32 See Rory Miller, *Britain and Latin America in the nineteenth and twentieth centuries*. 1993: 111.
33 Ana Célia Castro, 1979: 26, quoting J. Fred Rippy *British investments in Latin America: 1822-1949*, 1959: 25.
34 Correspondence of Minister Sérgio T. de Macedo to Lord Clarendon, 16 May 1859, cited in Apratto Tenório 1979: 28.
35 Apratto Tenório, op. cit., 1979: 42, translation.
36 William Summerhill, op. cit., 1998: 545
37 Rory Miller, op. cit., 1993: 134.
38 Josemir Camilo de Melo, *Ferrovias Inglesas e Mobilidade Social no Nordeste (1850-1900)*. 2008: 52.
39 Quoted in Gilberto Freyre, *Ingleses no Brasil: Aspectos da influência Britânica sobre a vida, a paisagem, e a cultura do Brasil*. 1948: 105.
40 For this correspondence and the exchange that follows, see: House of Commons Papers, *Correspondence with British ministers and agents in foreign countries and with foreign ministers in England relating to the slave trade, from April 1, 1856 to March 31, 1857*.
41 David Joslin, *A Century of Banking in Latin America*. 1963: 70
42 The British-built BARONESA locomotive has been preserved, and can be seen at the Museu do Trem in Engenho de Dentro, Rio de Janeiro.
43 Colin Lewis, op. cit., 1991: 36.
44 See Apratto Tenório 1979: 50 and Smith Duncan 1932: 31 for discussion of these statistics.
45 One 'conto de réis' was equivalent to 1,000 mil-réis, or 1,000,000 réis.
46 Taken from the *Quadro estatístico da viação férrea do Império do Brasil: Anno de 1883*. Published by the Primeira Secção da Diretoria das Obras Públicas da Secretaria de Estado dos Negócios da Agricultura, Commercio e Obras Públicas, 10 May 1884.
47 See 'Relatorio apresentado á Assembléa Geral Legislativa [...] pelo ministro e secretario de Estado interino dos negocios da Agricultura, Commercio e Obras Publicas, ministro Rodrigo Augusto da Silva, Rio de Janeiro'. Imprensa Nacional, 1887.

The Great Stronghold Of British Interests In Pernambuco
48 Henry Koster, *Travels in Brazil*. (1) 1817: 15
49 See Chapter 1 of *The Anglican Church in South America*, the Right Rev. Edward Francis Every, D.D. London: Society for Promoting Christian Knowledge, 1915.
50 The chamber of commerce's first title was *Associação Beneficiente Comercial*.
51 See Gilberto Freyre, *Ingleses no Brasil*, 1977: 50.
52 See Richard Graham, *Britain and the Onset of Modernization in Brazil 1850-1914*, 1972: 75.
53 Richard Graham, op. cit., 1972:117-8.
54 Alfredo J. Watts, "A Colônia Inglesa em Pernambuco." *Revista do Instituto Arqueológico, Histórico e Geográfico Pernambuco*, 1945: 167.
55 David Joslin, *A Century of Banking in Latin America*, 1963: 67.
56 David Joslin, op. cit., 1963: 82.
57 See Allen Morrison, *The tramways of Brazil. Recife, Pernambuco state, Brazil*, http://www.tramz.com/br/re/re.html, accessed 4 December 2005.

58 See, for example, Estevão Pinto, op. cit., 1949: 118.
59 Douglas Apratto Tenório, op. cit., 1979: 24.
60 See "Como surgiu a palavra bonde" http://www.casadorio.com.br/sites/default/files/pdf/ Como%20surgiu%20a%20palavra%20'bonde'.pdf (in Portuguese), accessed 4 December 2015.
61 See Lúcia Gaspar, *Football in Pernambuco*, Fundação Joaquim Nabuco, http://basilio.fundaj. gov.br/pesquisaescolar_en/index.php?option=com_content&view=article&id=1101:football-in-pernambuco&catid=39:letter-f&Itemid=1, accessed 4 December 2015.

Guaranteed Against All Risk

62 Josemir Camilo de Melo, *Ferrovias Inglesas e Mobilidade Social no Nordeste (1850-1900)*. 2008: 17 & 121, translation.
63 Aristides is buried in the British Cemetery in Recife.
64 Quoted in Medeiros de Santana, *Contribuição à História do Açúcar em Alagoas*: 355, translation.
65 Josemir Camilo de Melo, op. cit., 2008: 142.
66 For example, *O Diario Novo*, 26 August 1844.
67 C. B. Mansfield, *Paraguay, Brazil, and the Plate: Letters written in 1852-1853*. 1856: 4.
68 C. B. Mansfield, op. cit., 1856: 41.
69 *O Liberal Pernambucano*, 13 October 1852: 4, translation.
70 Moacir Medeiros de Santana, op. cit., 1970: 361.
71 See Estevão Pinto, op. cit., 1949: 59, footnote #80.
72 Jorge Caldeira, *Mauá: Empresário do Império*, 1995: 27, translation.
73 Cristiano Benedito Ottoni, *O Futuro das Estradas de Ferro no Brasil, 1859*: 16-17, translation.
74 Charles Waring, *Brazil and her railways*, 1883: 10.
75 The SS GREAT WESTERN was the first ship designed by Isambard Kingdom Brunel, built in 1838. In 1847, she was sold to the Royal Mail Steam Packet Company and was scrapped in 1856 after serving as a troop ship during the Crimean War in 1854.
76 See House of Commons Papers: *Correspondence with British ministers and agents in foreign countries and with foreign ministers in England relating to the slave trade, From April 1, 1856 to March 31, 1857*.
77 Their two other brothers, Charles and Frederick, stayed on in Brazil.
78 Josemir Camilo de Melo, "Escravos e moradores na transição para o trabalho assalariado em ferrovias em Pernambuco". *Dossiê História e Africanidades* 2011: 124-5.
79 Reported in the *Daily News*, 13 April 1860. The company of Waring Brothers was later awarded by imperial decree a concession in 1882 for "The construction, use, and enjoyment of a railway between the city of Victoria, capital of the Province of Espírito Santo, and the port of Natividade, on the banks of the River Doce, in the Province of Minas Gerais." (translation).
80 Report carried in *The Morning Chronicle*, 15 October 1861.
81 Josemir Camilo de Melo, op. cit., 2011: 125-6.
82 Cristiano Benedito Ottoni, op. cit., 1859: 36-37, translation.
83 Cristiano Benedito Ottoni, op. cit., 1859: 41, translation.
84 Cristiano Benedito Ottoni, op. cit., 1859: 77, translation.
85 Estevão Pinto, op. cit., 1949: 63, footnote #95.
86 Benício Guimarães, *O Vapor nas Ferrovias do Brasil*. 1993: 161.
87 Benício Guimarães, op. cit., 1993: 27.
88 Cyro Pessôa Junior, *Estudo descriptivo das estradas de ferro do Brasil, precedido da respectiva legislação*. 1886: 100.
89 See *The Railway Record*, 11 April 1857.
90 See report carried in the *Daily News*, 21 December 1861.
91 Ana Célia Castro believes that the final agreed figure came to £1,842,202. See *As Empresas Estrangeiras no Brasil: 1860-1913*. 1979: 52.
92 From the half-yearly report given to shareholders, carried in the *Daily News* on 8 April 1862.
93 Report carried in the *Daily News* on 9 April 1861.
94 Reported in the *Daily News* on 25 October 1865.
95 See the *Daily News'* account of the company's half-yearly report published on 10 October 1866.

96 Manoel da Cunha Galvão, *Noticia sobre as estradas de ferro do Brasil*. 1869: 233, translation.
97 Manoel da Cunha Galvão, op. cit., 1869: 235.
98 Report carried in the *Daily News* on 28 April 1870.
99 Half-yearly report presented on 26 April 1872, and carried in the *Daily News* on 27 April 1872.
100 Colin Lewis, op. cit., 1991: 8.
101 Josemir Camilo de Melo, op. cit., 2011: 126.
102 The terrible drought in the years 1877 to 1889, while not the only factor, certainly contributed to the government's decision to build this railway. The government formed 'frentes de trabalho' (workers' gangs), and labour was now cheaper given the exodus from the rural areas. This was true of the Sul de Pernambuco, the Central de Pernambuco, the Paulo Afonso, and two lines in Ceará, the Sobral and Baturité railways.
103 *Herapath's Railway Journal*, 2 April 1887, copied in *The Rio News* of 15 May 1887, page 3.
104 Directors' report for the year ending 30 June 1888, summarised in *The Times*, 'Railway and other companies', 8 October 1888.
105 Estevão Pinto, op. cit., 1949: 65.
106 Estevão Pinto, op. cit., 1949: 65.
107 Josemir Camilo de Melo, op. cit., 2008: 123.
108 Archivo Público Estadual de Pernambuco, Recife, *Great Western of Brazil Railway Petições*, fl. 02, translated from English into Portuguese.
109 *The Graphic*, 23 November 1878, issue no. 469.
110 The construction company responsible for the Great Western of Brazil line from Recife to Limoeiro was Wilson, Sons & Company. Historians sometimes confuse this company with the firm of Hugh Wilson & Son, which built railways in Alagoas. The company was founded by the brothers Edward and Fleetwood Pellew Wilson in 1837, in Salvador, Bahia, and still exists in Brazil under the name of Wilson Sons. The company set up in Recife in the 1850s, where they developed the business in navigation and in railway construction. The *Almanak Administrativo, Mercantil, Industrial, e Agricula de Pernambuco*, 1881, page 131: gives "Great Western of Brazil Railway Company (Limited). Constructors: Wilson, Sons & C. (Ltd)."
111 The *Diário de Pernambuco*, 25 October 1881, translation.
112 Tagore Villarim de Siqueira, "As Primeiras Ferrovias do Nordeste Brasileiro: Processo de implantação e o caso da Great Western Railway". 2002: 180.
113 Ana Célia Castro, op. cit.,1979: 45.
114 Manuel Correia de Andrade, *História das Usinas de Açúcar de Pernambuco*. 1989: 28.
115 For example, in *The Birmingham Daily Post*, 9 July 1883.
116 The Usina Tiúma had been founded in 1881 by Jovino Bandeira de Melo under the name of Engenho Central São Lourenço da Mata before changing its name when The North Brazilian Sugar Factories Company took over the running of this mill.
117 Jason Rigby held the post of general manager of the Great Western of Brazil Railway until 1890.
118 See Pernambuco State Public Archive, *GWBR Petições*, fl. 47.
119 See Pernambuco State Public Archive, *GWBR Petições*, fls. 86 – 87, translation.
120 See Pernambuco State Public Archive, *GWBR Petições*, translation.
121 Pernambuco State Public Archive, *GWBR Petições*, fls. 82-83, translation.
122 *Jornal do Recife*. 11 March 1883.
123 Pernambuco State Public Archive, *Estrada de Ferro Timbaúba-Goiana*, fls. 30–33, translation.
124 Pernambuco State Public Archive, *GWBR Petições*, fls. 96 – 100, translation.
125 See *Diário de Pernambuco* 10 October 1884.
126 Pernambuco State Public Archive, *Estrada de Ferro Timbaúba-Goiana*, fls. 10 – 11.
127 *The Brazilian Review*: 4 June 1901, page 400.
128 Estevão Pinto 1949: 94, quoting Great Western of Brazil Railway *Reports of the Directors: 1879 to 1900*.
129 Benício Guimarães (1993: 27) quotes an unnamed source. Dübs & Company in Glasgow became part of the North British Locomotive Company in 1903.
130 Cotton remained important to the economy of north east Brazil until the 1980s decade, when

the cotton weevil (*anthonomus grandis boheman*) ravaged plantations, and provoked a great exodus of labourers to the urban centres. It is estimated that more than 1,200 textile industries closed, and that half a million jobs were lost. The north east then became an importer of cotton.

131 See João Martins da Silva Coutinho, *Estradas de Ferro do Norte*, 1888.
132 See Estevão Pinto, op. cit., 1949: 97, footnote #147 for full table on the period 1882 to 1900.
133 *Report of the Proceedings at the Annual General Meeting of the Company*, 1891: 3-4. Quoted in Estevão Pinto, op. cit., 1949: 99, footnote # 150.
134 Estevão Pinto, op. cit., 1949: 99-100, translation.
135 Estevão Pinto, op. cit., 1949: 106.

A Man Of Probity And Integrity

136 Estevão Pinto, op. cit., 1949: 123, translation.
137 Douglas Apratto Tenório, op. cit., 1979: 107.
138 One *conto de réis* was the equivalent of 1,000,000 réis, the currency in use in Brazil until 1942.
139 Apratto Tenório, 1979: 108, translation.
140 *The Rio News*, 5 October 1888: 33.
141 See Apratto Tenório, op. cit., 1979: 109.
142 Apratto Tenório, op. cit., 1979: 110.
143 Apratto Tenório, 1979: 111, translation.
144 John Charles Morgan was awarded this concession by imperial decree n° 3,590, of 17 January 1866. This railway was known as the Estrada de Ferro do Paraguassú in Brazil.
145 *Correio Paulistano*, 28 October 1883, translation.
146 Apratto Tenório, op. cit., 1979: 188, translation.
147 Quoted in Apratto Tenório, op. cit., 1979: 193.
148 Alagoas State governor's annual report on 1889: 18, translation.
149 *Revista de Engenharia*, edition 213: 150, translation.
150 Reported in *The Times*, 'Railway and other companies', 2 April 1888.
151 Félix Lima Júnior, *Delmiro Gouveia: O Mauá do Sertão Alagoano*. 1963: 113, translation.
152 Decree 6,941 of 19 June 1878, translation.
153 Quoted in Félix Lima Júnior, op. cit., 1963: 114, translation.
154 The railway station constructed at Jatobá disappeared with the flooding caused by the Itaparica dam in Pernambuco.
155 Cyro Pessôa Junior, op. cit., 1886: 170.
156 *The Rio News*, 5 March 1886: 4.
157 *Revista de Engenharia*, 1886, edition 133: 57, translation.
158 *Revista de Engenharia*, 1888, edition 190: 164.
159 *Revista de Engenharia*, 1889, edition 222: 267, translation.
160 See Alagoas state president's report on 1889, page 18, translation.
161 *Relatório do Presidente da Província das Alagoas à Assembléia Legislativa Provincial*, 1882: 34.
162 Apratto Tenório, op. cit., 1979: 114, translation.
163 Medeiros de Santana, op. cit., 1970: 316, translation.
164 Apratto Tenório, op. cit., 1979: 212, translation.
165 Apratto Tenório, 1979: 212, translation.

A New Emotion Was Born

166 *Cartas sobre uma Estrada de Ferro na Provincia da Parahyba do Norte*, by "C. M.", 1872: 2, translation.
167 The present-day State of Paraíba has a capital called João Pessoa. Older documents refer to both the province and the provincial capital as Parayba, or as Parayba do Norte. João Pessoa was adopted as the name of the state capital from 1930, as a homage to the Paraíba State President, João Pessoa Cavalcanti de Albuquerque, assassinated that year in Recife.
168 C. M., op. cit., 1872: 2, translation.

169 C. M., op. cit., 1872: 5, translation.
170 Initially, the line worked with nine locomotives, thirteen passenger carriages, and 144 cargo wagons. Guimarães (1993: 27) quotes a survey of 1884: there were nine Black, Hawthorn & Company (Gateshead) locomotives on this line.
171 *The Manchester Guardian*, 18 September 1879, page 1.
172 See *Revista de Engenharia*, 1880, no. 8: 139.
173 Horácio de Almeida, *História da Paraíba*. (2) Impr. Universitária, 1978: 138, translation.
174 Cyro Pessôa Junior, op. cit., 1886: 97, translation.
175 Reported in *The Times*, 'Railway and other companies', 6 November 1883.
176 Obituary published in the *Minutes of Proceedings*, Institution of Civil Engineers, (XCV), 1889: 383.
177 See *The Times*, 'Railway and other companies', 18 October 1888.
178 For example, the advertisement carried in *The Leeds Mercury*, 17 October 1888.
179 Wagner do Nascimento Rodrigues. *Dos caminhos de água aos caminhos de ferro: A construção da hegemonia de Natal através das vias de comunicação (1820-1920)*. 2006: 89, translation.
180 See Rio Grande do Norte provincial president's report for 1877.
181 Estevão Pinto, op. cit., 1949: 112.
182 Some sources say that Reed, Bowen & Company started construction work on the Natal to Nova Cruz railway in July 1881, which seems unlikely.
183 *Revista de Engenharia*, 14 February 1883: 42, translation.
184 Lei Provincial no. 860 of 22 July 1882.
185 Cyro Pessôa Junior, op. cit., 1886: 93, translation.
186 Decree nº 9,695, of 8 January 1887.
187 In 1886, the railway had eleven locomotives, one saloon car, nine first class carriages, nine second class, fifty-six closed wagons, sixty-seven open wagons, and thirteen wagons for the transport of animals. (Cyro Pessôa, 1886: 92).
188 *The Rio News*, 24 May 1885: 5.
189 *The Rio News*, 'Railway Notes', 5 December 1885: 4.
190 *The Rio News*, 15 September 1886: 4.
191 The Rio Grande do Norte provincial president's report on 1888, page 7.
192 Estevão Pinto, op. cit., 1949: 114, translation.

Setting A Good Example

193 *Pall Mall Gazette*, "Brazilian Guaranteed Railways – II: Commutation of the guarantee", 29 October 1900.
194 While there is some disagreement over exactly when the spelling of the name of the country changed from 'Brazil' to 'Brasil' in Portuguese, decree no 20,108 of 22 July 1931 explicitly asserts that the correct spelling is with <s>.
195 Douglas Apratto Tenório, op. cit., 1989: 214, translation.
196 See Josemir Camilo de Melo, op. cit., 1989: 65.
197 Josemir Camilo de Melo, op. cit., 2008: 161, translation.
198 Douglas Apratto Tenório, op. cit., 1979: 215.
199 Josemir Camilo de Melo, op. cit., 1989: 67, translation.
200 Julian Smith Duncan, *Public and Private Operation of Railways in Brazil*. 1932: 8.
201 See Lamounier 2000: 14, quoting P. Eisenberg, *The Sugar Industry in Pernambuco: Modernisation without change, 1840- 1910*. Berkeley, University of California Press, 1974: 34, table 2.
202 Manuel Correia Andrade, op. cit., 1989: 33, translation.
203 See Medeiros de Santana, op. cit., 1970: 341.
204 See Josemir Camilo de Melo, op. cit., 1989: 66-67.
205 Josemir Camilo de Melo, op. cit., 1989: 67, translation.
206 The London firm of N.M. Rothschild, as agents to the imperial government in London, had the monopoly of flotation of Brazilian central government loans in London from the mid-1850s to 1907.

207 See Dr. Veiga Filho, *Monographia sobre o Convenio Financeiro do Brazil (Funding Loan)*, 10 December 1889. http://www.revistas.usp.br/rfdsp/article/viewFile/64973/67585, accessed 4 December 2015.
208 Marcelo de Paiva Abreu, *British Business in Brazil: Maturity and demise (1850-1950)*. 2000: 387.
209 *The Investors' Review*, "The Brazilian Railways and the Default", 24 June 1898: 888.
210 See *The Brazilian Review*, 2 May 1899: 287.
211 *The Brazilian Review*, 16 May 1899: 1899.
212 *The Pacific Line Guide to South America* of 1895: 34.
213 Great Western of Brazil Railway directors report for 1898.
214 *The Brazilian Review*, 25 July 1899: 494.
215 *The Brazilian Review*, 1 August, 1899: 511.
216 *The Brazilian Review*, 31 October 1899: IV.
217 See Estevão Pinto, op. cit., 1949: 111.
218 See Estevão Pinto, op. cit., 1949: 117.
219 A. H. A. Knox-Little was general manager of The Great Western of Brazil Railway from 1900 to 1905. He took over from Follett Holt, who had extensive experience in managing railways in Argentina. Knox-Little was followed by J. A. Lorimer (1905 - 1909), A.T.Connor (1909-1913), and H. O. Jungstedt (1913-1919).
220 This meeting was held on 28 August 1901. See *The London Gazette*, 20 September 1901, issue 27357: 6,185.
221 Apratto Tenório, op. cit., 1979: 216, translation.
222 See Apratto Tenório, op. cit., 1979: 219.
223 Apratto Tenório, op. cit., 1979: 216, translation.
224 Quoted in Apratto Tenório, op. cit., 1979: 221.
225 Quoted in Apratto Tenório, op. cit., 1979: 219, translation.
226 Quoted in Apratto Tenório, op. cit., 1979: 222, translation.
227 Report carried in *The Brazilian Review*, 3 June 1902: 273-4.
228 Reported in *The London Gazette*, 23 September 1902, issue 27476: 6,108.
229 Reported in *The Brazilian Review*, 13 March 1900: 176.
230 *Rio Grande do Norte* newspaper, 2 September 1891:3.
231 Reported in *The Rio News*, 6 June 1893: 4.
232 Reported in *The London Gazette*, 7 January 1902, issue 27395: 173.
233 See '*Instrucções para estudos e construcção de obras contra os effeitos da secca no Estado do Rio Grande do Norte*', Portaria da Comissão de Estudos e Obras contra a Secca no Estado do Rio Grande do Norte, 23 February 1904, quoted in Rodrigues, op. cit., 2006: 100.
234 *The Economist*, 30 December 1899: 1838-39. Also *The Brazilian Review*. 30 January 1900: 81.
235 *The Brazilian Review*. 28 November 1899: 783.
236 See *The Times*, "Railway and other companies", 25 April 1900.
237 *Pall Mall Gazette*, "Brazilian Guaranteed Railways, II: Commutation of the guarantee", 29 October 1900.
238 *Pall Mall Gazette*, "Brazilian Guaranteed Railways: The question of commutation", 19 November 1900.
239 *The Brazilian Review*, 25 December 1900: 862.
240 *The Brazilian Review*, 26 February 1901: 163.
241 Note: share vs. debenture. The share of a company provides ownership to the shareholder. Debenture-holders are creditors of a company who provide loans to the company, and cannot take part in the management of the company, while a shareholder is one of the owners of the company.
242 See *The Brazilian Review*. 12 March 1901: 196.
243 *The Brazilian Review*. 15 May, 1901: 357.
244 *The Brazilian Review*. 9 July 1901: 480.
245 *The Brazilian Review*, 13 August 1901: 587, provided a translation into English of the official publication in the *Diário Official* [Official Gazette] on 3 August of Decree n° 4,111.

246 See *The Times*. "Railway and other companies", 30 October 1901.
247 Reported in *The Brazilian Review*. 5 November 1901: 765.
248 *The Brazilian Review*, 26 November 1901: 813.
249 *The Brazilian Review*. 24 May 1903: 312.
250 *The Brazilian Review*. 31 May 1904: 327.
251 Decree n° 5,257 of 26 July 1904. "Condições regulamentares e tarifas da rêde de estradas de ferro a cargo de The Great Western of Brazil Railway Company", published in the *Diário Official da União* of 16 September 1904: 4232.
252 Decree n° 7,632 of 28 October 1909.
253 See Tagore Villarim de Siqueira, op. cit., 2002: 191, tabela 6.
254 Reported in *A Provincia*, 3 October 1901: 1.
255 Reported in *A República*, edição 225, Curitiba, 4 de outubro de 1901.
256 *The Brazilian Review*. 27 May 1902: 263.
257 *The Brazilian Review*. 10 February 1903: 69.
258 *The Brazilian Review*. 24 April 1906: 340.
259 Reported in *The Brazilian Review*, 26 May 1908: 552-53.
260 A 6% dividend continued to be paid in the following years: 1909, 1910, 1911, and 1912.
261 *Diario do Natal*, 13 January, 1909: 2, translation.
262 *The Brazilian Review*, 19 January 1909: 66.
263 *A Província*, 20 January 1909, translation.
264 Federal decree 8,112 of 28 July 1910, published in the *Diário Oficial da União* on 30 July 1910, section 1, page 2.
265 Federal decree 0,727 of 17 May 1911, published in the *Diário Oficial da União*, 20 May 1911, section 1 page 2.
266 See The Great Western of Brazil Company annual general report for 1911, published in *The Railway Times* on 29 April, 1911: 412.
267 The statutes published in 1857 were approved by decree n° 2,324 of 29 December 1858.
268 A copy of this contract was consulted in the Museu do Trem in Recife.
269 Authorised by decree nº 10,030, de 29 de Janeiro de 1913. See *The Brazilian Review*, 'The Alagoas and Northern Railway Company', 20 May 1913: 511.
270 In 1913, the general manager was A. T. Connor. Appointed on 1 May 1909, he had started as a book-keeper on the Conde d'Eu line. The area managers were C. H. Howe (Alagoas), W. J. Knox-Little (Paraíba and Rio Grande do Norte), and L. M. Howe Manager (Paulo Afonso Railway). David Simson was the company chairman until early 1914, when Follett Holt succeeded him. (See Reginald Lloyd, op. cit., 1913).
271 Reported in *The Times*, "Great Western of Brazil Railway Company (Limited): Gradual development of the whole business", 30 April 1913.
272 See Rippy, op. cit., 1947: 226.

We Fall Between These Rival Parties

273 Extract from Jorge de Lima, 'G.W.B.R.', in *Novos Poemas*, Rio de Janeiro, Editora Pimenta de Melo & Cia., 1929. Author's translation.
274 Frederic Halsey, *Railway Expansion in Latin America*. 1916: 88.
275 Estevão Pinto, op. cit., 1949: 7-8, translation.
276 Estevão Pinto, op. cit., 1949: 152.
277 See *The Times*, "Great Western of Brazil Railway Company (Limited): Improved prospects – Negotiations for adjustment of tariffs", 5 June 1915.
278 Ordinary general meeting, June 1916. Reported in *The Times*, "Great Western of Brazil Railway Company (Limited): The tariff negotiations, message of good will from the Brazilian government," 6 June 1917.
279 See *The Times*, "Company Meetings. Great Western of Brazil Railway Company (Limited). The 1909 contract: the tariffs", 5 July 1918.
280 See *The Times*, "Great Western of Brazil Railway Company (Limited). Pauperized transport undertakings in Brazil. Inadequate tariffs – Negotiations for revision of the lease contract," 14 July

1919.
281 Decree n° 14,326 of 24 August 1920.
282 See *The Times*, "Company meetings. Great Western of Brazil Railway Company, Limited. Revision of tariffs. New contract approved," 10 March 1921.
283 See *The Times*, "Great Western of Brazil Railway Company, Limited. The new contract with the government," 15 July 1921.
284 *Wileman´s Brazilian Review*, 24 August 1921, page 1,344.
285 See *The Times*, "The Great Western of Brazil Railway Company, Limited. Revision of contract. Delay in negotiations," 26 May 1922.
286 See *The Times*, "Great Western of Brazil Railway. Negotiations with new government," 1 March 1923.
287 President of Pernambuco State, annual report on 1923, page 31, translation.
288 See *The Times*, "Company meetings. Great Western of Brazil Railway. The present position. Negotiations with new government," 21 June 1923.
289 Published in the *Diário Oficial da União*, 19 September 1923, Section 1, page 14.
290 See Alagoas state president's report for 1923.
291 H. O. Jungstedt was general manager from 1913 to 1919. J. G. Castles from June 1919 to December 1924. Joaquim de Assis Ribeiro from December 1924 to June 1932. Arlindo Luz from 1932 to 1936. Frank Bennett Fellows was interim general manager from June to September 1936. Manuel de Azevedo Leão took over from September 1936 to March 1946.
292 *The Times*, "Company meetings. Great Western of Brazil Railway. Company's serious position. Federal government and tariff question," 10 July 1924.
293 Portaria of the Ministro da Viação published in September 1924, reviewed by *Wileman´s Brazilian Review*, 29 October 1924, page 1441.
294 Ordinary general meeting of the Great Western of Brazil held on 11 June 1925. See *The Times*, "Great Western of Brazil Railway. Result of negotiations with the government. The new tariffs," 12 June 1925.
295 See the President of Pernambuco's report on 1924, page 57.
296 Alagoas State president's report for 1924, translation.
297 See *The Railway Gazette*, 6 December 1926: 85-86.
298 Ordinary general meeting held on 23 May 1927. See *The Times*, "The Great Western of Brazil Railway. The new government and tariff revision. President's declaration," 24 May 1927.
299 Ordinary GM in London, Follett Holt presiding, held on 19 June 1928. See *The Times*, "Great Western of Brazil Railway. Inadequate tariff and burden of liabilities. The contract with the federal government," 20 June 1928.
300 See *The Times*, "Great Western of Brazil Railway. New arrangement with the government. Improved position," 5 June 1929.
301 T. C. Hanson, op. cit., 1989: 15.
302 The most common version of what happened differs from Hanson's account; most historians believe that the heads were placed in kerosene tins that contained *aguardiente* and lime.
303 T. C. Hanson, op. cit., 1989: 16.
304 The ordinary general meeting held on 7 May 1930, Follett Holt presiding. See *The Times*, "The Great Western of Brazil Railway. First ordinary dividend for 16 years," 8 May 1830.
305 The ordinary general meeting in London held on 22 April 1931, Follett Holt presiding. See *The Times*, "Great Western of Brazil Railway. Factors affecting the year's working", 23 April 1931.
306 Annual general meeting in London, Follett Holt presiding, held on 30 May 1933. See *The Times*, "Great Western of Brazil Railway. The exchange problem". 31 May 1933.
307 Ordinary General Meeting in London, Harrisson presiding, held on 15 May 1934. See *The Times*, "Great Western of Brazil Railway. Anomalies of tariff system", 16 May 1934.
308 Félix Lima Júnior, *Delmiro Gouveia: O Mauá do Sertão Alagoano*, 1963: 115, author's translation.
309 See Chapter 14 of *Lampião na Bahia*, Oleone Coelho Fontes, 1937: 96-99; quoted in Bonfim 2001: 105, author's translation.
310 Author's translation of:

Tem duas coisas no mundo
Que eu vejo e me admiro:
É o trem lá de Piranhas,
E o carro de Delmiro.

311 The ordinary general meeting held on 17 July 1935, G. H. Harrisson presiding. See *The Times*, "Great Western of Brazil Railway. Continued difficult conditions", 18 July 1925.

312 The ordinary general meeting held on 24 June 1936, G. H. Harrisson presiding. See *The Times*, "Great Western of Brazil Railway. Need of revised working conditions", 25 June 1936.

313 This was duly published in the *Diário Oficial da União* on 12 March 1936, section 1, page 27.

314 See the *Diário Oficial da União*, 30 April 1937, section 1, page 37.

315 The ordinary general meeting held on 26 May 1937, G. H. Harrisson presiding. See *The Times*, "Great Western of Brazil Railway. Difficult operating conditions. Necessity for government assistance", 27 May 1937.

316 Ordinary general meeting, G. H. Harrisson chairman presiding, held in London on 21 June 1938. See *The Times*, "Great Western of Brazil Railway. Difficult operating conditions", 22 June 1938.

317 Minutes of the ordinary general meeting in London, held on 21 June 1939.

318 See T. C. Hanson, *A railway engineer in Brazil*, 1989: 182.

319 The ordinary general meeting held in London on 22 September 1943, W. M. Codrington chairman. See *The Times*, "Great Western of Brazil Railway. Improved results", 23 September 1943.

320 Decree nº 5,299 of 3 March 1943. "Autoriza a supressão da Estrada de Ferro Paulo Afonso e dá outras providências."

321 The ordinary general meeting held in London on 18 October 1944, chairman W. M. Codrington. See *The Times*, "Great Western of Brazil Railway. Record gross receipts", 19 October 1944.

322 The ordinary general meeting held on 15 August 1945, W. M. Codrington presiding. See *The Times*, "Great Western of Brazil Railway. Record receipts", 16 August 1945.

323 See *Diário Oficial da União*, 4 May 1946: 6,718, translation.

324 Ordinary general meeting held in August 1947, actual date not given. See *The Times*, "Great Western of Brazil Railway: Intense activity in all departments", 25 August 1947.

325 Ordinary general meeting held in London on 15 August 1948. See *The Times*, "Great Western of Brazil Railway: Mr. W. M. Codrington on the acquisition question", 16 August 1948.

326 D. Trevor Rowe provides a useful overview of the locomotives connected with the network based on a stock list dated 1 January 1949 in his article entitled 'The Great Western of Brazil Railway' (1996). The railway tried a Baldwin 2-8-0 (of 1879) and seven Baldwin 2-6-0s (1891-1895) from the United States. From Britain, they acquired a Black Hawthorn 4-4-0T (1883), three Sharp Stewart 2-6-2Ts (1892), and four Neilson 4-6-0s (1880). Trevor Rowe adds that two Hunslet 0-6-0s (1894) were rebuilt into 2-6-2Ts, and a Baldwin 2-8-0 (1895) was rebuilt as a 2-6-2T as late as 1945. He reported that in 1977 it was still possible to see a Robert Stephenson 2-4-0T no. 3 on the seafront in Boa Viagem, Recife, but in poor condition, and in fact this locomotive no longer exists.

According to Trevor Rowe, the first large batch of line locomotives was a class of 2-6-0s manufactured by the North British Locomotive Company in Glasgow between 1904 and 1914. The original numbers were 1-25, 43-48, 162-177, and 187-219, which later became numbers 209-288. In 1906, the North British provided three 4-4-0s, and the first of fourteen 4-8-0s that arrived in 1906 (five), 1910 (two), 1914 (three) and in 1929 (four). The latter order of 1929 was built by the Armstrong Whitworth company, which also supplied two Garratt 2-6-2+2-6-2s in the same year. In the 1920s decade, the Great Western received three Baldwin 4-6-0 (1921), two Swiss Locomotive and Machine Works 2-6-2Ts (1922), four Henschel 4-6-0s (1927), and four 4-6-0s built by Armstrong Whitworth (1929). With the increase in traffic during the Second World War between Recife and Natal, the company took delivery of three American-built ALCO 2-8-2s.

Adeus!

326 Extracts from the poem *Trem de Alagoas* by Ascenso Ferreira in *Poemas*, 1951. Author's translation.

327 See the minutes of the extraordinary general meeting published in *The London Gazette*, 3 November 1950, issue 39059, page 5501.

328 See Marcelo de Paiva Abreu, op. cit., (54), 4, 2000, translation.

329 See "Histórico das ferrovias no Brasil," Instituto do Patrimônio Histórico e Artístico Nacional (IPHAN), http://portal.iphan.gov.br/portal/montarDetalheConteudo.do?id=15833&sigla=Institucion al&retorno=detalheInstitucional, accessed 4 December 2015. Translation.

330 Lei Ordinária no. 1,180 of 17 August 1950, translation.

331 *The London Gazette*, 26 January 1951, issue 39133, page 494.

332 See D. Trevor Rowe, "The Great Western of Brazil Railway," *Locomotives International*, 7/34, August 1996: 21.

333 Decree no. 3,277 of 7 December 1999, further altered by Decrees no. 4,109 of 30 January 2002, no. 4,839 of 12 September 2003, and no. 5,103 of 11 June 2004.

334 Article 9 of Federal Law 11,483: "It will be the responsibility of the Instituto do Patrimônio Histórico e Artístico Nacional [IPHAN – the institute of national historic and artistic heritage] to receive and administer the assets and real estate of cultural, historical, and artistic value originating from the extinct RFFSA, as well as watch over its keep and maintenance."

A 36 seater tram that once ran along Rua da Aurora in Recife with the number 104, now on display at the Museu do Homem do Nordeste, Recife, Pernambuco.

Author's Collection

Bibliography

Archive Resources

- Digital archive *The British Newspaper Archive*, http://www.britishnewspaperarchive.co.uk/, accessed 4 December 2015.
- Digital archive *Diário de Pernambuco*, University of Florida Digital Collections, http://ufdc.ufl.edu/AA00011611, accessed 4 December 2015.
- Digital archive *Folha de São Paulo*, http://acervo.folha.uol.com.br/, accessed 4 December 2015.
- Digital archive *Hemeroteca Digital Brasileira da Fundação Biblioteca Nacional* http://memoria.bn.br/hdb/periodico.aspx. For example, *The Rio News*, http://memoria.bn.br/DocReader/docreader.aspx?bib=349070&pesq=Great Western of Brazil, accessed 4 December 2015.
- Digital archive *Provincial Presidential Reports 1830-1930*, Center for Research Libraries, Global Resources Network, http://www-apps.crl.edu/brazil/provincial, accessed 4 December 2015.
- Digital archive *Wileman's Brazilian Review*, 1898-1940, <http://memoria.org.br/wbr1.php>, accessed 4 December 2015.
- Documentary archives of the Fundação Joaquim Nabuco, Recife, Pernambuco: the Instituto de Documentação and the Acervo Fotográfico da Biblioteca Central Blanche Knopf.
- Documentary archive *Centro-Oeste*. For example, the Paulo Afonso Railway, http://vfco.brazilia.jor.br/estacoes-ferroviarias/1960-nordeste-RFN/Linha-Paulo-Afonso.shtml, accessed 4 December 2015.
- Documentary archive *Estações ferroviárias do nordeste*, http://www.estacoesferroviarias.com.br/index_ne.htm, accessed 4 December 2015.
- Pernambuco State Public Archive, Arquivo Público de Pernambuco, Anexo Rua Imperial 1069, Recife, Pernambuco. (The valuable collection of GWBR documents catalogued by the historian Josemir Camilo de Melo).
- *The Times* digital archive: reports on board meetings of railway companies: http://www.thetimes.co.uk/tto/archive/, accessed 4 December 2015.
- Facebook community, *Projeto Memória Ferroviária de Pernambuco*, https://www.facebook.com/ProjetoMemoriaFerroviariaDePernambuco?pnref=story, accessed 4 December 2015.
- Facebook organization, *Estradas de Ferro do Nordeste*, https://www.facebook.com/EstradasFerroNordeste?ref=stream, accessed 4 December 2015.
- *Railway Age*. Some editions are available in digital format on the internet, such as *Railway Age*, Seventieth Quarto Volume, January to June, 1921, https://archive.org/stream/railwayage70newy#page/n3/mode/2up, accessed 4 December 2015.
- *The Railway News and Joint-Stock Journal*. Some editions are available in digital format on the internet, such as *The Railway News*, Vol. VII, June 1867, https://books.google.com.br/books?id=8-E0AQAAIAAJ&printsec=frontcover&source=gbs_ge_summary_r&cad=0#v=onepage&q&f=false, accessed 4 December 2015.
- *The Railway Times*. Some editions are available in digital format on the internet, such as *The Railway Times*, Vol. XCIV, July to December 1908, https://archive.org/stream/railwaytimes94londuoft#page/n3/mode/2up, accessed 4 December 2015.

Steam Locomotive Lists

- Baker, Allan C., & T. D. Allen Civil. *Bagnall Locomotives: A pictorial album of Bagnall narrow gauge locomotives*. Burton-On-Trent: Trent Valley Publications, 1990.
- Baker, Allan C. *Black, Hawthorne & Co., Works List*. Richmond: The Industrial Locomotive Society, 1988.
- Garratt locomotives. http://www.beyerpeacock.co.uk/loco%20list/List%20of%20Beyer%20

Peacock%20Locomotives.html, accessed 4 December 2015.
- Jux, Frank. *John Fowler & Co. Locomotive Works List*. Richmond: The Industrial Locomotive Society, 1985.
- _____, *Kerr Stuart & Co. Ltd., light railway engineers*. Richmond: The Industrial Locomotive Society. 1992.
- Mabbott, Fred. *Hunslet Locomotives List*. Unpublished.
- _____, *Dübs Locomotives List*. Unpublished.
- Neale, Andrew. *Kerr, Stuart's Locomotives. List C., 1924*. Norwich: Plateway Press, 1991.

Books and articles consulted

- Abreu, Marcelo de Paiva. "British Business in Brazil: Maturity and demise (1850-1950)". *Revista Brasileira de Economia*, 54 (4): 2000.
- Andrade, Manuel Correia de. *História das Usinas de Açúcar de Pernambuco*. Recife: Fundação Joaquim Nabuco, Editora Massangana, 1989.
- Apratto Tenório, Douglas. *Capitalismo e Ferrovias no Brasil*. Coleção Estudos Alagoanos, no. 2. Maceió: Editora da Universidade Federal de Alagoas, 1979.
- Araujo, Antônio Amaury Corrêa de, & Luiz Ruben F. de A. Bonfim. *Lampião e a Maria Fumaça*. Paulo Afonso, Alagoas: Edit. Graf Tech, 2013.
- Bardi, P. M. *Lembrança do Trem de Ferro*. São Paulo: Banco Sudameris Brasil S. A., 1983.
- Barroso Braga, Napoleão. *Cartas Recifenses*. Coleção Recife, vol. XLVI. Recife: Prefeitura da Cidade do Recife, 1985.
- Benévolo, Ademar. *Introdução à História Ferroviária do Brasil: Estudo Social, Político e Histórico*. Recife: Edições Folha da Manha, 1953.
- Bethell, Leslie. "A Presença Britânica no Império dos Trópicos". *Acervo*, Rio de Janeiro, 22 (1) (Jan/June 2009): 53-66.
- _____, "Britain and Latin America in historical perspective". Victor Bulmer-Thomas [ed.] *Britain and Latin America: A changing relationship*. The Royal Institute of International Affairs. Cambridge: Cambridge University Press, 1989: 1-24.
- Bonfim, Luiz Ruben F. de A. *A Estrada de ferro Paulo Afonso: 1882-1964*. Paulo Afonso, Alagoas: Graf Tech, 2001.
- Bôtto Targino, Itapuan. *As Estações de Trem da Paraíba*. João Pessoa: Idéia, 2001.
- Branner, John Casper. *The railways of Brazil: a statistical article. Reprinted from the Railway Age, with notes and additions*. Chicago: Railway Age Publications, 1887.
- Burton, Richard F. *The Highlands of the Brazil*. Vol. II. London: Tinsley Brothers, 1869.
- Caldeira, Jorge. *Mauá: Empresário do Império*. São Paulo: Editora Companhia das Letras, 1995.
- Cararo, Aryane. "O Apito do Trem no Nordeste". *Caminhos do Trem: Apogeu, Decadência e Retomada da Ferrovia no Brasil*, 2: 14-19. São Paulo: Duetto Editorial, 2008.
- Castro, Ana Célia. *As Empresas Estrangeiras no Brasil: 1860-1913*. Rio de Janeiro: Zahar Editores, 1979.
- Catchpole, Paul. *A Very British railway: The São Paulo Railway*. St. Teath: Locomotives International Publications, 2003.
- "C. M." *Cartas sobre uma Estrada de Ferro na Provincia da Parahyba do Norte*. Parahyba: Typ. Liberal Parahybana, 1872.
- Cooper, Martin. *Brazilian Railway Culture*. Cambridge Scholars Publishing, 2011.
- Correia de Andrade, Manuel. *História das Usinas de Açúcar de Pernambuco*. Recife: Fundação Joaquim Nabuco, 1989.
- Côrtes, Eduardo. *Da Great Western ao Metrô do Recife*. Recife: Persona, 2004.
- Costa, Francisco Barreto Picanço. *Viação férrea do Brasil*. Rio de Janeiro: Typ. E Lith. De Machado & Cia., 1884.
- Coutinho, João Martins da Silva. *Estradas de Ferro do Norte: Relatorio apresentado ao Exm.*

Snr. conselheiro Antonio da Silva Prado, ministro e secretario dos negocios da agricultura, commercio e obras publicas. Ministério da Agricultura: Imprensa Nacional, 1888.

- Dantas Silva, Leonardo. (Ed). *O Monitor das Famílias: Facsimile da primeira edição*. Recife: FUNDARPE, 1985.
- Darwin, Charles. *Journal of researches into the natural history and geology of the countries visited during the voyage of H.M.S. "Beagle" round the world, under the command of Capt. Fitz Roy, R.N.* Vol. III. "Journal and remarks. 1832-1836", London: Henry Colburn, 1839.
- Duarte, José Lins. *Recife no Tempo da Maxambomba (1867-1889): O Primeiro Trem Urbano do Brasil*. Masters dissertation. Universidade Federal de Pernambuco, Centro de Filosofia e Ciências Humanas, Programa de Pós-graduação em História. Recife: 2005.
- Duncan, Julian Smith. *Public and Private Operation of Railways in Brazil*. New York: Columbia University Press, 1932.
- Edmundson, William (Eddie), (collaborator). *Inventário das Locomotivas a Vapor no Brasil/ Inventory of Steam Engines in Brazil*. Regina Perez. Rio de Janeiro: Notícia & Companhia, 2006.
- _____, "The Great Western of Brazil Railway". *Brazil Handbook*. Bath: Footprint Handbooks, 2002: 468.
- _____, (collaborator) *A presença britânica em Pernambuco, Brasil (1808-1950)/ The British presence in Pernambuco, Brazil (1808-1950)*. Antônio Paulo Rezende. Recife: Secretaria de Ciência, Tecnologia e Meio Ambiente, 2000
- _____, "Surviving steam locomotives in north east Brazil". Part 1, *Locomotives International*, 50, July-August 1999: 14-17. Part 2, *Locomotives International*, 51, September-October 1999: 20-26. Part 3, *Locomotives International*, 52, January-February 2000: 23-25. Part 4, *Locomotives International*, 53, March-April 2000: 24-27.
- _____, "The British influence in 19th century Pernambuco". *Exploring Olinda*. Gaynor Barton. Recife: Editora Bagaço, 1997: 171-5.
- _____, "Calle Exeter and Rua Charles Darwin: British Studies on Your Doorstep". *British Studies Now*. London: The British Council, 1994. Reprinted in *British Studies Anthology*, Nick Wadham-Smith (Ed.), London: The British Council, 1995: 66-68.
- Eisenberg, Peter L. *The sugar industry in Pernambuco, modernization without change, 1840-1910*. Berkeley: University of California Press, 1974.
- Ferrez, Gilberto. *Velhas Fotografias Pernambucanas: 1851-1890*. Rio de Janeiro: Campo Visual, 1988.
- Freyre, Gilberto. *Ingleses no Brasil: Aspectos da influência Britânica sobre a vida, a paisagem, e a cultura do Brasil*. Coleção Documentos Brasileiros, 58, 2nd. edition. Rio de Janeiro: José Olympio, 1977. (1st. edition, 1948).
- Fundação Roberto Marinho & Lloyds Bank. *A Presença britânica no Brasil (1808-1914) /The British presence in Brazil (1808-1914)*. São Paulo: Editora Paubrasil, 1987.
- Galloway, J. H. "The Sugar Industry of Pernambuco during the Nineteenth Century". *Annals of the Association of American Geographers*, 58 (2) (1968): 285-303.
- Gerodetti, João Emilio & Carlos Cornejo. *Ferrovias do Brasil nos cartões postais e álbuns de lembranças*. São Paulo: Solaris Editorial, 2005.
- Gouveia, Fernando da Cruz. *Perfil do Tempo*. Recife: Fundação de Cultura, 1990.
- Graham, Richard. *Britain and the Onset of Modernization in Brazil: 1850-1914*. Cambridge Latin American Studies. Cambridge: Cambridge University Press, 1968.
- Guimarães Benício. *O Vapor nas Ferrovias do Brasil*. Petrópolis: Editora Gráfica Jornal da Cidade, 1993.
- Galvão, Manoel da Cunha. *Noticia sobre as estradas de ferro do Brasil*. Rio de Janeiro: Typ. Do Diario do Rio de Janeiro, 1869.
- Graham, Maria. *Journal of a Voyage to Brazil, and Residence There, During Part of the Years 1821, 1822, 1823*. London: Longman, Hurst, Rees, Orme, Brown & Green, 1824.

- Graham, Richard. *Britain and the Onset of Modernization in Brazil 1850-1914.* Cambridge Latin American Studies. Cambridge: Cambridge University Press, 1968.
- Hahmann, Carlheinz, & Charles S. Small. *Brazilian Steam Album: Plus & Minus Two Footers.* Greenwich: Railhead publications, 1985.
- Halsey, Frederic M. *Railway Expansion in Latin America.* New York: The Moody Magazine and Book Company, 1916.
- Hanson, T. C. *A Railway Engineer in Brazil.* London: Excalibur Press, 1989.
- Joslin, David. *A Century of Banking in Latin America.* London: Bank of London & South America/Oxford University Press, 1963.
- Koster, Henry. *Travels in Brazil.* London: Longman, Hurst, Rees, Orme, and Brown, 1816.
- Lamounier, Lucia. *The 'Labour Question' in Nineteenth Century Brazil: Railways, export agriculture and labour scarcity.* Working paper no. 59, Department of Economic History, London School of Economics, 2000.
- Lewis, Colin M. *Public Policy and Private Initiative: Railway Building in São Paulo 1860-1889.* Institute of Latin American Studies Research Papers no. 26. London: University of London, 1991.
- Lima Júnior, Félix. *Delmiro Gouveia: O Mauá do Sertão Alagoano.* Maceió: Editora Depto. Estadual de Cultura, 1963.
- Lloyd, Reginald. *Impressões do Brasil no Século Vinte.* London: Lloyd's Greater Britain Publishing Company, Ltd., 1913. http://www.novomilenio.inf.br/santos/h0300g42b.htm, accessed 4 December 2015.
- Manchester, Alan K. *British Preëminence in Brazil: Its rise and decline.* Chapel Hill: University of North Carolina Press, 1933.
- Mansfield, C. B. Paraguay, *Brazil, and the Plate: Letters written in 1852-1853.* Cambridge: Macmillan, 1856.
- Martins, Graciliano. "Viação Férrea no Nordeste". *Livro do Nordeste. Comemorativo do primeiro centenário do Diario de Pernambuco.* Gilberto Freyre, et. al., Recife: Diário de Pernambuco, 1925.
- Medeiros, Gabriel Leopoldino Paulo de. *As cidades e os trilhos: Resgate histórico da implantação das ferrovias no Rio Grande do Norte e inventário de suas estações.* Graduation monograph in the course of Arquitetura e Urbanismo of the Universidade Federal do Rio Grande do Norte. Natal: November 2007.
- Melo, Josemir Camilo de. "A República e a Mania Ferroviária". *Repensando a República,* Revista do Arquivo Público, Recife. Recife: Arquivo Pública Estadual. 39/42 (1989): 62-72.
- _____, "O papel dos investimentos ferroviários ingleses no nordeste, 1852 – 1902 (Notas para um estudo da história ferroviária)". *Revista Sitientibus,* Feira de Santana, 15 (1996): 363-88.
- _____, *Modernização e Mudanças: O trem inglês nos canaviais do Nordeste (1852-1902).* Doctorate thesis, Universidade Federal de Pernambuco, Recife, 2000.
- _____, *Ferrovias Inglesas e Mobilidade Social no Nordeste (1850-1900).* Campina Grande, Paraíba: Editora da Universidade Federal de Campina Grande, 2008.
- _____, "Escravos e moradores na transição para o trabalho assalariado em ferrovias em Pernambuco". *Dossiê História e Africanidades.* João Pessoa: SÆCULUM – Revista de História, 25 (July/ Dec. 2011): 115-30.
- Mello, José Antonio Gonsalves de. *Ingleses em Pernambuco.* Recife: Instituto Arqueológico, Histórico e Geográfico Pernambucano, 1972.
- Mendonça, João Hélio. "Cronistas Ingleses em Pernambuco no Século XIX". *Arrecifes,* 6 (July/December 1992): 83-98.
- Miller, Rory. *Britain and Latin America in the nineteenth and twentieth centuries.* Longman Studies in Modern History. London: Longman, 1993.
- _____, "The decline of British interests in Latin America." *History Today,* 41 (12) (1991):

42-58.

- Morrison, Allen. *The tramways of Brazil. Recife, Pernambuco State, Brazil.* http://www.tramz.com/br/re/re.html, accessed 4 December 2015.
- Ottoni, Cristiano Benedito. *O Futuro das Estradas de Ferro no Brasil.* Rio de Janeiro: Tipografia Nacional, 1859.
- Paraíso, Rostrand. *Esses Ingleses.* Recife: Edições Bagaço, 1997.
- Perez, Regina. *Inventário das Locomotivas a Vapor no Brasil/Inventory of Steam Engines in Brazil.* Rio de Janeiro: Noticia & Co., 2006.
- Pessôa Junior, Cyro Diocleciano Ribeiro. *Estudo descriptivo das estradas de ferro do Brasil, precedido da respectiva legislação.* Rio de Janeiro: Imprensa Nacional, 1886.
- Pinto, Estevão de Menezes Ferreira. *História de uma Estrada de Ferro do Nordeste.* Coleção Documentos Brasileiros, 61. Rio de Janeiro: Editora José Olympio, 1949.
- Platt, D. C. M. "Bibliographical Aids to Research. XX. The British in South America". *Bulletin of the Institute of Historical Research*, 38 (1965): 172-191.
- Rezende, Antônio Paulo. *The British presence in Pernambuco, Brazil (1808-1950)/ A presença Britânica em Pernambuco, Brasil (1808-1950).* Secretaria de Ciência, Tecnologia e Meio Ambiente. Recife: 2000.
- Rippy, J. Fred. *British investments in Latin America, 1922-1949: A Case Study in the Operations of Private Enterprise in Retarded Regions.* Minneapolis: University of Minnesota Press, 1959.
- _____, "British investments in Latin America: End of 1913". *The Journal of Modern History*, 19 (3) (September 1947): 226-234.
- Rodrigues, Wagner do Nascimento. *Dos caminhos de água aos caminhos de ferro: A construção da hegemonia de Natal através das vias de comunicação (1820-1920).* Dissertation presented in post-graduate programme in Arquitetura e Urbanismo of the Universidade Federal do Rio Grande do Norte as part of the prerequisites for obtaining a Masters degree in Arquitetura e Urbanismo. Natal: 2006.
- Sampaio, Marcos Guedes Vaz & Felipe Amorim Campos. "Hugh Wilson: Um capitalista britânico na Bahia oitocentista". *Revista Crítica Histórica*, III (6) (December 2012). http://www.revista.ufal.br/criticahistorica/attachments/article/145/Hugh%20Wilson_Um%20Capitalista%20Britanico%20Na%20Bahia%20Oitocentista.pdf, accessed 4 December 2015.
- Santana, Moacir Medeiros de. *Contribuição à História do Açúcar em Alagoas.* Recife: Instituto do Açúcar e do Álcool, Museu do Açúcar, 1970.
- Siqueira, Tagore Villarim de. "As Primeiras Ferrovias do Nordeste Brasileiro: Processo de implantação e o caso da Great Western Railway". *Revista do BNDES*, Rio de Janeiro: 9 (17) (June 2002): 169-220.
- Souza, Alcindo de. *Antologia ferroviária do nordeste.* Recife: Editora Bagaço, 1988.
- Summerhill, William R. "Market Intervention in a Backward Economy: Railway Subsidy in Brazil, 1854-1913". *The Economic History Review*, New Series, 51 (3) (Aug., 1998): 542-568.
- Telles, Pedro C. da Silva. "A história das ferrovias brasileiras: Parte 1, As primeiras ferrovias". *História da Engenharia no Brasil (Séculos XVI a XIX).* Rio de Janeiro: Ed. Livros Técnicos e Científicos Editora, 1984 (capítulo 6). Tran. *A History of Brazilian Railways: Part 1, The First Railways.* Paul E. Waters. Bromley, Kent: P. E. Waters & Associates, 1987.
- Trevor Rowe, D. "The Great Western of Brazil Railway". *Locomotives International*, 34 (7) (August 1996): 18-22.
- Waring, Charles. *Brazil and her railways.* Montreal: Gazette Printing Company, 1883.
- Watts, Alfredo J. "A Colônia Inglesa em Pernambuco". *Revista do Instituto Arqueológico, Histórico e Geográfico Pernambuco*, (XXXIX) 163-70. Recife: Instituto Arqueológico, Histórico e Geográfico Pernambuco, 1945.
- Wells, James W. *Exploring and travelling three thousand miles through Brazil, from Rio de Janeiro to Maranhão.* London: Sampson Low, Marston, Searle, & Rivington, 1886.